Democracy's Dharma

A

Philip E. Lilienthal

BOOK

The Philip E. Lilienthal imprint
honors special books
in commemoration of a man whose work
at the University of California Press from 1954 to 1979
was marked by dedication to young authors
and to high standards in the field of Asian Studies.
Friends, family, authors, and foundations have together
endowed the Lilienthal Fund, which enables the Press
to publish under this imprint selected books
in a way that reflects the taste and judgment
of a great and beloved editor.

Democracy's Dharma

Religious Renaissance and
Political Development in Taiwan

Richard Madsen

UNIVERSITY OF CALIFORNIA PRESS
Berkeley · *Los Angeles* · *London*

University of California Press, one of the most
distinguished university presses in the United States,
enriches lives around the world by advancing
scholarship in the humanities, social sciences, and
natural sciences. Its activities are supported by the UC
Press Foundation and by philanthropic contributions
from individuals and institutions. For more information, visit www.ucpress.edu.

University of California Press
Berkeley and Los Angeles, California

University of California Press, Ltd.
London, England

Library of Congress Cataloging-in-Publication Data

Madsen, Richard, 1941–.
    Democracy's dharma : Religious renaissance and
political development in Taiwan / Richard Madsen.
        p.   cm.
    Includes bibliographical references and index.
    ISBN 978-0-520-25227-1 (cloth : alk. paper)
    ISBN 978-0-520-25228-8 (pbk. : alk. paper)
    1. Buddhism and politics—Taiwan.   2. Buddhism—
Taiwan—History—20th century.   I. Title.

    BQ649.T32M33   2008
    294.3'3720951249—dc22   2007002242

Manufactured in the United States of America
16   15   14   13   12   11   10   09   08   07
10   9   8   7   6   5   4   3   2   1

This book is printed on New Leaf EcoBook 50, a
100% recycled fiber of which 50% is de-inked post-
consumer waste, processed chlorine-free. EcoBook 50
is acid-free and meets the minimum requirements of
ANSI/ASTM D5634-01 (Permanence of Paper).

Contents

Illustrations

Acknowledgments

My interest in pursuing this project began almost a decade ago, when I was privileged to take part in a delegation to China and Taiwan of experts in voluntary, non-profit associations. The delegation was organized by the National Committee on U.S.-China relations, which over the past thirty-five years has played a major role in facilitating exchange between the U.S. and China. The organizer of our trip was Jan Berris, whose warmth, creativity, and leadership have made a major contribution to dialogue between the United States and Asia. When our delegation reached Taiwan, our introduction to the religious organizations studied here was arranged by Allen Choate of the Asia Foundation, one of the many unsung Americans who builds bridges of understanding across the Pacific.

To finance my research, I turned, first, to the Academic Senate of the University of California, San Diego, which provided a small grant for exploratory research. I was then given a generous grant from the Chiang Ching-kuo Foundation, which enabled me to do five months of fieldwork in Taiwan. Later, I was able to do some follow-up work with the help of funding from the Pacific Rim Research Program at the University of California.

In Taiwan, I was hosted by the Institute of Sociology of the Academia Sinica. I am grateful for the kindness of the director of the Institute at that time, Chiu Hei-yuan. I am especially grateful to Hsiau A-chin—a former student who is now a major scholar at the Academia Sinica and who has taught me at least as much as I taught him.

My research assistants were Kuo Ya-yu and Ho Hua-chin. I am grateful not only for their help and counsel—which went far beyond the call of duty—but also for their friendship. Finally, I am most grateful to all of the people who opened their communities and trusted me with their stories. In my final follow-up visit, Mark Moskowicz—another former student who has turned into my teacher—let me stay in his apartment and showed me parts of Taiwan that I had not seen before. He also arranged for me to meet with David Schak, who has read the manuscript and given valuable advice.

My wife and I were also embraced by our old colleagues in the Maryknoll Fathers and Sisters in Taiwan, especially Al Doyle and Mary Ellen Kerrigan. They made us feel as if we had returned home.

Much of the intellectual framework for this book—as for all of my other books—was developed through three decades of conversation with Robert Bellah, William Sullivan, Steven Tipton, and Ann Swidler. Thomas Wong, of Hong Kong University, invited me to present the last part of this book's conclusion as a keynote speech at the Hong Kong Sociological Association, and he gave me important ideas about how to frame that conclusion.

Thanks, finally, to Tom Gold and Bonnie Adrian, who critiqued an earlier draft of the manuscript, to Chris Pitts, who did a superb job of copyediting, and to Reed Malcolm, who guided the book through the University of California Press.

My wife, Judy Rosselli, has been a patient and intrepid companion throughout this intellectual journey, and indeed throughout the whole journey of life. Words cannot adequately express my gratitude for her companionship.

A Note on Romanization

The international standard for romanizing Chinese characters—that is, representing them phonetically with the Western European alphabet—is the pinyin method used in the People's Republic of China. Generally, pinyin romanization is the best available guide for English speakers on how Chinese words are actually pronounced.

In Taiwan, however, other romanization methods are commonly used, most of them derived from the Wade-Giles system developed over a century ago. The Taiwanese romanization systems are further complicated because many words, especially proper names, are commonly rendered in ways that inconsistently depart from the Wade-Giles system.

Standard academic conventions would have led me to reproduce all Chinese names in pinyin. However, a desire to make this book as useful as possible to a wide range of non-Chinese speaking audiences has led me to depart from standard academic conventions. I have thus rendered all proper names in the form in which they are commonly romanized in Taiwan. Likewise, the names of Taiwanese authors of English language publications retain the spelling they use in print. All other Chinese words, as well as proper names of people and places in the People's Republic of China, have been romanized in pinyin. It is my intention that this inelegant and somewhat schizophrenic policy will make it easier for non-Chinese speaking readers to search libraries and the Internet for further English language information on the groups studied here.

For example, the Chinese name of the Buddhist Compassion Relief

Association is written as *Tzu Chi,* because this is how it is spelled in Taiwan and in English language literature put out by Tzu Chi itself. In pinyin, this name would be rendered as *Ci Ji*. However, if one searches the Internet for *Ci Ji,* almost nothing related to the Buddhist Compassion Relief Association appears. In contrast, searching for *Tzu Chi* results in many pages of relevant websites, including the official website of the organization itself. The same is true of the other organizations and their leaders studied here. For further reference, I have provided a glossary at the end of the book, which lists all proper names and places with their Chinese characters, Taiwanese romanization, and pinyin romanization.

Preface

Shortly before 2:00 A.M. on September 21, 1999, a devastating earthquake (7.9 on the Richter scale) struck central Taiwan, killing about 2,400 people, injuring tens of thousands, and leaving over one hundred thousand homeless. In Puli, a midsized town close to the epicenter, the chairman of the local section of the Buddhist Compassion Relief Association, commonly called Tzu Chi, was shaken out of bed. His house had almost collapsed and would later have to be torn down. Because there was neither electricity nor phone service, he did not know the full extent of the disaster. But he knew what he had to do: he went immediately to the Tzu Chi headquarters, a small wooden building next to the Puli high school. Twenty or thirty other Tzu Chi members had also spontaneously come to the center. Using emergency supplies stored there, supplemented with food brought from their own homes, they began cooking hot breakfasts for earthquake survivors. By dawn, a long line of people had gathered in front of the center for comfort and meals. There had been no way for the Tzu Chi center to announce that it was going to carry out earthquake relief work, but people knew that the organization was the natural place to turn to for help.[1]

By 5:00 A.M. a specially equipped truck had arrived from the larger Tzu Chi branch in the central city of Taichung and began to report on the extent of the damage by radio telephone (ordinary cell phones did not work) to the Tzu Chi headquarters in Hualien. Later in the morning Tzu Chi began delivering medical supplies and personnel. Eventually, Tzu

Figure 1. Earthquake destruction, September 21, 1999, Taichung County.

Chi would raise more than 250 million U.S. dollars for earthquake relief. In addition, it mobilized almost two hundred thousand volunteers
to help with rescue, cleanup, and reconstruction.[2]

I myself was shaken out of bed by the quake and forced to flee to an
empty parking lot, where I stood in the rain for several hours as succes-
sive aftershocks shook the ground. It was only my second night in
Taipei—a terrible but ironically appropriate beginning for a project to
study the role of religion along the social, political, and cultural fault
lines of modern Asia. As it turned out, the rupture in the geological fault
line helped to bring into sharper relief some of the sociological fault lines,

even as the response of Taiwan's religious groups demonstrated Asian cultural resources for repairing the ensuing damage.

Thus, in the name of participant observation research—and out of a more basic desire to do something to respond to this human tragedy—my wife and I soon found ourselves taking part in a Tzu Chi project to build a "Great Love Village" for people who had lost their homes in the quake. Tzu Chi is a philanthropic foundation that claims four million members. The minimal qualification for membership is a commitment to contribute a certain amount of money (which could be as low as a few U.S. dollars) every month. But the members are differentiated into circles with different levels of responsibility and commitment. At the lowest level are the volunteers (zhigong—a term that conveys more of a sense of moral dignity than the ordinary word for volunteer, yigong), who commit themselves to regular work on one of Tzu Chi's projects, such as visiting the poor and sick, helping with the moral education of children, or cleaning up the environment. A more exclusive group is the faith corps, which consists of men responsible for logistics and security during Tzu Chi events. A still more exclusive group consists of the approximately seventeen thousand commissioners (originally all women, but now about one-third male) who solicit contributions, organize volunteers, and generally promote the Tzu Chi spirit. At the top of all of this is Dharma Master Cheng Yen, a Buddhist nun, and her convent of about one hundred nuns located in the city of Hualien.

The Tzu Chi foundation has branches in the major cities of Taiwan, and each branch is divided into various districts. Responsibility for the particular building project that I participated in was allocated to the Taipei branch (even though the project itself took place near the central city of Taichung), and different districts within Taipei supplied workers on different days. Each group of workers included commissioners, faith corps members, regular volunteers, and ordinary members who had been moved by the magnitude of the emergency.

Tzu Chi mobilized one hundred and eighty thousand volunteers and spent over US$100 million to construct new temporary housing for earthquake victims. Even more money and volunteer effort were deployed to provide medical care and social welfare services, as well as to rebuild schools destroyed in the quake. The relief housing was built in clusters throughout the central part of Taiwan, which had borne the brunt of the earthquake damage, and was meant to provide earthquake victims with a comfortable community environment until they could rebuild homes of their own. (Most people in these temporary houses have now successfully made the transition to homes of their own.) Our site was designated "Great Love Village 17" and consisted of 116 houses built upon land donated by a local businessman. Most other such housing developments were built on land allocated by the government, and consisted of up to 340 houses.

At first glance, the building site reminded me of a Habitat for Humanity project in the United States. There were piles of prefabricated building materials and well-organized teams of volunteer workers pouring cement, erecting walls, building roofs, and installing doors. A closer look revealed significant differences, however. First of all, there were uniforms. The great majority of workers were Tzu Chi volunteers, who all wore identical navy blue shirts, white pants, and white athletic shoes. They even had identical hardhats, white with a blue logo. Tzu Chi likes uniforms because they suppress individual differences in worldly wealth and status. (It even requires the faculty at its university to wear uniforms.) The uniforms, however, bear the marks of Tzu Chi's internal status system. Insignia on the shirts indicate if the wearer is a commissioner, faith corps member, or ordinary volunteer; and within these ranks, whether one is a group leader or not. Tzu Chi is thus more than an efficient organization for collecting money and mobilizing volunteers: it is a religious and social movement. The Tzu Chi flag (a blue logo of a lotus flower and a ship sailing the sea on a white background) was displayed at the entrance of the worksite, and in the center of the site a large sign proclaimed that this was the "Tzu Chi world."

The Tzu Chi world is full of joy (*xiqi*—a term they use to describe the happiness that comes with enlightenment. Its usual English translation would be "bliss," but I avoid the term here because to Westerners it may connote more of a self-absorbed satisfaction rather than the extroverted engagement with the world that is characteristic of Tzu Chi Buddhists). Buddhist hymns with sprightly modern melodies played constantly in the background. There were slogans in all central places about working happily together, giving with gratitude, and receiving with joy. The Tzu Chi world is a world of gentleness and tolerance (the distinctive dress that Tzu Chi members wear is called the "garment of gentleness and patience"), which is expressed in the quiet and considerate tones with which the workers addressed one another—this contrasted markedly with the profane gruffness of some heavy equipment operators who had been hired for the project. Their world is above all about "great love," which is the resonant amalgamation of the little love in many hearts working together.[3]

Figure 2. Building a Great Love Village.

The Tzu Chi volunteers undoubtedly had their normal share of human frailties. Many of them were managerial or professional workers, whose success depended on prevailing in the endless competition that is part of a dynamic market economy. But while they were at the Tzu Chi worksite, on Tzu Chi business, they usually behaved in a remarkably cooperative way and adopted the demeanor of cheerful generosity. This was true for all Tzu Chi events that I attended in Taiwan.

Indeed, maintaining a positive attitude was neither a prerequisite nor a byproduct of their work—it was an integral part of their work. The volunteers treated their work not simply as an instrument to achieve some good end, but as an expression and actualization of their Buddhist sense of interconnectedness with all beings. Work was a kind of ritual, the right performance of which was more important than its efficiency. There was no Tzu Chi way of swinging a hammer, but there was a Tzu Chi way of serving food. The kitchen workers handed out chopsticks with two hands and a bow. The recipient was supposed to bow too. When eating, one was supposed to hold the rice bowl with the index finger and thumb, to sit straight, and to consume every last grain of one's rice. (When I did not do this, my companions gently but firmly pointed out the proper etiquette.) Regardless of what they are doing, the Tzu Chi members are expected to maintain a graceful bearing and a calm, deliberate manner.

Figure 3. Great Love Village completed.

Tzu Chi was the largest and most sophisticated non-governmental contributor to the earthquake relief, but it was by no means alone. Monks, nuns, and many lay volunteers from the organization called Buddha's Light Mountain, or Foguangshan, were also a highly visible and effective presence. A somewhat smaller community, Dharma Drum Mountain, set up "comfort the heart service teams" to provide psychological counseling from a Buddhist perspective. The Daoist Enacting Heaven Temple (Hsing Tien Kung) in Taipei donated US$6 million for earthquake relief.

Besides providing material help, some of these organizations played a crucial public role in providing meaning for a stunned population. Huge pictures of Dharma Master Sheng Yen of Dharma Drum Mountain were posted in Taipei subway stations and printed as full-page ads in newspapers, together with the slogan "Get going Taiwan!" In widely broadcast television lectures, Sheng Yen encouraged Taiwanese not to think of the disaster as the result of bad karma from previous sins, but instead as an important opportunity to make Taiwan safer and better for future generations. Meanwhile Master Hsing Yun of Buddha's Light Mountain was offering similar reassurance, while Master Cheng Yen of Tzu Chi was urging Taiwanese to show one another compassionate care in this time of trial.

Such activities were a powerful public display of a remarkable religious renaissance that has been taking place in Taiwan from the mid-1980s up to the present—one part of a resurgence of public religious belief and practice that has been taking place throughout the world within the past generation.[4] It came as a great and pleasant surprise to me, for both personal and scholarly reasons.

The personal reasons first. I started out my adult career as a Catholic missionary—a member of the Maryknoll Fathers—in 1968 in Taiwan. Full of idealism, I hoped to bring the Christian message to the island. As I saw it at the time, this primarily meant trying to spread a message of love and hope that would help people in Taiwan to care for each other and to wisely confront the challenges of their time. If this led to an increase in converts to the Catholic Church, fine, but, in my mind at least, it was not the main goal. As it turned out, I never made a single convert. After three years in Taiwan I left my missionary society and undertook an academic career, with the goal of helping myself and others gain a better understanding of the Asian cultures that I had come to see as so intriguing, so important, and so overwhelming. Now, three decades later I was returning home, as it were, to the scene of some of my most formative experiences. And I was finding modern expressions of love and hope in places I would never have dreamed of in 1968. Thirty years ago, Buddhist and Daoist temples undoubtedly forged bonds of compassion and solidarity among their followers—but they had seemed premodern, remnants of an agrarian past in a society that was just starting to undergo rapid modernization. Thirty years before, I had assumed that a spirit of love and hope appropriate to the modern world would have to come from outside, from Christianity. The religious renaissance that I witnessed at the beginning of the twenty-first century showed that I had been wrong. But by now, I was delighted to see love and hope emerge anywhere, in any guise, no matter what the origin.

I was pleasantly surprised not just because of the idiosyncratic mixture of idealism and naïveté that had been part of my own biography. Much that I had learned in my academic career had failed to prepare me for the religious transformations that I was seeing in Taiwan. Most scholars whose work I read in the 1970s assured me that modernization inevitably entailed secularization, which meant that traditional religions would decline as modernization proceeded. This set of assumptions, dressed up in the jargon of social science, has now fallen apart in the face of vigorous religious movements all over the world.[5] The emperor of secular social science turned out to have no clothes. But then new sets of secular scholarly assumptions coalesced in the 1980s and 1990s. One group of such assumptions held that religious movements were inherently reactionary—attempts by losers to take revenge on the winners in the modern political economy. One sees this line of argument often in discussions of Islamist movements.[6] Other assumptions held that some religious or moral revitalization movements represent an alternative form of modernity that is incompatible with the democratic forms supposedly achieved in the West. One sometimes sees this line of argument in discussions about Confucian cultures in East Asia.[7]

In the 1990s, not only influential Western scholars (Samuel Huntington), but also influential Asian leaders (Lee Kuan Yew, the former prime minister of Singapore) agreed that the cultural traditions of East Asian societies were not conducive to democratic governance. It was said that these cultures were based on a Confucian tradition that subordinated the individual to society and emphasized the prerogatives of authority over the rights of the citizen. As Lee Kuan Yew put it, "The Confucianist view of order between subject and ruler helps in the rapid transformation of society. . . . I believe that what a country needs to develop is discipline more than democracy. Democracy leads to undisciplined and disorderly conditions."[8] Apologists of "Asian values" like Lee Kuan Yew claimed that such communitarian and authoritarian values made Asian societies superior to Western societies because only Asian values could maintain the social stability necessary for economic growth in an interdependent modern world. Apologists for Western (i.e., American) values like Samuel Huntington suggested that Asian civilizations were morally inferior to Western democratic traditions, but politically threatening enough to bring about a "clash of civilizations."[9] From this point of view, the spread of democratic freedoms would necessitate "modernizing" Asian societies by replacing their traditional values with Western values. Either way, both sides shared the consensus that Asian values were not compatible with liberal democracy.

The religious movements I encountered in Taiwan demolish both sets of assumptions. The people introduced in this book are by no means malcontented losers in the modern world. They are successful middle-class citizens who have contributed to and who rejoice in modern high-tech economic development. Nor are they anti-democratic. I will show, in fact, how these religious transformations have played very positive roles in the consolidation of democracy in Taiwan.

As a sociologist who has spent the last thirty years studying modern social theory and doing studies of East Asian societies, I found these groups surprising. I also think they will surprise most American and European

readers whose intellectual worlds have been formed by these theories—
and it is a pleasant surprise. The groups I will discuss here have helped
bring about a democratic modernity, but one somewhat different than
what we know in the West. It suggests the possibilities of a fruitful dialogue between civilizations: a genuine, mutually enriching learning rather
than competition and conflict. I like to think that a few of the best of my
naïve, good intentions as a Catholic missionary three decades ago were
small seeds that fell on fertile soil and produced good fruit—a different
kind than I would have imagined, but well worth tasting.

Another contribution I hope this book will make is to direct much-
needed and deserved attention to religious developments in East Asia.
As a participant in a series of dialogues sponsored by the Ethikon Institute on secular and religious (Christian, Jewish, Islamic, Buddhist, and
Confucian) perspectives on the moral constitution of civil society, I have
become all too familiar with the temptation to focus these discussions
on the relative clarity of dead doctrines rather than the messy contemporary practices of living traditions. The temptation is exacerbated by
the dearth of materials about the political implications of these living
traditions, especially in Asia. Some excellent monographs in English have
recently been published on several of the religious movements discussed
in this book, and there is a small flood of Chinese language dissertations
and research reports about them emerging in Taiwan.[10] As far as I know,
however, there is not one work that introduces these religious developments to the wide range of public citizens who are concerned with the
changing interactions between religion, civil society, and politics in the modern world. Those who consider such issues have been focusing most of
their attention on Islamic revivals in the Middle East and Africa, the spread
of evangelical Christianity in Latin America and Africa, and the religiously
driven "culture wars" in the United States. One reason for the lack of attention, perhaps, is that the public influence of East Asian religious movements has been quieter than those cited above—they have not been im-
plicated in as much dramatic social conflict or political violence.[11]

Yet in many cases the influence of these movements has nonetheless
been profound, with long-term consequences. Although in Taiwan (as I
shall argue in this book) the consequences have been basically benign,
this is no reason to ignore them. They give us hope that we can accept
the benefits of a globalized modernity, while finding peaceful resolution
to some of its social dislocations.

These dislocations are certainly visible in Taiwan, which sits on top
of some of some the most dangerous political, social, and cultural—not

to mention geological—fault lines in Asia. There is, first of all, the political fault line which pits an independent-minded Taiwan against an increasingly powerful People's Republic of China (PRC), which threatens to go to war, if necessary, to reunite the two. This is a war that could ultimately engage both the United States and Japan, and which could lead to catastrophic consequences for the whole world.

This political fault line intersects with powerful social and cultural fault lines. Taiwan is a vigorous but fragile democracy that emerged less than twenty years ago from an authoritarian regime, and the rules of the game for political contests keep changing.[12] Politics is often marred by corruption. Bickering, intrigue, and general ineptitude often result in legislative gridlock. And under the messiness of Taiwanese politics was a tectonic shift in public opinion that, in early 2000, led to an unprecedented defeat of the ruling Nationalist Party (KMT) and the accession to the presidency of Chen Shui-bian, whose Democratic Progressive Party (DPP) openly advocated Taiwan's independence from China—an event that has increased the threat of war in the Taiwan Strait.[13]

Taiwan's unstable political fault line is further connected with deep social cleavages, divided between Mainlanders, the group that immigrated to the island after the defeat of the KMT in China's civil war in 1949, and native Taiwanese. The Taiwanese are further divided into ethno-linguistic groups—the majority Hoklo, the Hakka, and various tribes of indigenous aborigines.[14]

Finally, all of the above divisions are complicated by fault lines within Taiwan's culture, which are derived from the confusions and ambiguities caused by the island's rapid transition—within little more than a generation—from an agrarian society, dominated by extended families living within farming villages, to an urban society, driven by mobile professionals within a high-tech economy.

Everyone should be concerned about the fate of Taiwan. Although it is a small island with only 23 million inhabitants, it is worth close attention because it sits on top of a highly unstable political, social, and cultural Asian fault zone. The rise of Asia as the world's most dynamic center of wealth, power, and cultural creativity is perhaps the single greatest challenge for a global order that has for centuries been dominated by Europe and now the United States. A breakdown along some of the fault lines centered on Taiwan could, in the worst-case scenario, become the epicenter for a catastrophe of global proportions. The stories I tell in this book give some hope for the ways in which such breakdowns might be avoided. In addition, as I have indicated in the preceding pages, they raise general issues that go well beyond specific concerns about Taiwanese society.

THEMES

We can summarize the general issues around two main themes. By studying several prominent religious groups in Taiwan, I want to show more generally how religion affects movements toward democracy. I also want to demonstrate how progressive forms of religion grow.

First, *religion and democracy*. A remarkable religious renaissance—a revitalization, reform, and renewal of Buddhism and Daoism to meet the needs of the new middle classes in a modernizing society—has taken place in Taiwan. This renaissance has coincided with Taiwan's transition to democracy. I think that the coincidence is evidence of causation—mutual causation. Taiwan's religious renaissance was not only encouraged by the early phases of transition to democracy, but it also helped to make that transition successful. Although, as I have suggested in the preceding paragraphs, Taiwan's democracy has often seemed on the verge of chaos, it has not fallen into chaos, and one important reason that it has not done so has been the moderating, healing, and solidarity producing influence of the religious groups that I will describe in this book.

The Taiwan case has implications that go well beyond the country. The positive contribution of Taiwan's religious renaissance has gone largely unnoticed by Western experts on Taiwanese politics. The reason may have to do with a general skepticism among mainstream scholars about the capacity of religion to play a positive public role in the building of modern, liberal democratic institutions. This case, however, is another piece of evidence for what my coauthors and I argued in *Habits of the Heart* and *The Good Society*: A purely secular liberalism—a liberalism founded simply on the rational self-interest of individual citizens—is not a viable basis for a stable, robust polity. It is evidence for the notion that all coherent states rest on holy ground.[15]

But if this is so, they—we—rest on shaky ground. Religion in history has often been the source of tribal and ethnic conflict, a justification for political oppression, and a crusading impulse behind imperialist aggression, while at the same time enabling the self-transcendence that makes civilization possible. This leads to the second, and for me the more important, theme of this book: *a search for hope that the progressive promises of religion will overcome the regressive perils of religion in the modern world.*

The regressive and progressive aspects of most forms of religion are intimately interconnected. One formulation of this interconnection can be based on Robert Bellah's scheme of "religious evolution."[16] Bellah argues that religious symbolism and practice is at the base of all human culture and that more differentiated and complex forms of religious symbolism and organization are built upon simpler forms. Religious practice is a way in which humans come to terms with the "ultimate conditions of existence." In its simplest "primitive" forms, religion is thoroughly fused with all aspects of the moral order of small communities. Religious rituals celebrate the moral bonds that give the small group its fundamental identity, set it apart from others, affirm its members' particular responsibilities for one another, and ensure its continuity over time. When a social world organized in terms of small groups gives way to larger kingdoms, dominated by rulers who set themselves apart from ordinary people and dominate their kingdoms through specialized staffs of administrators and priests, religious teaching and practice becomes more complex. It usually refers to gods who stand apart from ordinary people, and to moral rules that need to be interpreted and enforced by priests. Often, rulers themselves are seen as divine, or at least as the privileged emissaries of the gods. Yet, even at this stage of "archaic" religion, the earlier, primitive forms remain. The myths and rituals celebrating the special identity of smaller groups—clans, tribes—remain. And subjects of a kingdom usually see the kingdom as a whole (not just the ruler and his court) as uniquely sacred, set apart from all other kingdoms and groups.

A major breakthrough in religious symbolism and organization came in the middle of the first millennium B.C.E. During this period—which the German philosopher Karl Jaspers called the axial age, because it was an axis of world history, the time when "Man as we know him today came into being"[17]—there arose transcendent religious visions based on universal principles applicable to all tribes and nations. The major initiators of these visions of transcendence were Confucius, Mencius, Laozi (Lao-tzu), Gautama Buddha, the Hebrew prophets, and the classic Greek philosophers.[18] According to Jaspers, the spiritual movements associated with these thinkers had important features in common. Though "widely divergent in their conviction and dogma," these paths all enabled humans not to accept the world as it appears, but to judge themselves and their surrounding world according to universal, transcendent principles.[19] This set the stage for radical, creative questioning of the visible world. People gained the capacity to criticize established social and political arrangements and to imagine alternatives. By recognizing their limitations, they could seek higher goals. Part of the axial breakthrough was the recognition that humans needed rational reflection to understand these higher goals, even though in each case the form of this reflection was somewhat different, and, in the case of ancient Israel, reasoned discourse was to be directed by divine revelation.[20]

The axial breakthroughs to what Robert Bellah calls modern religion were built upon the legacies of primitive and archaic forms of religious thought, indeed, they were to an important degree dependent on them, and these earlier forms are still with us. The great religious and moral reformers of the axial age saw themselves as fulfilling the ultimate meaning embedded within their traditions. The power of the axial breakthroughs came from the way that they paradoxically connected radical innovation with the affirmation of traditions.

The religious innovators of the axial age did not so much abandon the myths and rituals that made people members of particular bounded communities, such as families, lineages, kingdoms, or city-states. They reinterpreted them so as to enable people to see them as partial representations of a higher moral order. The universalistic visions of a spiritual elite could then find a connection to the sacred stories and ritual practices of ordinary people bound to their particular communities. The axial visions gained world transforming power because of their dynamic tension with popular practices.

The breakthrough to transcendence that one sees in the origins of Buddhism, Daoism, Confucianism, monotheistic Judaism, and later in Christianity and Islam, is always tentative. Most of the actual communities and institutions that currently base themselves on the teachings of Gautama Buddha, Laozi, Confucius, the Hebrew prophets, Jesus, or Mohammed are actually forms of primitive or archaic religion. To cite just a few examples, when people identify a certain type of Christianity with the "American way of life," such appeals are more like evocations of a primitive religious impulse than they are responses to the call of Jesus to subordinate all human attachments to the unconditional love of God and neighbor. Similarly, when bishops or mullahs demand absolute obedience in the name of God, they are more like archaic religious leaders than prophets in the tradition of their religions' founders. In an interdependent world, the zealous fragmentation produced by primitive religious impulses is obviously extremely dangerous, even deadly. In a post-Enlightenment world in which human dignity is based on the freedom of individuals to shape their lives in accordance with their critically informed consciences, the authoritarian submission demanded by archaic religion is a defeat for human aspiration.

If it really is true, as Bellah argues, that "nothing is ever lost" in human religious consciousness, we cannot expect that these primitive and archaic impulses will disappear. What we might hope for is that the progressive quest for transcendent meaning and universal morality that was the founding impulse of the great world religions will continue. For there to be a sustainable liberal peace in a world as interdependent as ours, we will need various forms of prophetic reinvigoration of this axial quest.

The religious groups I introduce in this book each seem to represent some degree of creative reinvigoration of the search for universal human interconnection that is often buried within the primitive and archaic layers of the legacy of the great world religions. They are fragile, progressive religious breakthroughs that show the way toward a more hopeful, peaceful world in which human differences will be respected while the basis for a deeper human solidarity is simultaneously affirmed. I want to show how such good things grow.

Before introducing the groups further, I will first briefly describe the environment in which they grew and tell how I studied them.

CHAPTER I

The Taiwanese Religious Context

RELIGIOUS TRADITION
AND TRANSFORMATION IN TAIWAN

The Taiwanese religious renaissance studied here is mainly a renaissance of Buddhism and Daoism. Despite (or perhaps because of) having received privileged treatment by Taiwan's Nationalist (KMT) government during the 1950s and 1960s, most Christian denominations in Taiwan, which at most only accounted for about 7 percent of the population, seem to be losing practicing members and declining in influence, except among the Taiwanese aborigines, who remain mostly Christian.[1] Today it is large, rapidly growing Buddhist organizations (and to a lesser extent some Daoist temples) that are finding innovative ways of helping the poor and the sick, educating the young, and providing spiritual guidance for middle-class people trying to set priorities for their lives amid the myriad choices presented by a modern consumer society.

However, as we shall demonstrate below, the Buddhist and Daoist beliefs that provide the formal identity of these organizations are thoroughly intertwined with Confucian moral ideals. This involves a modern continuation of a long history of creative transformation of the Buddhist and Daoist traditions. Buddhism, for example, teaches that the best way to live is to "leave one's family" *(chujia)* and to become a monk. At face value this is at odds with Confucian insistence that filial piety is central to a morally good life. Yet despite persisting tensions throughout most of the past two millennia, orthodox Buddhism and Daoism have generally made peace with the Confucian tradition by incorporating key elements of the latter into their own practices. They not only accepted the centrality of filial piety, at least for those who were not monastics, but also legitimized and reinforced family commitments.

The groups studied here continue this process of adaptation, but in a modern form. They, and the Confucianism they are adapting to, represent changing, modernizing forms of old traditions. These modernizing Buddhist and Daoist groups are indeed helping to modernize Confucianism in such a way as to make it compatible with a modern, democratic political economy. To readers who may have been taught that Confucianism supports hierarchical authoritarianism rather than egalitarian democracy (and therefore constitutes a basis for a clash of civilizations with the Western democratic tradition), it will come as a surprise to see the extent that the groups studied here develop and popularize forms of the Confucian tradition that not only tolerate democracy, but also actively support it.

By this tradition, I do not mean "Confucian*ism*," a canonical set of fixed doctrines from which clear moral rules can be derived. I refer instead to a broad, flexible way of moral discourse that can be used to discuss current moral dilemmas in the light of long, diverse traditions of Asian scholarship. This "Confucian persuasion" (as Tu Wei-ming calls it) seeks a holistic vision of the world, in which self, community, nature, and the ultimate principles of things are integrated in a mutually interdependent harmony. It aims to achieve this harmony by cultivating certain virtues, certain habits of mind and heart, which are developed through the practice of rituals of social propriety and through study of the reasons behind such rituals. The most important virtues are those that bolster strong family relations, which are seen as based on interdependent, hierarchically structured roles: parent-child, husband-wife, and older-younger sibling. These primary family relationships become a model for all other social relations, for instance, between political authorities and subjects, or employers and employees. Confucian moral discourse assumes that there is no fundamental conflict between the family and wider society. Apparent conflicts should be resolved by cultivating the self to understand one's familial responsibilities in the broadest possible context.[2]

This way of thinking about moral order is different from the logic of Western-style liberal philosophy, which is more concerned with protecting the autonomy of individuals than with ensuring the integrity of a societal whole. Rather than assuming that there are certain virtues that all good persons should strive to cultivate, classical liberalism would allow each person to pursue his or her own version of the good, so long as this does not harm others. The starting point for the liberal imagination is not the family—and especially not the hierarchical, unchosen relationship between children and parents—but the autonomous individual, whose significant relationships are based on voluntary contracts with other autonomous individuals. Liberalism assumes that there are indeed fundamental conflicts between different components of society and seeks to protect individuals by attributing to them inalienable rights. The most basic rights constitute a sphere of privacy, protected from the demands of the state and other public institutions.[3]

Many Americans believe that the liberal tradition, based on the philosophy of John Locke and enshrined in the Declaration of Independence and the Constitution, is the universal foundation for modernity. As the 2002 National Security Strategy of the United States declared, "The great struggles of the twentieth century between liberty and totalitarianism ended with a decisive victory for the forces of freedom—and a single sustainable model for national success: freedom, democracy, and free enterprise. . . . These values of freedom are right and true for every person in every society."[4]

If one takes this point of view seriously, one would have to argue that, for Asian societies to successfully modernize, they must replace Confucian ways of thinking with Western liberal ones. Many Asians, including those discussed in this book, disagree. They may accept, even embrace, the idea that individuals should have more autonomy than they had in premodern societies—that they should choose where and with whom they want to live, their lifestyle, their religion, and their form of government. They want economies and governments that increase opportunities for such choices. Yet they are often worried about the insecurity, irresponsibility, and general disorientation that accompany modernization. The Taiwanese people discussed here think that they can enjoy the benefits of modernity while avoiding its liabilities, by creatively adapting Confucian ways of thinking to contemporary conditions.

They are doing this through their participation in newly emerging Buddhist and Daoist associations. On one level these associations seem to fit traditional religious practice into a modern, liberal model. They are less like traditional temples and monasteries, and more like religious denominations in the United States—that is, they are not public institutions that hold sway over people by custom, but private voluntary associations that people join by consent. But they are also unlike most "Americanized" Buddhist and Daoist associations in the United States (as opposed to those formed by recent immigrants), which seem mostly oriented toward individual enlightenment or spiritual consolation, and do not systematically promote engagement in public life. The Taiwanese associations studied in this book transcend the role of private voluntary association. They aspire not just to provide social fellowship and personal salvation to their members, but to influence society as a whole, to shape the way their society takes care of its sick and vulnerable members, and to influence the way it confronts public problems. The general way in which they want to undertake this shaping is to expand the sense of shared responsibility that, in the Confucian tradition, is supposedly at the basis of good, harmonious family life.

At the same time, in ways that will be discussed in individual chapters, they seek to expand Confucian, Buddhist, and Daoist discourse in such a way as to accommodate desires for individual freedom and equality. They discourage blind submission to authority and encourage individual initiative. They encourage equality between men and women. They also encourage scientific research and technological innovation. The result is the promotion of social practices that are superficially similar to those of middle-class people in most urban industrial societies around the world, but with different understandings of the moral basis of these practices, understandings that lead to subtle differences.

THE RESEARCH PROCESS

The information used in this book comes from a combination of participant observation, interviews with leaders and followers, and archival research conducted on four religious organizations that have become popular among Taiwan's emerging middle classes. If I had had more time and resources, I could have made a case for considering other groups.[5] But these four organizations could be widely recognized as important and influential examples of popular middle-class religious engagement. I was aided in my research by two outstanding Taiwanese assistants, Kuo Ya-yu and Ho Hua-chin. I conducted my interviews in Mandarin Chinese, which is officially the national language of Taiwan. My two assistants were native speakers of Taiwanese (Hoklo or *Minnan yu*), the preferred idiom of most native Taiwanese, which compensated for my own lack of fluency.

Three of the four religious organizations are Buddhist: Tzu Chi, whose headquarters are in the city of Hualien; Buddha's Light Mountain, head-quartered near Kaohsiung; and Dharma Drum Mountain, headquartered near Taipei. All of these organizations have branches not only in other parts of Taiwan, but also in other parts of the world. These are three of the largest and best-known organizations that have become popular among Taiwan's middle classes since the 1980s, when Taiwan began to make its transition to democracy. I gratefully acknowledge the advice of the distinguished sociologist Hsin-huang Michael Hsiao in selecting them. To these three Buddhist organizations, I added a case study of a Daoist association in Taipei, Enacting Heaven Temple (Hsing Tien Kung), which is also very popular among the urban middle classes and is well known for its efforts to build a public library, hospital, and university.

These four groups share several common characteristics. On a super-ficial level, they have all developed extensive organizations of laypeople (in addition to the core of monks, nuns, and priests), accumulated ex-tensive financial assets (in some cases reaching the billions of dollars), made sophisticated use of the media (books, magazines, videos, and web-sites), and share doctrines and practices that come from a common wrestling with the dilemmas of Taiwan's modernization.

On a deeper level, another common characteristic that all of these groups share is at least partially demythologized traditional beliefs. That is, instead of taking these beliefs as a solid, literal representation of a world beyond the one of ordinary experience, they see their beliefs as symbolic expressions of the challenges of common human life. Reminis-cent of the quest of the Protestant theologian Dietrich Boenhoffer for a "religionless Christianity,"[6] some of the members of these Taiwanese or-ganizations describe their faith as non-religious. There is much talk about "cultivating behavior" (xiu xing), a term well known from books on Con-fucian philosophy, but one that I had never heard much in ordinary con-versation until I became engaged with these groups. The term refers to the process of spiritual development that enables one to understand how to apply them in the broadest possible contexts. Each of the groups' nu-merous multimedia publications aim to facilitate this understanding.

The norms of filial piety, for instance, have to be adapted to a world of high-tech occupations in which, to be successful, children have to learn to think critically for themselves, and may eventually have to move far away from their parents. The religious groups that I have studied all say that one should still hold on to the principle of filial piety under these circumstances, but that one must understand it in a deeper way and ex-ercise it using new methods. To be truly filial, one must not blindly obey one's parents, but thoughtfully assimilate the lessons they have taught and carry on their legacy in a cosmopolitan world that they may no longer be able to comprehend.[7] The collective work of these religious groups is an example of how to do this. They devote themselves to reworking the lessons that Taiwanese parents typically impart to their children and encourage followers to help strangers in need as a grown child would help his or her own parents. For example, those living far from home can fulfill filial duties by generously caring for another's parents—and in the process gain confidence that other members of the religious community will be on hand to take good care of their own parents. Self-cultivation, then, is not just improvement of one's individual self (the "small self"—*xiao wo*), but a broadening of vision that generates affiliations to a wider community (the "big self"—*da wo*).

Another common characteristic of the groups studied here is a devaluation of ritual. Though all of them still regularly practice rituals, they all claim to subordinate external ritual practice to internalized morality. Along with a devaluation of ritual comes a dilution of hierarchy. In their formal structure they remain authoritarian, not democratic. The dharma master in the Buddhist organizations is a supreme leader whose decisions are final. The priests of Enacting Heaven Temple have unchallenged authority in interpretations of ritual and practice. But if rituals led by Buddhist monks or nuns, or by Daoist priests, are no longer as important as the good intentions harbored in a well-cultivated heart, then laypeople can be just as important as ordained masters. All of the organizations studied here have created dynamic associations of lay followers that have rapidly expanded and are carrying out much of the public work of the organization. One secret of the success of these lay associations is that their members are encouraged to take initiative. Even though formal hierarchy remains, its power is diluted by, as well as disseminated through, the active initiatives of the lay associations.

A final common characteristic of all these groups is the rationalization of their organizations. Events in all of the Buddhist organizations run on extremely precise schedules. Even Enacting Heaven Temple seems more orderly than most Daoist temples, and its foundation offices, with their neatly attired professional staff working at banks of computers, seem a very model of rational efficiency.

Yet these organizations are not bureaucratic. "We are not an apparatus," says a Tzu Chi commissioner. "People don't come to work every day. So everybody has to know what has to be done and how to fit in." Authority is not passed down from top to bottom through layers of specialized offices. Since these organizations depend so much on volunteers, they have to elicit their goodwill, not enact their obedience, and rely on their general skills rather than any specialized training. The religious organizations do this by putting great effort into educating their key volunteers to understand the vision of the organization and to articulate this to each other. A key part of the vision is that work should be carried out in a self-conscious, disciplined, efficient way, and that members should constantly discuss this with one another and encourage one another to act accordingly.

RELIGION AND MIDDLE-CLASS STATUS DIFFERENCES

All of the previously mentioned characteristics fit well with the experiences of mobile middle classes. But the emerging middle classes of Taiwan—and for that matter, of most of modernizing East Asia—are not unified social groupings. They have a number of different segments, and in Taiwan they are also divided by ethnicity. The four organizations discussed here represent the wide range (though not necessarily the full range) of middle-class segments in Taiwan.

By reputation, these four religious organizations correspond to different fractions of Taiwan's middle class. There was considerable consensus among my interviewees about the following distinctions: Enacting Heaven Temple is the most downscale of the four. It is most attractive to shopkeepers, clerical workers, and retail clerks. Buddha's Light Mountain attracts fairly affluent business owners as well as government officials and politicians. Tzu Chi has especially strong attraction to people in modern managerial and service professions. Dharma Drum Mountain has special appeal to intellectuals.

Survey data, however, indicates that actual membership is more fluid than these imputed distinctions.[8] Yet the distinctions made in popular discourse provide a good map to the complexities of Taiwan's emerging middle classes. Their prosperity has arisen from a number of different sources: globalized technology, which is heavily dependent on research and development; small-scale, entrepreneurial manufacturing, which is networked with counterparts throughout greater China; government patronage (especially connected with the KMT); and local service industries. People whose path to success stems from different sources usually acquire different ways of thinking and feeling that leads them toward different religious affiliations.[9]

Middle-class Taiwanese utilize the distinctions in reputation of the different religious groups to provide a map of relative social status, and individuals try to celebrate or enhance their status by moving between different religious groups.[10] Religious affiliations intersect with and reinforce status distinctions created by consumer advertising.

Besides providing a map of different status stemming from occupation and education, the distinctions commonly made between the different religious groups also provide a map of the ethnic divisions that intersect class divisions in Taiwan. Enacting Heaven Temple is thoroughly Taiwanese. Its ceremonies and sermons are all in the Taiwanese language and its practices remain rooted in the folk customs of Taiwanese village life. Tzu Chi is also Taiwanese—its founder is Taiwanese, the language most commonly used in its ceremonies is Taiwanese, and many of its followers take great pride is saying that Tzu Chi represents the best in Taiwanese culture—but a more refined and cosmopolitan Taiwanese identity than that associated with Enacting Heaven Temple. Buddha's Light Mountain is Mainlander.[11] Its founder was from the mainland and has been associated with Mainlander political factions in the KMT. Dharma Drum Mountain is also Mainlander.

With the exception of Enacting Heaven Temple, whose membership is almost entirely Taiwanese, however, the religious groups have become quite mixed ethnically. Although neither Hsing Yun of Buddha's Light Mountain nor Sheng Yen of Dharma Drum Mountain speak Taiwanese, many of their associates do. Their dharma talks are often given half in Mandarin, half in Taiwanese. Participants in their rituals are a mixture of Taiwanese and Mainlander in rough proportion to the mixture in the general population (with perhaps a slight over-representation of Mainlanders). Master Cheng Yen of Tzu Chi speaks both Taiwanese and Mandarin (some interviewees told me that her Mandarin has improved significantly in recent years), and in recent years there have been increasing numbers of Mainlanders participating in the organization, some in high positions.

This gap between what the four organizations *represent* and what they *are* is of great importance sociologically and politically. Taiwan's rapid economic development has produced a middle class full of conflicts. Meanwhile, the island's delicate geopolitical position and conflicted history sets up potentially devastating conflicts between Mainlanders and native Taiwanese. The differences between popular religious organizations could provide a frame of reference for thinking about such social and political divisions. When this happens in other societies, religious groups cán become the agents of violent social polarization. But this has not happened in Taiwan. The groups that I have described have encouraged the blending of different segments of the population and facilitated reconciliation between potentially warring factions. This undoubtedly has helped Taiwan make a relatively peaceful transition to democracy since the end of martial law in 1987.[12]

Though these groups reflect divisions of class and ethnicity, they do so in a way that has kept differences among these interests from becoming antagonistic. To understand how this has happened, we need to consider how the historical development of these organizations has intersected with the particular political history of Taiwan and with the general forces of globalization.

Each of the following chapters in this book thus offers a description of how different segments within Taiwan's middle classes are creatively adapting traditional Asian moral discourse to make sense out of modern conditions. I hope that they give the reader some sense of the flexibility and adaptability of these traditions, as well as some understanding of why these particular forms of revival and adaptation have been taking place in Taiwan and how they are different from movements originating in other parts of Asia. The cases are presented in such a way as to highlight the contributions of these movements to Taiwan's transition to democracy.

To assess these contributions, we need to take a broader look at the sociopolitical history of Taiwan in the late twentieth century.

THE TAIWAN CONTEXT

There is much more to contemporary Taiwanese culture, of course, than Buddhism, Daoism, and creative adaptations of Confucian traditions. Besides a rich and varied folk religious tradition, there are all sorts of practices and values derived from the West.[13] Politicians invoke the ideals of Western liberalism—human rights, democratic competition. Social scientists use the latest economic and "rational choice" theories for political analysis. Entrepreneurs espouse the need for minimally regulated competition. The advertising industry promotes an incessant competition for status within an ever-expanding consumer society. Taiwanese nationalists celebrate the rough-hewn, somewhat belligerent ethos of native Taiwanese culture. Immigrants from mainland China speak of the glories of a common Chinese heritage. In the midst of all these contending voices, all of these pushes and pulls, it is difficult to isolate the exact influence of the middle-class Buddhist and Daoist associations studied here. However, one can plausibly argue that these groups have, at the least, helped Taiwan avoid the kind of religious conflict that has aborted democratic transitions elsewhere, and, at the most, have contributed to the stock of social capital—bonds of trust and capacities for civic cooperation—that is commonly assumed to be the basis of a sustainable democracy.

The Taiwanese trajectory has been full of surprises. When I first arrived in Taiwan in 1968, the island hardly seemed to be a likely candidate for a democratic transition. At the time, the country was under the dictatorial rule of the Nationalist Party (KMT) led by Chiang Kai-shek. The KMT government had assumed control over Taiwan in 1945, following fifty years of colonial rule by Japan. To secure their power, they ruthlessly suppressed the local Taiwanese intellectual and political elite through a "white terror" of widespread killing and imprisonment. When the KMT lost the civil war with the Chinese communists in 1949, many of its leaders and soldiers subsequently fled to Taiwan, with the hope of using the island as a base for a counterattack. In the early 1950s, under the cold war strategy to contain communism, the United States gave the KMT economic and military support, although it discouraged its leaders from making a major effort to roll back China's communist regime. In the name of anti-communist struggle, Chiang Kai-shek's government imposed a martial law that justified dictatorship. The United States government acquiesced in this, sometimes with the rationalization that, because of their "Confucian values," the people of Taiwan were not suited to democracy.[14]

By the early 1970s, however, the government began to lose its grip. Economic development had given rise to an entrepreneurial middle class, which was beginning to become difficult to subject to tight government control. For geopolitical reasons, the United States, Taiwan's principal international sponsor, began a rapprochement with the Maoist regime in mainland China. Chiang Kai-shek had become increasingly infirm, and eventually died in 1975. Chiang Ching-kuo, his son and successor, opened a small political space for opposition, and non-KMT candidates began to contest local elections. By the late 1970s, a loosely networked political opposition began to emerge and found its voice in the magazine *Formosa* (Meilidao zazhi). The opposition picked up strength because of the sense of national crisis brought about when the United States officially normalized diplomatic relations with the People's Republic of China (PRC) in January 1979 and severed its formal ties with Taiwan. Then, in the infamous Kaohsiung incident of December, 1979, the KMT government crushed the nascent opposition movement and put eight of its key leaders on trial.[15]

What appeared to be a defeat for the opposition in the long run turned out to be a victory. The trial of the "Kaohsiung Eight" stirred up public opinion against the KMT's heavy handed methods. It also provoked concerns from the American human rights lobby, at a time when Taiwan's government continued to rely heavily on the United States for military support. Pressures mounted on the KMT to relax controls on political dissent. Opposition candidates became increasingly well organized and successful in local elections.[16]

The opposition also began to emphasize an explosive new theme: Taiwanese self-determination. They had previously focused on the issue of lack of democratic freedom, and had not directly challenged the notion that Taiwan would someday be reunited with mainland China, ideally on terms favorable to Taiwan. There was widespread, if subterranean, resentment among native-born Taiwanese, who constitute about 85 percent of the total population, over their repressive and exploitative treatment by a KMT government composed of Mainlanders, who had seen Taiwan mainly as a staging ground for an attempt to win back political control over China. It was only after Chiang Ching-kuo assumed power in 1975 that the KMT began to invest more in improving the lives of native Taiwanese and recruiting native Taiwanese into its ranks. But the memories of exploitation continued, and there emerged long-repressed desires to construct an authentically Taiwanese national identity, based upon the Taiwanese dialect and local history and cultural traditions. Besides exposing Taiwan to the danger that the PRC would use force to overcome any possibility of Taiwanese self-determination, this new Taiwanese nationalism threatened to open up deep ethnic divisions within Taiwan's society.[17]

Under Chiang Ching-kuo, the KMT for its part tried to counter the incipient Taiwanese nationalism by co-opting more Taiwanese into the KMT, even making Lee Teng-hui, a Taiwanese of Hakka origin, its vice president. In 1987, an ailing Chiang Ching-kuo lifted martial law, which made possible all manner of voluntary associations, including the formation of rival political parties. The following year Chiang Ching-kuo died and Lee Teng-hui became president of Taiwan's government.[18]

These events brought about a new era for Taiwanese civil society. A rich variety of new associations were born, associations representing every imaginable brand of social, cultural, religious, and political interest. The main opposition political party, the Democratic Progressive Party (DPP), began to put together a coalition that played an increasingly important role in Taiwan politics. One product of the new democratic freedoms was an intensification of Taiwanese nationalism, although only a minority of the population seemed willing to risk war by calling for outright independence from mainland China.[19]

It is precisely during this period that there was an explosion in the size and ambitions of the Buddhist and Daoist organizations studied here. Why Buddhist and Daoist rather than Christian? The answer may lie in the KMT's policies of controlling and stifling Buddhism and Daoism during its first three decades of rule on Taiwan.

Part of the KMT's dictatorship entailed the suppression of religion. Although it did not try to eliminate peasant folk religion, the government imposed strict controls on any kind of Buddhist or Daoist organization that might have the potential to mobilize citizens against the government. The KMT aimed to legitimize itself as a secular, modernizing government. While promoting classic Confucian moral virtues (interpreted so as to justify obedience to authoritarian government), the KMT's public education attempted to make students critical of traditional "superstitions." Meanwhile, the government made it difficult for religious leaders to develop more sophisticated understandings of their practices or to use modern forms of organization to expand their influence.[20]

A partial exception to this effort to control and suppress was the KMT's policy toward Christianity. Some of its key supporters in the United States were old China missionaries. Unwilling to alienate such supporters, the KMT gave special privileges to Christians. While it refused to allow Buddhists or Daoists to establish universities, for example, it allowed Catholics to establish Fu Jen University and Protestants to establish Tunghai University. During the 1950s and early 1960s, it also used Protestant and Catholic missionaries as conduits for American donations of food and clothing. During that period, the Christian denominations underwent steady growth. With the exception of the Taiwanese Presbyterian Church, which had long been an incubator of Taiwanese nationalism, most Christian organizations, both Protestant and Catholic, either cooperated with or remained neutral toward the KMT's agenda. In retrospect it is not surprising that, when government restrictions on religious association were lifted and sentiments for a Taiwanese national identity (if not for outright independent statehood) were on the rise, the Taiwanese would favor religious organizations that had a greater claim to be indigenous and that had not been privileged during the years of

KMT dictatorship. Meanwhile, most Christian organizations (the Taiwan Presbyterian Church being an important exception) seem to have declined in membership and influence.[21]

The democratization of Taiwan has been by no means a smooth process, and, in spite of impressive, high-tech-driven economic growth during the 1990s, Taiwanese society has often seemed on the verge of chaos. Ethnic politics have been increasingly contentious. A faction of Mainlanders who strongly favored reunification with China broke off from the KMT and formed the New Party, which regularly garnered about 14 percent of the vote (roughly corresponding to the percentage of Mainlanders in Taiwan) in elections. The KMT itself became split between one faction, led by then President Lee Teng-hui, that increasingly pushed toward the greater autonomy of Taiwan and another faction that advocated a more accommodating stance. The DPP was divided into a core group that strongly supported declaring outright independence from China and a more pragmatic group that did not want to push independence to the point that would bring war. Further factionalization and political maneuvering have resulted in two large coalitions, a "pan-blue" coalition, centered on the accommodationist part of the KMT, and a "pan-green" coalition, centered on the DPP.

Politics, meanwhile, have remained incompletely institutionalized. The rules of the game for political contests have continued to change, and informal norms of political conduct remain instable. Vote-buying and other forms of corruption have been prevalent, in the 1990s especially among KMT politicians, who had more resources than the DPP to engage in such misbehavior—but now the DPP is by no means immune to such corruption. Bickering, infighting, and general ineptitude often lead to legislative gridlock.

In 1996, the PRC tried to use crude intimidation—it conducted "missile tests" off the coast of Taiwan—to pressure voters to reject Lee Teng-hui. The move backfired and Lee won handily. In the 2000 presidential elections, the DPP presidential candidate, Chen Shui-bian, won a plurality in a three-way race and assumed the presidency. Of the multiple factors that made his victory possible, one was widespread disgust at the corruption and incompetence of the ruling KMT.[22] And one factor in the perception of KMT incompetence was their slow and disorganized response to the 1999 earthquake—an incompetence that that was highlighted by the efficiency of Buddhist relief organizations. In public opinion polls taken shortly after the earthquake, only 33 percent agreed that the government's response had been good. This was in contrast to 95 percent who thought that Buddhist relief organizations had done a good job. (The only complaint that might have led to the 5 percent disapproval rate was that the Buddhists served only vegetarian food in their relief operations.)

Chen Shui-bian's administration has not gone smoothly, however, and he has had a difficult time passing any significant legislation. Problems have ranged from the economy, which remained mired in recession throughout the first few years of the twenty-first century (although it has since made a sluggish recovery), to hard-line independence advocates within the DPP who have blocked the relatively pragmatic Chen from making significant progress in easing tensions with the PRC.

As perhaps a desperate move to gain enough votes to win reelection in 2004, Chen, in the fall of 2003, held rallies to push for a new constitution, one that would make Taiwan a "normal, complete, great country"—code words for increased national sovereignty. Beijing warned that any such moves would bring "a disaster for Taiwan."

Chen won reelection by less than thirty thousand votes after having survived an assassination attempt—which his opponents claimed that he staged himself in order to gain a sympathy vote. Beijing responded to Chen's reelection with escalated vitriol and increased threats of military action. Chen continued to have a difficult time passing any significant legislation, and in 2006 he was politically crippled by allegations that members of his family had engaged in political corruption.

One sometimes hears Western experts call Taiwan a "dysfunctional democracy," with free elections but no democratic culture that would enable the various parties to coexist cooperatively. By this definition, most societies that have made the transition from authoritarian rule to democracy within the past two decades could probably be called dysfunctional democracies. Taiwanese political culture continues to have many rough edges and the government sometimes teeters on the brink of disaster. However, there is a more optimistic way of looking at this picture. Despite a history of atrocities committed by Mainlanders against the Taiwanese, the legacy of a harshly authoritarian regime, a "Confucian" cultural tradition that many experts have considered incompatible with democratic values, tensions with mainland China, and a lack of political recognition on the global stage, Taiwan has carried out peaceful transitions of power, managed enough order to sustain a vigorous high-tech economy, maintained the high level of education necessary to develop that economy, instituted a progressive universal health care system, supported a free press, and encouraged a high level of artistic and cultural creativity—this is perhaps the true "Taiwan miracle." In some parts of the world, religion intensifies ethnic conflict, deepens feelings of historical grievance, and turns political causes into crusades. It pours gasoline on the kinds of fires that have afflicted Taiwan. But I will show that just the opposite effect has come from the patterns of religious belief and practice embodied in the four organizations studied here. Their net effect has been to soothe conflict, reconcile differences, and calm political passions. It is too early to tell if they will be sufficient to sustain Taiwan's troubled democracy, but one can make a persuasive argument that without their important contributions, Taiwan's troubles would have been much worse.

CHAPTER 2

Tzu Chi

The Modernization of Buddhist Compassion

Let us begin with the builders of the Great Love villages described in the opening of this book. In terms of size and visible social impact, Tzu Chi, the Buddhist Compassion Relief Association, is the most impressive of the organizations I studied. Its foundress and leader, Master (*shangren,* literally "Above Person") Cheng Yen, has been called the "Mother Teresa of Asia."[1]

Cheng Yen's collection of spiritual writings, *Still Thoughts,* was the basis for most of the slogans displayed at the Great Love Village worksite.[2] Her authority was absolute. When she came to inspect the first houses being built for the earthquake victims, she noted that streets in the housing complex were being paved with asphalt and that one of the bedrooms in the basic model house had no windows—aspects of design that increased the cost-effectiveness of the projects. Cheng Yen, however, declared that the asphalt made the developments feel more like refugee camps than true homes and that it was not good for the human spirit to have to live in windowless rooms. There could be no arguing with a declaration like that; the first houses were torn down and the asphalt was dug up. All Great Love villages now have attractive tiled streets (it lets the earth breathe, say Tzu Chi members) and all rooms have a window.

The intervention was typical of Cheng Yen. She strongly insists on putting a certain vision of human flourishing—one that emphasizes social cooperation and harmony with the environment—ahead of economic efficiency, and she sees this insistence as a way of teaching Buddhism. As

Figure 4. Master Cheng Yen. Permission courtesy of the Buddhist Compassion Relief Tzu Chi Foundation.

an Above Person, the Master's teaching is definitive and her authority is not questioned, which is typical for the heads of Buddhist monasteries. But although Cheng Yen does indeed have charismatic authority and Tzu Chi members quote her words constantly, they do not display her pictures or carry out other such aspects of a personality cult.

TZU CHI AND DEMOCRACY

A tightly knit organization with a religious ideology led by a charismatic leader wielding absolute authority does not seem like a promising foundation for an emerging democracy. Yet I will argue that Tzu Chi has indeed served as such a foundation—even though our Western political theories would have difficulty explaining this. In accounting for the constructiveness of Tzu Chi's contributions to Taiwanese democracy, we will have to expand the scope of our theories of democracy to take into account Asian cultural perspectives and cultural capacities.

The members I spoke with did indeed see Tzu Chi as a vehicle for a spirit of democratic freedom. After dinner on my first day at the house-building worksite, some of the men (who tend to be less pious than the women) commented on the growth of Tzu Chi. An organization like this would never have been allowed during the Chiang Kai-shek regime, they said. Its full growth had only become possible with the relaxation of the martial law that had institutionalized Taiwan's political authoritarianism. Previously, Tzu Chi would not have been allowed because it was too effectively organized. As one of the men said, "It does things its way rather than the government's way."

From their point of view, Tzu Chi was a product of Taiwan's newly found democratic freedom—a self-governing voluntary association, one of tens of thousands of such associations that came into existence after the end of martial law, proof of a hunger on the part of citizens to manage their own affairs rather than take orders from the government.[3] Although in form Tzu Chi is an autonomous free association in a liberalizing democratic society, in spirit it represents something other than the classic Western liberal understanding of what a free association is and what it should do.

In Western liberalism, a free association is an expression of the autonomous choices of its constituent individuals. But according to the Buddhist philosophy that is the foundation of Tzu Chi, individual autonomy is an illusion—the truth of our existence is radical interdependence. One manifestation of this is the wearing of uniforms which obscure all indications of worldly distinctiveness. Another is the Tzu Chi word for "volunteerism"—*zhigong*, rather than *yigong*.[4] The latter term, which is the one most commonly used in Chinese, connotes a freely chosen activity, while the former term connotes an activity taken up as part of a professional responsibility. Voluntary association is seen not so much as an exercise of an individual's free choice as it is an enlightened acceptance of one's duties toward others.

If its ultimate concerns are Buddhist, Tzu Chi's social vision is largely based on classical neo-Confucian themes. The key metaphor Tzu Chi members use to talk about their association is that most non-voluntary of institutions, the family. They are constantly talking of themselves as if they were members of a large extended family, and their master, Cheng Yen, is spoken of as a common mother. In this vision, members are bound together not by freely accepted contracts, but by fulfillment of mutual responsibilities.

Moreover, in keeping with this Confucian form of social imagination, the boundaries between their own small families and the Tzu Chi family become blurred—as do the boundaries between the Tzu Chi family and the world as a whole, including the Taiwanese state. In the classic Western liberal vision, voluntary associations preserve individual freedom by putting limits on the reach of the state. For Tzu Chi members, however, their association is not seen as independent from the state, but connected to it through an expansive web of interdependent responsibilities.

Such a vision is expressed in Tzu Chi's practical interactions with the government. Some of the free associations that flourished after the end of martial law certainly have had an oppositional spirit and have struggled against the encroachment of the government in general, against the ruling party, or against specific policies. But Tzu Chi, one of the largest of these associations, is by no means anti-government. This can be seen in its approach to the earthquake reconstruction. It built its houses mostly on government land. Later on, it would take responsibility for rebuilding fifty public schools that had been destroyed in the earthquake. Though built with privately raised money, these would be public schools, with standard government-approved curricula—an approach directly opposite to that of "faith-based" organizations in the United States that want to use public money to build private, religiously oriented schools.

Moreover, Tzu Chi has always had positive relations with the Taiwanese government. As we will see in more detail later, it has gained government awards for its welfare work, received government land for some of its major enterprises, and accepts government advice about where to direct its charity efforts. But its cooperation with the government is based on moral conviction, not on bureaucratic constraint, and the strength of its convictions can force the government to make compromises with it. One example is in the procedures for allocating the houses its volunteers constructed for earthquake victims. Local governments wanted to allocate the houses. The leaders of Tzu Chi were concerned that government officials might distribute houses as a form of patronage to their supporters. After discussions with Master Cheng Yen, the government allowed Tzu Chi to allocate a third of the houses. The moral authority of Cheng Yen, and for that matter, of the whole Tzu Chi organization, is such that the government would not dare to totally ignore her request for a role in the allocation.

If Tzu Chi blurs the boundaries between free association and government, it seems to build up boundaries between free association and the market economy. For Western liberalism, it is the freedom of individual choice produced by the open market that underlies the freedom to join voluntary associations. But Tzu Chi is ambivalent about market freedom. Some officials in the Taiwanese government wanted to simply give each family that had lost a house a cash payment that would allow them to rent new housing and begin to purchase a new house. Many Taiwanese citizens also seemed to prefer this market-based strategy. Tzu Chi resisted this. Instead of giving individuals the freedom to rent or buy their own housing, which under the circumstances would have led to an inflation in housing prices, Tzu Chi wanted the interdependent Taiwan community—led by those whose spiritual enlightenment enabled them to more fully appreciate that interdependence—to directly provide houses to those in need.

Although in its internal organization Tzu Chi recognizes the absolute authority of a charismatic head, espouses a social vision based on social duty rather than individual rights, blurs the boundary between free association and government, and promotes skepticism about the benefits of the market, it promotes in practice a great deal of individual initiative, of respect for the dignity of the individual, and it inspires in many of its members a strong sense of agency.

Immediately after the September 21 earthquake occurred, Cheng Yen is said to have given a simple one-sentence directive: "Go rescue the disaster victims." This mobilized an enormous amount of creative endeavor: teams were established to bring food and medicine into afflicted areas, architects organized to design emergency housing, and building projects were prepared. The scope and flexibility of these efforts came from the creative efforts of a great many individuals inspired to put the single general directive into effect.

Where Cheng Yen did intervene in specific projects, it was generally to insist on the dignity of those whom the projects were to serve. The recipients were, first of all, seen as individuals who needed to express their personal grief. When comforting earthquake victims, Cheng Yen told her disciples, they should hold them in their arms (contrary to traditional Taiwanese notions of propriety toward strangers) and wipe their tears. Cheng Yen insisted that recipients get houses with windows in every room and a warm pleasant environment, "like a home rather than a refugee camp." Tzu Chi further insisted that allocation of houses be based on need rather than personal affiliation with Buddhism. While articulated in terms of Buddhist beliefs, the atmosphere of joy that permeated the building sites seemed to be based on the participants' sense of personal efficacy in an important cause. Tzu Chi thus promotes a liberal form of life without the underpinnings of a Western liberal philosophy.

To explore this paradox, we will tell how Tzu Chi's religious, moral, and institutional development intersected with Taiwan's social and political modernization.

Figure 5. Hall of Still Thoughts, the Tzu Chi administration building in Hualien.

RELIGIOUS DEVELOPMENT

Dharma Master Cheng Yen, the founder of Tzu Chi, was born near Tai-chung in central Taiwan in 1937, the third daughter of a family of small business owners. When she was eleven months old, Wang Chin-yun, as she was named, was adopted by her aunt and uncle (her father's younger brother), who up to that point had been childless. Her adoptive father became wealthy by building a chain of theaters in Taichung. In 1960, however, he died suddenly of a stroke. Plunged into a personal crisis at her father's death (which she partially blamed on herself by unwittingly giving him improper medical treatment), Chin-yun began to intensively study Buddhism under the direction of a young nun, Hsiu Tao, the master of a small temple near Taichung.[5]

Hsiu Tao had spent time in Japan and learned a form of Buddhism that emphasized service to society in addition to praying and teaching, which contrasted with the forms then prevalent in Taiwan. Influenced by Hsiu Tao, Wang Chin-yun resolved to become a Buddhist nun herself. Her mother, however, was at the time not particularly devout and, like most Taiwanese parents, would have been very reluctant to permit such an action—all the more so since Chin-yun had shown herself very capable in managing the family business in her father's absence. Chin-yun ran away from home and tried to join a temple in Taipei. Her mother located her and brought her back. Displaying the determination that has marked her whole career, Chin-yun ran away again, this time with her first mentor, Hsiu Tao, who wanted to start a new kind of temple devoted to the socially oriented practice learned in Japan. The two traveled to the remote eastern part of Taiwan, where they endured malnutrition and illness from exposure to winter cold. They lived in a series of temples in small towns. They refused donations of money and survived on foraged food. After almost two years, they ended up in the Pu Ming Temple, a small, vacant temple newly constructed by Mr. Hsu Tsung-ming, a local businessman. Hsu allowed them to stay in his house until they got established, and they supported themselves by giving lectures on Buddhism to local villagers. Chin-yun distinguished herself as an excellent lecturer, albeit with a message that emphasized current events and social service to an extent that upset some traditional Buddhists.[6]

Partly because her health had suffered during their years of wandering, Hsiu Tao returned to her temple in Taichung. In 1963, Chin-yun traveled to Taipei to try to become ordained as a Buddhist nun. At one point in her wanderings she had shaven her own head and declared herself a nun, but, according to the rules of Mahayana Buddhism, legitimate induction as a nun would require an ordination by a monk. (Taiwan has been quite liberal in this regard. In many branches of Buddhism, it is not possible for women to be ordained at all.)[7] An ordination ceremony was scheduled to take place at the Lin Chi Temple in Taipei, and Chin-yun hoped to find a monk to take her through this ceremony.

Unfortunately, she had great difficulty finding a monk who was willing to do so. The proper procedure for becoming a nun was to undertake a two-year discipleship with a qualified monk, after which he would shave the novice's head and carry out her ordination. There was no place in the regular tradition for a woman who had already shaven her head to show up and say that she wanted to be a nun immediately. But just as Chin-yun was preparing to leave Taipei, she met Master Yin-shun.[8] At the time in his late fifties, Yin-shun had been a pioneer in developing the tradition of the early-twentieth-century reformist monk Tai Xu, who had advocated a form of "humanist Buddhism."

Humanist Buddhism was part of a response of Asian Buddhist communities as a whole to the challenges of an imperialist-driven modernization at the beginning of the twentieth century. Even as these movements strove to revitalize Buddhist practice to meet the challenge of Christianity, they adapted Buddhism to fit the assumptions of late-nineteenth-century mainstream Western Protestantism. Among these assumptions was the idea that true religion should be free from "superstition" and "magic"— belief in direct forms of supernatural intervention gained automatically through ritualistic prayer (allegedly found in premodern Catholicism)— and should aim at systematic ethical conduct aimed at improving the social world. Monks like Tai Xu strove to interpret Mahayana Buddhism in this-worldly terms. Instead of hoping to go to some heavenly pure land after death, Buddhists should place their hope on making this world a pure land by devoting themselves to eliminating social suffering. Nor was Buddhism just for monastics. In carrying out the mission to create a pure land on this earth, the sangha (monastic community—although the term *sangha* can also be used to refer to the broad community of Buddhist practitioners) should work closely with an engaged lay community. Tai Xu's reform program attracted devoted followers, but was disrupted by war and revolution. In the period of reasonable stability in Taiwan following 1949, some Buddhists tried to revive Tai Xu's hopes, although this was discouraged by the sangha under the control of the Buddhist Association of the Republic of China (BAROC). Yin-shun, a Mainlander from southern China who was somewhat of a maverick within the Buddhist community, was one such person.[9]

Chin-yun was suddenly inspired to ask Yin-shun to accept her as his disciple, and he spontaneously agreed to ordain her—an hour before the scheduled ceremony at Lin Chi Temple. Chin-yun was given the religious name Cheng Yen ("orthodoxy and strictness"). After thirty-two days at Lin Chi Temple, during which she learned the basic rules for life as a Buddhist nun, Cheng Yen returned to Hualien and took up residence in a small hut (120 square feet) built for her by Mr. Hsu, the devout businessman, behind the Pu Ming Temple. Within about a year she had taken in five new disciples, who would themselves eventually become ordained nuns at the Lin Chi Temple.[10]

In the hut, Cheng Yen devoted herself to studying the Lotus Sutra, a foundational text of Mahayana Buddhism, reciting it every day and hand copying it every month.[11] When she took in her candidate nuns, she lectured them on the Lotus Sutra, the four books of Confucian learning, and the *Lament by a Liang Dynasty Emperor*. The group continued to grow and by 1967 they needed a larger home. Cheng Yen's mother, Wang Yue-kuei, donated money to build a convent—the Abode of Still Thoughts, which (after several additions) has remained the spiritual home of the Tzu Chi organization.[12]

When Chin-yun (Cheng Yen) left home to be a nun in 1960, she didn't even say goodbye, because she knew that she would meet with opposition. This caused no end of grief for her mother. Chin-yun took every effort to hide her whereabouts from her mother. When she finally wrote her a letter, she said: "There is an old saying: a proud horse will not return from the field from which it had already fled. I am proud, and I will not return . . . until I become a success."[13] When Wang Yue-kuei finally did locate her daughter, thin, hungry, and wearing a worn-out nun's robe in a remote temple in Taitung, Mrs. Wang exerted as much pressure as she could to in order to have her daughter return home to Taichung. Chin-yun pretended to comply, but as her mother boarded a bus for the return trip, Chin-yun stepped aside and let the bus move on. It was only after she had already shaven her head that she returned home for a brief visit; afterwards she engaged in frequent correspondence with her mother.[14] After Chin-yun became the nun Cheng Yen, her mother visited her frequently and became one of her strongest supporters.

In this rather odd but dramatic narrative of how the rich, young woman Chin-yun ran away from home, sojourned in the wilderness, shaved her own head, managed to become ordained, and finally established a convent on land her mother bought, we see the main outlines of the religious vision that underlies Tzu Chi. It has many different dimensions. It is first of all a distinctively modern version of the classic Mahayana Buddhist vision, based on the Lotus Sutra. The Mahayana vision has always directed its followers to follow the bodhisattva path—the path toward becoming an enlightened person by relieving suffering of all living beings on this earth. The preeminent way to do this is by leaving behind one's family to become a monk or nun. (One common word for monk or nun is *chujia ren*—literally, "a person who leaves the family.") But the leaving of family is usually followed by immediate entry into a disciplined monastic community. The young Chin-yun left her family, not to directly enter a monastery, but to wander in the wilderness for three years. It was the gesture of a spiritual entrepreneur, a seeker—a gesture that seems quite common in the modern individualistic West, but not at all common in the Taiwan of 1960. Although Chin-yun studied Buddhism intensively with her friend Hsiu Tao while in the wilderness, it was hardly a standard Buddhist education. She was largely self-taught. Although she was an excellent lecturer, she was criticized from the beginning for speaking more about current events than about classical Buddhist doctrines.[15] To this day, she seems defensive about her lack of formal education. "The Master doesn't like to talk with scholars," one of her nuns told me. Cheng

Yen's ideal is a simple, practice-oriented version of the Buddhist vision, without the baggage of its complicated, traditional metaphysics.

What began with an exceptionally individualistic gesture, however, ended with a rather exceptional embrace of the family. Few major Buddhist leaders remain so closely bound to their mothers.[16] Besides being a major contributor to the building of her daughter's convent, Wang Yue-kuei has helped with many of Cheng Yen's charitable enterprises. She is an active member of the Tzu Chi organization and widely revered by Cheng Yen's followers.

As an adopted daughter, Cheng Yen entered into her family in a somewhat unconventional way. She left the family when a key part of the family left her, through the sudden death of her father. Having come to terms with that loss through her days in the wilderness, she returned to a strong relationship with her mother. Or perhaps more accurately, her family returned to her, as her mother helped her build the Abode of Still Thoughts, which has become the center of a spiritual family for many.

Classical Mahayana Buddhism came to terms with Chinese Confucian values, especially with norms of filial piety. In both her life and her teaching, Cheng Yen promotes these norms with new strength and creativity, in an urbanizing Taiwanese world that makes fulfillment of these norms increasingly difficult.

The "family"—envisioned in classical Confucian terms as an interdependent system of social roles bound together by hierarchically ordered moral responsibilities—is a central metaphor in Cheng Yen's rhetoric. "Filial piety," writes Cheng Yen, "is the gate to all other good deeds. If we do not cultivate this virtue, it will be impossible to cultivate the mind of a Buddha."[17] But the kind of filial piety practiced by monks and nuns, the best kind of filial piety, is to increase the "wisdom life" of one's parents.[18] The way to do this is to "abandon the selfish, temporary love we give only to our relatives and close friends and expand our love to include all living beings."[19] "Tzu Chi is like an extended family," writes Cheng Yen in one of her books, "and we have to treat all commissioners and members who come to us as family. Yet, to treat them as family does not mean merely to provide them a place to pay tribute to the Buddha, but to help them understand the Buddha's spirit."[20]

Several Tzu Chi members remarked to me that they are "both liberal and conservative at the same time." Tzu Chi seems liberal in action, but is conservative in principle. The vision of Cheng Yen is certainly liberal in its insistence on treating everyone in the world, regardless of religion, ideology, lifestyle, or ethnicity with respect, and in its insistence that respecting others involves increasing their agency, their ability to take control of their lives. It is conservative, though, in insisting that the path to this universal respect is through recognizing the social embeddedness of individuals, especially within the corporate family.

In Cheng Yen's vision, the family is not a voluntary association based on a contract entered into by a man and a woman aiming to maximize their individual happiness. The family is an institution that transcends the self-interests of its individual members. Cheng Yen counsels family members to maintain the integrity of their families even when other members of the family are causing them grief. For example, in *Rebirth,* a series of testimonies by Tzu Chi members about their personal transformations, there are several stories by women who discovered that their husbands were unfaithful. They claim that their association with Cheng Yen helped them to get over their anger toward their husbands and even to love the mistresses.

In one story, the Master told one woman, "Since you love your husband so much, you should love the one your husband loves."[21] And in another, she says, "Both you and [your husband's mistress] are women, yet she has to hide her life in the dark and is unable to see the sunlight. Isn't her life even more miserable?"[22] At the conclusion of this story, the wife treats the mistress with more magnanimity and tolerance, and has won respect from the husband, gratitude from the mistress, and esteem from her children and stepchildren. By no means does Cheng Yen countenance adultery. She urges her male followers not only to remain faithful to their wives but to share more fully in domestic responsibilities than Taiwanese men have been accustomed.[23] But she believes that (up to a point) a person on the bodhisattva path should sacrifice individual happiness for the sake of maintaining the integrity of the family—or more precisely that individual happiness will be the result of diligent efforts to maintain the stability of the family.

Cheng Yen's path toward promoting the liberal ideal of universal respect for the dignity of each individual, no matter what background or belief, is different from the classic Western liberal path. Classic Western liberals hold that persons can gain control over their lives only by liberating themselves from any social obligations that they have not freely chosen and by making voluntary contracts the basis for community life. For the Western liberal, even the family becomes like a voluntary association, whose members have an easy exit and the ability to affiliate or not if they so please. In contrast, Cheng Yen insists that individuals gain control over their lives only by surrendering to family obligations. In the neo-Confucian perspective, as I have written elsewhere, "freedom comes from creatively contextualizing the commitments which fate has assigned. It involves more deeply understanding one's roles as parent/child, ruler/minister, husband/wife, older sibling/younger sibling, and friend—so that one can flexibly, even playfully, reconcile these with each other and all the roles that one must play in an evolving, modern world. This task can provide wide latitude for action and immense challenges for personal creativity, and it can lead to a plethora of individualized responses to particular situations."[24]

But how does one achieve this contextualization? For Cheng Yen, it is through the practice of Buddhist compassion. This is achieved not through self-absorbed meditation, but rather through the outward-looking work of helping others in need. Just as one progresses toward achieving enlightenment in Buddhist meditation by steadily pushing beyond one's limits (for instance by sitting in the lotus position longer than feels comfortable, and when one has gotten comfortable with that, sitting even longer), so does one make progress toward achieving enlightenment in compassionate work by pushing beyond one's limits—by being generous not just toward the family but also neighbors, and when one is used to that, striving to go further still by being generous toward one's countrymen, and then beyond that toward one's enemies.

In classic Western liberalism, it is assumed that if individuals are given maximum freedom of choice in a world free of traditional hierarchy and open to any kind of economic and intellectual transaction, most such individuals will naturally have sentiments of sympathy for one another and will use their freedom for mutual benefit. For Cheng Yen's synthesis of Buddhism and Confucianism, humanitarian moral sentiments need to be cultivated through systematic moral practice, and this is best done by balancing individual freedom with the individual's need to make a commitment to a firm path. Echoing her own experience and following a long tradition of Mahayana Buddhist teaching, Cheng Yen insists that there are many valid paths toward enlightenment, but only a few of these are right for any particular person. So a person must search among the different paths. But when someone finds their path, he or she must stay with it. Finding a path means searching far and wide for the teacher who is right for you. Following the path means remaining loyal to that teacher throughout the rest of your life.[25]

Cheng Yen's particular blend of liberal action and conservative principle has turned out to be remarkably appealing to many Taiwanese because of the ways in which their social and political context has evolved over the past forty years.

When Cheng Yen began her spiritual journey in 1960, Taiwan was within the grip of an authoritarian government. The KMT tried to block the formation of any independently organized associations that could even remotely support a challenge to its rule. This included religious associations. Through the Buddhist Association of the Republic of China (BAROC), the KMT kept the sangha under surveillance and kept it from expanding in a way that would enable the systematic cultivation and organization of large numbers of lay followers.[26] At the same time, through its compulsory education, the KMT, like its rival, the Chinese Communist Party, heir to the anti-religious May 4 movement, promoted a secular scientific worldview. With respect to social morality, and to distinguish itself from its communist rivals on the mainland, the KMT also promoted a conservative form of state Confucianism, defined mainly in terms of Confucian norms of respect for authority.[27]

By the early 1960s, however, Taiwan was undergoing the stirrings of economic development that would lead to a full fledged economic take-off in the late 1970s. A small urban middle class was beginning to develop. Increased mobility, including mobility abroad, was putting a strain on the rural extended family and limiting the ability of such families to take care of their members. The aspirations of an emerging middle class were being shaped by an international discourse of modernization that defined progress in terms of more mobility and more individual freedom, even as the middle class was subjected to a political education that emphasized the timeless glories of Confucian virtues (especially those that enjoined respect for authority).

In short, the slowly emerging middle classes were becoming modern in practice while remaining embedded in a rigid version of a traditional Confucian ideology. Cheng Yen's emerging vision began to link modern practice with traditional theory. It did this partly by making Confucian theory more flexible, not by blending it directly with Western ideology, but by confronting it with Buddhism, a religious form that could claim to be a firm part of Asian traditions (even though the humanistic Buddhist form that Cheng Yen espoused had itself absorbed some Western elements). In this way, Cheng Yen was providing Taiwanese with a model for becoming socially modern and remaining morally Asian at the same time.

She was doing this in a remote place, outside of the government's (and most of the Buddhist religious establishment's) field of attention. Yet through her mother and friends like Mr. Hsu whom she had met during her wanderings, she had a source of support, a base within which to nurture the sprouting seeds of her vision.

Although it was a vision with a great deal of subtlety, it did not have a great deal of complexity—this too is a good condition for giving mass appeal to an innovative vision. With little formal education in Buddhist metaphysics, Cheng Yen had to teach through the example of practice rather than learned dialectics. She found a vehicle for this teaching-through-doing in her Tzu Chi foundation.

THE TZU CHI FOUNDATION

At the Pu Ming Temple in Hualien, where Cheng Yen began her career as a Buddhist nun after her ordination in 1963, she and her disciples lived an extremely austere life. In the tradition of "agricultural Buddhism," established by the tenth-century Chan (Zen) Master Baizhang with the principle, "no work, no food," Cheng Yen and her disciples strove to create a self-sufficient community, supported by their own labor. Unlike other Buddhist monastic communities, they refused to live off contributions from laypeople, even contributions given in exchange for religious services like chanting sutras for the dead. They planted a small field behind the temple with peanuts, rice, and yams, and relied upon their crops for food. They would continue this tradition of self-sufficiency after they moved to their new dwelling, the Abode of Still Thoughts, in 1967. To this day, Cheng Yen's monastic community does not accept any outside contributions for its sustenance. The nuns currently grow beans, which are ground into a popular food additive and sold in the stores connected with each Tzu Chi branch office. They also manufacture candles. At earlier points in their history they produced baby shoes, gloves, and electric circuit breakers.[28]

A way for lay followers of other monasteries to gain merit (which would allow them to be reborn into a heavenly pure land after this life) was to contribute money to temples. When Cheng Yen started to attract lay followers, especially women from the Hualien area, she could not provide them with this means of merit. She came up with the idea of establishing a foundation through which lay followers could gain merit not by donating money to nuns, but to the poor. She founded this organization in April 1966, calling it the "Buddhist Compassionate Relief Association" (Ciji Gongdehui). Since Buddhist cultivation relies on the constant—not just occasional—practice of meritorious deeds, she asked her thirty lay followers, mostly housewives, to put the equivalent of two

Figure 6. Abode of Still Thoughts.

cents per day into a bamboo receptacle and then to deposit the accumulated sixty cents at the end of each month with the association. "Even though the [two cents] you save daily is not of great value, you accumulate the spirit of helping and loving others every day." In the first year, Tzu Chi had accumulated enough to distribute the equivalent of US$435 to thirty-one people. In 1967, the association put out the first edition of a monthly magazine, which reported on its work and solicited more donations. This attention not just to doing good works, but also to publicizing them, has continued to the present.[29]

The flair for publicity has been key to Tzu Chi's mission. Cheng Yen saw the association not simply as a charity association but also as an educational association—a way to "educate the rich and help the poor." Implicit in this mission was a powerful impetus to expand. It was not enough simply to give to the poor whatever one could afford. One had to convince more rich people (at this time, for the most part not truly wealthy, but people who had enough for adequate food and housing) to understand the nature of Buddhist compassion by contributing their money and time. The contributions of time were as important as money. Cheng Yen named the first group of dedicated lay followers "commissioners" and gave them the job of expanding the association by recruiting their friends and neighbors to make regular contributions. Since the mission of Tzu Chi was fundamentally educational, the commissioners were not to be content simply with soliciting money. They were supposed to help the contributors become more aware of the spiritual significance of generosity. They played the role of counselors, listening to contributors' problems and offering comfort and advice. If the contributors were moved to dedicate themselves more fully to the Buddhist path, they could be recruited to become commissioners themselves and go forth to recruit even more contributors and commissioners.[30]

The official accounts of the founding of Tzu Chi say that Cheng Yen was inspired to establish this charitable work following a visit from three Catholic nuns. The nuns tried to prove that Catholicism was superior to Buddhism by showing how Catholics had established hospitals, schools, and churches to help the poor while Buddhists were content simply with their own self-cultivation.[31] No one has ever been able to locate these three nuns to get their account of the encounter with Cheng Yen, but it is tempting for Christians to see in this story an acknowledgement that Tzu Chi's charity work was simply copied from Christians. A closer look at the development of Tzu Chi, however, suggests that Tzu Chi was the result of something more like competitive adaptation. The initial encounter with the nuns looks less like a dialogue than a debate. To get the upper hand on Christians who tried to spread their faith by carrying out organized works of charity, Cheng Yen established her own charitable enterprise.[32] But although some of the forms of the charitable work would be the same as Christian efforts, the spirit of these works was thoroughly Buddhist.

As a way of educating the rich in the very meaning of Buddhism, Tzu Chi's work placed greater emphasis than Catholic Christians on the role and initiative of the laity. For most Catholic groups at the time, works of charity were carried out primarily by priests and nuns, with some help from laypeople; one important aim of these works was to attract the poor into the faith. Protestants would have relied more on the help of laypeople to deliver services, but the impetus and direction would still come from ordained clergy. Tzu Chi, on the other hand, made laypeople the prime movers in charitable work. Tzu Chi was to educate the "rich" in the compassionate spirit of Buddhism by having them *practice* compassion. True compassion was not supposed to be used as a means to get the needy to do one's will—so, unlike most Christians, Tzu Chi has made little effort to use its good works to proselytize the poor. A truly educative practice was not simply carried out for the charitable designs of others. An educative practice was one in which the Tzu Chi member used "skillful means" to respond to the needs of others and to encourage others to do likewise. In Cheng Yen's vision, Tzu Chi members were to educate themselves by creatively expanding their organization and thinking up new ways of helping those in need.

Cheng Yen uses religious doctrine to give meaning to the compassion that Tzu Chi members practice, but as someone not highly trained in the infinite intricacies of Buddhist philosophy, she preaches a rather simple message that lays emphasis on the experience that comes from creative, generous giving. Although Tzu Chi members see their compassionate giving as being inspired by the teaching of Cheng Yen and the example of the nuns in her monastic community, their compassion comes from within their lay organization, not from any formal relationship with the monastic community.

Thus, in Tzu Chi, the secular becomes sacred. Tzu Chi members go through a number of evocative ceremonies as they join the Tzu Chi foundation, a lay organization. But they do not undergo the rite of "taking refuge" in Cheng Yen's monastery, the Abode of Still Thoughts. Nor does the Abode, which is self-sufficient, get any money from the Tzu Chi association.

The members of the other Buddhist groups discussed in this book all "take refuge" in a particular monastery. The ceremony of taking triple refuge in the Buddha, the dharma, and the sangha is the basic rite of formal initiation into Buddhism, somewhat akin to baptism in the Christian church. But whereas baptism makes one a member of the Christian church as a whole, taking refuge makes one a lay member of a particular monastery—for example, Buddha's Light Mountain or Dharma Drum Mountain—and in doing so one also assumes a responsibility for financially supporting the monastery. For Tzu Chi members, the cultivation of a spirit of compassionate giving is a sacred act in itself; it does not gain its sacredness through formal connection with the sangha. In other words, one does not have to become a Buddhist to be a member of Tzu Chi. Some Jesuit priests in Taiwan told me that they thought that a Catholic could be a full member of Tzu Chi without in any way compromising his or her faith.

The energy for constant growth was built into the constitution of Tzu Chi, with its requirement that commissioners constantly seek out new members and new commissioners. After its founding in 1966, the Tzu Chi foundation grew steadily, at first slowly but later with increasing speed. Following networks of personal connections, commissioners began to recruit new members in communities around Taiwan, and when a sufficient core of new members and commissioners was built up, Tzu Chi branches were established in various cities.[33]

Along with the expansion of members, there was an expansion of missions. In the first years, Tzu Chi mainly helped the poor and sick. It first gave emergency gifts of food and clothing to the needy, especially in the Hualien area, and its commissioners visited the sick and lonely. A special concern was for elderly people who had no families to support them. In 1969, as its resources grew, Tzu Chi began to carry out a regular winter distribution of food and clothing in Hualien. It also began to provide long-term financial assistance to the poor. Besides the accumulation of money, this work required the development of an effective system for identifying and keeping track of the needy—work which was carried out by commissioners making home visits.

By 1970, Tzu Chi's reputation began to spread because of its response to disasters like fires, typhoons, and earthquakes. Tzu Chi members were often faster and more effective than government agencies in providing aid to victims—testimony not only to Tzu Chi's accumulation of material resources, but also to its development as a sophisticated organization.

A logical outgrowth of such work was medical care. With the help of several doctors and nurses from Hualien's hospital, Tzu Chi set up a free clinic in 1972, and later a mobile clinic that traveled to remote locations. The need for such services—as well as the desire of some people to voluntarily provide these services—became increasingly important as Taiwan began to develop into an industrialized society in the 1970s. On the one hand, industrialization was generating new wealth and the growth of a new urban middle class—people moderately rich in material resources, but somewhat cut off from their roots in rural extended families and therefore in search of spiritual meaning.

On the other hand, industrialization was generating new forms of poverty. Even though almost all levels of society gained more money to spend, many people lost crucial sources of social support. The elderly used to be able to rely on their extended families to take care of them. Now, increased mobility meant that some old people were left alone. The most pitiable people I encountered when I accompanied Tzu Chi volunteers on visits to the sick were elderly rural people, disabled by illness, whose children had moved away—to the cities and perhaps even abroad—and wanted nothing to do with them. All the while, rising expectations—for improved medical care, for example—brought a painful experience of relative deprivation to those at the bottom of society. As was typical in other East Asian developing countries, the government continued to hold to the belief that families should take care of each other, and it was reluctant to invest in welfare programs.[34]

In this newly industrializing environment, Tzu Chi appealed to the newly rich who needed meaning and the newly poor who needed help. By the time it had grown large enough to be noticed, the government had become more interested in using religious groups to take care of emerging social welfare needs rather than in trying to stifle them. In 1976, under Chiang Ching-kuo, who had taken over as president when his father Chiang Kai-shek died the previous year, the Taiwanese government instructed all temples to carry out charity work. Tzu Chi won an award for being the best provider of such charity—it was the first official government recognition of Tzu Chi.[35]

Thereafter, Tzu Chi's expansion proceeded with government help. In 1979, Cheng Yen launched Tzu Chi on a major expansion into medical care. There was no first-rate hospital in Hualien, and the one hospital that did exist charged fees that were too high for the local poor, especially the aborigines, to afford. Distressed by this lack, Cheng Yen made a vow to build a six-hundred-bed hospital in Hualien. Though they admired the nobility of her humanistic Buddhist intentions, practical-minded people—even some of her own nuns—thought that she was being unrealistic. Tzu Chi still had only modest resources, nowhere near the US$20 million that such a hospital would cost. There were only about one hundred Tzu Chi commissioners and ten thousand members who could help with the fundraising. Moreover, there were real practical reasons why there was no decent hospital in Hualien. Most people living in the area could not afford the fees that would make such a hospital self-sustaining. And the area was so much of a backwater that it would be difficult to attract doctors and nurses to work there.

Cheng Yen, nonetheless, persisted. She worked so hard seeking support that some of the nuns in the Abode worried about her health. In the end, however, crucial help came from the government. President Chiang Ching-kuo offered some military-owned land for the project. Although the military balked and the offer had to be rescinded, the government eventually provided another suitable plot of land. The government obviously saw the value of providing help to a religious organization striving to fulfill an important welfare need, and the government's support helped to encourage private donors to step forward. Tzu Chi was no transmission belt linking government policies to the grassroots—it remained too independent and it mobilized too much bottom-up initiative. But it was, and would continue to be, like a belt buckle linking popular initiative with government concerns.

For her part, Cheng Yen traveled throughout Taiwan raising funds.

Perhaps the sheer novelty of a Buddhist nun's attempt to build a large hospital attracted the attention of the public. Perhaps the rapidly increasing affluence of Taiwan in the early eighties coupled with new opportunities for public awareness created a favorable atmosphere for philanthropy. Seemingly against all odds, Cheng Yen raised US$26 million for her project and the Tzu Chi General Hospital opened in 1986.[36]

The fundraising effort and its improbable success made Tzu Chi famous. By the mid-1980s the number of commissioners had increased to five hundred and its members to fifty thousand. Tzu Chi was now on the brink of an explosive expansion.

In 1987, Chiang Ching-kuo ended the martial law that had formed the foundation of the KMT's dictatorial rule. The years following the end of martial law, when most restrictions on free association were swept away, were a true springtime for Taiwan's civil society. People flocked to all manner of associations representing an extraordinary wide range of causes, from politics and social reform to community improvement and philanthropy. Many of these groups remained small, while others grew quickly but soon died. Tzu Chi was poised to grow rapidly and steadily precisely because it had good, if somewhat detached, relations with the government before 1987. Participating in Tzu Chi was a respectable and safe way of taking private initiative to help address Taiwan's public social problems.

Tzu Chi began to undergo exponential growth. Within a decade, it would claim four million members and fifteen thousand commissioners. As it expanded it rapidly added new missions. Since it was difficult to attract doctors and nurses to the remote hospital, Tzu Chi built its own institutions for medical education—a nursing school in Hualien in 1989, a medical school in 1994, and a comprehensive university in 2002. Another obstacle to attracting good doctors is the relatively low quality of the public schools in Hualien. So Tzu Chi opened a private school in Hualien, based on its vision of Buddhist principles, that it hopes will be a model for other such schools in Taiwan. Tzu Chi has also developed a series of textbooks and teacher's manuals for teaching moral education in Taiwan's public schools—a compulsory course that used to be based on Sun Yat-sen's Three Principles of the People, but can now be taught in a variety of formulations.

Attentive from the beginning to the importance of the media, Tzu Chi has developed new popular magazines, radio programs, videos, and websites, and has now even built its own cable television station.[37]

In 1989, Tzu Chi established its first branch in the United States, located in southern California. Since then it has established at least forty more branches in the United States, and dozens more around the world. The international branches are established wherever there are substantial communities of Taiwanese, and although open to all, the membership consists mostly of Taiwanese. Each international branch raises its own money and mobilizes its own volunteers for charitable or educational works in its area. However, in the event of a large humanitarian disaster, the central organization in Taiwan will send aid around the world.

In 1991, Tzu Chi began its first relief efforts beyond Taiwan's borders. In response to devastating floods in the PRC, Tzu Chi raised money in Taiwan and sent a team of volunteers to deliver relief supplies to mainland China. Setting an important precedent, they insisted on delivering the supplies in person. Volunteers paid their own way to go on the relief mission. The next year they carried out their first "international" relief mission (in its official accounts, Tzu Chi does not consider help for mainland China to be international) to Mongolia. Since then they have delivered food, clothing, and medicine and built emergency housing in disaster sites around the world. (In the United States, for example, they provided aid in the aftermath of the Los Angeles riots of 1992, the destruction of the World Trade Center in 2001, the southern California wildfires of 2003, and Hurricane Katrina in 2005.) Indeed, Tzu Chi seems to take pride in responding to the most difficult and controversial situations. They have, for example, given humanitarian aid to North Korea, Rwanda, Kosovo, Chechnya, and, after U.S. invasions, Afghanistan and Iraq (where they delivered medical supplies to a hospital in Fallujah that had been looted).[38]

Tzu Chi currently receives about US$150 million per year in regular contributions from its members, not counting special money raised in response to emergencies like the Taiwan earthquake. The total value of its assets—its hospitals (four more have been built in addition to the one in Hualien), schools, and other buildings—is in the billions of dollars.

Tzu Chi has thus become a huge, multifaceted organization, no longer the group of devout Buddhist housewives that it was in the 1970s, or even the 1980s. It now has a relatively small but efficient professional staff that employs the latest technologies to communicate with members and the general public, as well as to coordinate Tzu Chi's operations. It enters into cooperative relationships with other international relief organizations, like Doctors Without Borders. It has youth groups on college campuses around the world.

Tzu Chi has multiple layers of members with multiple layers of motivation. At any Tzu Chi site, one can still see the earnest, middle-aged Taiwanese women who have been with Tzu Chi from near the beginning. They proudly display the name badges which indicate the order in which they became commissioners, and their numbers are below one hundred. They are eager to talk about the early history of Tzu Chi, but they often do so in the stereotyped terms of the true believer. Such women were the backbone of Tzu Chi in the 1970s and 1980s. Typically, they never had jobs outside the home, had become bored as their children had grown up, and discovered a new outlet for their energies in Tzu Chi. As the anthropologist Lu Hwei-syin has written, the Tzu Chi ethos was traditionally based on the virtues of Taiwanese mothers.[39] The older commissioners ply visitors with tea and cookies, and reprimand them for not holding their bowls properly.

But one also sees many younger women with professional degrees—teachers, social workers, accountants, and managers. They do not necessarily tie their hair in the tidy bun that is the standard style for Tzu Chi commissioners. Sometimes they even wear fancy diamond rings in violation of norms that forbid displaying signs of one's worldly status. Membership in the Tzu Chi commissioners has come to have high status in Taiwanese society, and the desire for status begins to interfere with the quest for spiritual cultivation. Tzu Chi leaders acknowledge that they have had to pay more attention to commissioner training as the motives of prospective commissioners have changed.

As Tzu Chi expanded in the 1990s, its core membership grew to include more men. After the Hualien hospital was built, Tzu Chi's public events began to become larger and more complex. To meet the security requirements posed by such activities, a men's security team was formed, which in 1990 was named the Tzu Cheng Faith Corps.[40] Dressed in neat white shirts and blue ties, Faith Corps members can be seen at every Tzu Chi event, directing traffic, moving equipment, guarding money and supplies. About a third of Tzu Chi core membership is now male, many of them husbands of Tzu Chi commissioners. Many of these men come from business backgrounds, and they have brought a new insistence on organizational efficiency to Tzu Chi. Their business and social commitments also bring complexity into the single-minded devotion practiced by the older women commissioners. Once while I was traveling in a car with a foreign visitor, a male commissioner, and several female commissioners, the foreign visitor expressed interest in buying a bottle of Taiwanese wine. The male commissioner accompanied him into a wine shop to help with the purchase. Some of the female commissioners became upset, because Tzu Chi members are supposed to follow the Buddhist precept forbidding alcohol. After returning to the car, the male commissioner told me that he did indeed refrain from drinking whenever he was in his Tzu Chi uniform and doing official Tzu Chi business. But, he added, " I am a businessman, and when entertaining other businessmen, you are expected to drink. So I have a little wine, but I don't drink to excess."

Another influential, mostly male component to Tzu Chi is its "honorary board," a group of businesspeople whose contributions range from thirty-five thousand U.S. dollars up into the millions. First established in the early 1980s to help raise money for the hospital, the board now comprises some of the leading entrepreneurs in Taiwan. The endowment provided by the board finances all of the operating expenses of the foundation, to ensure that every dollar that an ordinary donor contributes goes directly to a charitable purpose. The board members are not necessarily committed devotees of Buddhism, just successful businesspeople who want to channel their philanthropic contributions through an organization that is respectable and effective. The functions of the honorary board in Taiwan are partially replicated in the groups of local Taiwanese businesspeople who support branches of Tzu Chi around the world. It is important for their long-term success to give something back to their local communities, and Tzu Chi provides an effective vehicle for this.

Professional men also play an increasing role in the overall leadership of Tzu Chi. The head of the "religious affairs committee," the leading body at the top of Tzu Chi's organizational chart, is Steven Huang, a Taiwanese businessman who built a successful import business in Los Angeles, but who now devotes full time to the work of Tzu Chi. Constantly traveling around the world—he told me that he takes at least one hundred trips a year—he was principally responsible for setting up Tzu Chi's global network. One of his main activities is meeting with local Taiwanese chambers of commerce to promote the work of Tzu Chi. He also played a major role in establishing Tzu Chi's international relief work. Other top leaders, both Mainlanders and native Taiwanese, came to Tzu Chi after careers in government.

Although the backbone of Tzu Chi remains its volunteers, there is an increasing role for a professional staff to edit its publications, run its television station, manage its hospitals and medical schools, and organize its international relief projects. Some international relief projects are planned and implemented by local Tzu Chi branches (with permission from Cheng Yen conveyed through the religious affairs committee in

Hualien). Programs that are particularly complicated and politically sensitive, however, are carried out by professional staff from Tzu Chi headquarters in Taiwan. In some of these projects, for example the provision of seed grain and fertilizer to North Korea, teams of volunteers travel to deliver the relief goods in person. In other cases, however, as in the provision of medical supplies to a hospital in Iraq, Tzu Chi sends some professional staff to make liaison with local relief organizations—in the Iraq case with a Jordanian relief organization—and the Tzu Chi supplies are delivered in cooperation with these organizations. [41]

Tzu Chi has thus evolved into a complicated (and wealthy) corporate organization even as it retains the characteristics of a religious community. It is this interpenetration of religious community and complex organization that makes a unique contribution to the modernization of Confucianism and Buddhism. Tzu Chi's mission makes no sense outside of the humanistic Buddhist vision and the Confucian ethic propagated by Cheng Yen. Not only its members, but also its professional staff, speak of it as a family bound together by ties of love and commitment, and dedicated to following the bodhisattva path of spreading compassion throughout the world. All of its members see Cheng Yen as a Confucian parent who needs to be consulted on all important issues and whose will is final. When going on international relief missions, for example, they send daily faxes to Hualien reporting their activities to the Master. But the Master does not necessarily have time to read all of these dispatches. Although she does intervene decisively on matters of principle, most of Tzu Chi's activities take place according to established organizational routines. Most of the volunteer work takes place in an egalitarian spirit with minimal division of labor. Members address one another as Teacher Brother and Teacher Sister (*shixiong* and *shijie,* using the term for "older brother" and "older sister" even if the addressee is not actually chronologically older), and wear uniforms that suppress any signs of worldly status. Volunteers do not have fixed jobs, but are ready to pitch in with whatever is needed. But planning for deployment of volunteers is done by experts (increasingly male) working within a flexible but well-articulated framework of responsibilities.

Tzu Chi is not an official religious organization. It is incorporated under Taiwan's law as a charitable foundation, on a par with secular foundations. Although there is a long tradition of Buddhist philanthropic work, there are no provisions in the regulations governing the Buddhist sangha for the establishment of a legally incorporated charitable foundation. Yet under Cheng Yen, this formally secular foundation has become sacred. Cheng Yen has not only set its broad goals, but she has intervened in the organization in such a way as to give its routines sacred significance.

An example is the way that the Tzu Chi medical school seeks to educate physicians both to meet high professional standards as well as manifest a humanistic Buddhist attitude. It is willing to embrace the core procedures of scientific medicine, even when these are contrary to Buddhist principles.

For example, the first of the Buddhist precepts forbids killing of any sentient being, and in the Abode of Still Thoughts, the nuns even refrain from killing mosquitoes and ants. But when asked if physicians at the Tzu Chi medical school and hospital performed experiments on animals, the superintendent of the hospital said, "Of course we do, it is a necessary part of scientific research." The Master says that medical researchers can sacrifice animals as long as this is done for worthwhile purposes and the animals are not made to suffer unnecessarily.

Yet although Tzu Chi medical training compromises traditional Buddhist ideals for advancement of modern science, it also tries to raise scientific medicine to the level of traditional Buddhist ethics. In addition to standard medical school courses, students are offered courses in flower arranging and the traditional Taiwanese tea ceremony—ritualized activities that aestheticize natural and social relationships. They also have a distinctive way of teaching basic anatomy, during which students learn to dissect human cadavers. Most medical schools teach this class in the basement. The Tzu Chi school holds the class on an upper story with a window that overlooks a peaceful garden. An image of the Buddha is in the front of the classroom, and the students pray to it before they begin their work. They address the cadavers as their "silent teachers," and on the wall of the classroom are short biographies of the people whose bodies they are dissecting—including pictures of the deceased with their families and the stories of their life accomplishments. There are also essays by the medical students expressing their gratitude to the deceased for contributing to their education. At the end of each semester when the students have finished their work on the cadavers, the families of the deceased are brought together for a funeral ceremony. The students put letters into the coffin of their silent teacher, expressing gratitude for all the lessons learned from the donation of the body. Nuns from the Abode of Still Thoughts solemnly chant prayers for the dead—and in at least one case where the donor was a Catholic, a priest says a funeral Mass. Acting as pall bearers, the students solemnly carry the caskets to hearses, which deliver them to a crematorium. Half of the ashes are returned to the family and half retained in crystal urns (shaped like the Abode of Still Thoughts) placed in a Buddhist chapel next to the anatomy classroom, where students and teachers can come to pray and meditate before and after their work. Cheng Yen herself was closely involved in developing these procedures for the anatomy class, even requiring a special machine that dips the cadaver into its preservative solution in a respectful reclining position rather than in the standard vertical position. Thus doctors are encouraged to develop, along with their technical competencies, a deep respect for the human body and attentiveness to the continuities between death and life.[42]

The Tzu Chi philanthropic organization itself thus becomes like a religious institution. Its instrumental routines take on a sacramental character. The organization does not simply accomplish things, it represents meanings. It teaches through structured, meaningful doing. If in its beginnings it approximated the sociological definition of a sect—a community of people united by common belief and devotion—it has become more like a church, a complex institution that embraces people with a wide range of belief and commitment but whose structured activities give them lessons in how to live their lives.[43]

TZU CHI AND TAIWANESE NATIONALISM

Cheng Yen built into Tzu Chi's design a general imperative to expand and to respond to the this-worldly needs of the Taiwanese people. The drive to expand has continued, but the needs have developed in ways that even Cheng Yen could not have envisioned. In ways unplanned by its founder, Tzu Chi has come to serve the needs of an emerging Taiwanese nationalism. But even as it has been shaped by that nationalism, it has shaped it in accord with Confucian and Buddhist principles.

The end of martial law in 1987 provided the freedoms that made it easier for Tzu Chi and other religious groups to recruit new members. It also opened the way to an emerging Taiwanese nationalism. As recounted in chapter 1, under Lee Teng-hui the government increasingly asserted its sovereignty, to the outrage of Beijing. The winner of the presidential election of 2000 was Chen Shui-bian, of the DPP, which from its very beginning has espoused Taiwanese independence. Underlying these political events were movements by artists, historians, and social scientists to build and assert a distinctive Taiwanese national culture.[44] There was a fundamental ambivalence to these political and cultural processes, however. The majority of the Taiwanese population, even those who were native Taiwanese as opposed to those descended from recent mainland immigrants, wanted to assert its cultural distinctiveness but did not want to risk the war that would probably ensue if Taiwan declared independence. Meanwhile, Taiwanese businesses steadily deepened their economic ties with mainland China.[45]

Tzu Chi was buoyed up by this strong but ambivalent nationalism. Cheng Yen was one of the few major Buddhist leaders who was a native Taiwanese. Her core followers from the beginning have been native Taiwanese. Although she speaks Mandarin well, most of the events at her Abode of Still Thoughts are conducted in Taiwanese. Even the architecture of the Abode and the monumental Hall of Still Thoughts that serves as Tzu Chi's headquarters in Hualien is in a vaguely Japanese rather than late-imperial Chinese style—an architecture that points to the Japanese cultural influences of the first half of the twentieth century, which helped to give a unique shape to Taiwan's culture.[46] As the Taiwanese developed a sense of cultural uniqueness, it seemed natural for them to express this in indigenous religious institutions like Tzu Chi. A number of my interviewees told me that they had become converted to Tzu Chi's mission because they recognized in it something deep inside their culture. A young woman who works in the central office told how she had cried the first time she attended morning prayers at the Abode. "Similar things must happen to European Catholics when they travel to the Vatican," she said.

Yet Tzu Chi represents a particular version of native Taiwanese culture— a cosmopolitan, ecumenical version. One of the traits that distinguishes Taiwanese culture, and which helps Taiwan receive international support for its cause from the United States and Europe, is the openness of Taiwan to outside influences. While the PRC remains somewhat xenophobic (though it has become much more open in the past two decades), Taiwan has been exceptional in its efforts to build cultural, economic, and political connections with the outside. It embraces every form of foreign popular culture and thrives on expansive networks of Taiwanese abroad. This openness is paradoxically a kind of boundary marker—it sets Taiwan off from its more opaque, assertively nationalistic neighbor, China.

There is also a belligerent, populist form of Taiwanese nationalism, which expresses itself in the passionate, uncompromising posture of Taiwan's more radical independence activists, as well as in such popular customs as betel nut chewing, which is popular among Taiwanese males eager to express their irreverent earthiness.[47]

One of Tzu Chi's requirements for its members is to abstain from betel nuts. Tzu Chi obviously represents the cosmopolitan form of nationalism, with its commitment to international relief work, its respect for dialogue with other cultures—and its sense of cultural superiority for being so heroically devoted to this openness. Tzu Chi claims, for example, that it is making Taiwan into an "Island of Great Love." Although it tries to disseminate its love around the world, and wishes to respect all cultures, nationalities, and religions, its leaders always make it clear that the source of that love is from Taiwan.

The nationalist appeal is not just based on the fact that Tzu Chi originated in Taiwan; the political and economic system of Taiwan gives it the freedom and economic resources needed to develop and disseminate its message. It is clear that Beijing would never allow such a large and independent religious organization to flourish.[48]

Other religions, particularly Christianity, preach universal love. But Christianity did not flourish after the end of martial law, perhaps because most Christian groups had received special privileges during the period of Nationalist dictatorship. As noted in chapter 1, Buddhists were forbidden to build universities and discouraged from developing social welfare institutions, while Christians were allowed to build major universities, as well as to establish hospital, clinics, and social welfare services (which in the 1950s and early 1960s served as conduits of U.S. foreign aid). When political freedom came to Taiwan it was perhaps not surprising that an emerging middle class turned to Buddhist organizations, because Buddhism represented more of an authentic expression of Taiwanese religious culture than Christianity. But it also seems natural that the middle classes would embrace Buddhist organizations that represented the concerns for social welfare that Christian organizations had taught them to expect from modernized religions.

One Christian denomination that has maintained a solid place in Taiwanese society after the end of martial law is the Taiwanese Presbyterian Church. But this is the exception that proves the rule, because the Taiwanese Presbyterian Church is the one Christian denomination that has long been associated with the cause of Taiwan's independence.[49] However, it is tempting to speculate that the Presbyterian Church has not had the spectacular growth of Tzu Chi because the Presbyterian Church has been associated with somewhat more belligerent forms of Taiwanese nationalism.

Tzu Chi's contribution to the debate on the meaning and destiny of Taiwan as a nation was manifest in an encounter I witnessed in the fall of 1999 between Cheng Yen and Annette Lu (Lu Hsiu-lien), the politician who was at the time running for election as vice president of Taiwan on the DPP ticket. Throughout her career, Lu, a pioneering feminist, Harvard-trained lawyer, and former political prisoner, has been one of the sharpest, most outspoken advocates of Taiwan independence. Both because of the steadiness of her commitment and the abrasive way in which she promotes it, Beijing has called her the "scum of the Chinese nation." During an important political campaign, all major candidates feel the necessity to visit Cheng Yen to have earnest discussions (with television cameras present) on the moral basis of Taiwanese society. Cheng Yen, for her part, forbids Tzu Chi from taking sides in partisan politics, but she welcomes all politicians who wish to visit her. The meeting between Cheng Yen and Annette Lu was a highly charged encounter between two powerful women, but powerful in different ways. Both participants seemed nervous—Annette Lu was uncharacteristically hesitant in her questioning; Cheng Yen's face was serene, but under the table she was constantly wringing her hands. "Master," said Annette Lu, "you have so much wisdom—you are so different from Jiang Zemin [then president of the PRC and Communist Party general secretary]. You send food and medicine to China when they have their natural disasters, but when we had our earthquake Jiang Zemin sent us nothing. It shows his lack of respect for us." Cheng Yen responded, "We believe that everyone has a place for love in their hearts. That includes Jiang Zemin. We should not denounce him."[50]

Certainly, not everyone in Tzu Chi is as magnanimous as its founder. Many, especially those on the margins, have doubts about Tzu Chi's gifts to mainland China, especially insofar as those gifts help a corrupt and incompetent government avoid the consequences of its mismanagement. These donations were initially very controversial. But as more and more Taiwanese businessmen have set up enterprises in China, the attitude is changing. (Many of them seem to see the sponsorship of Tzu Chi charity as a way to gain goodwill from their Chinese hosts.) Most would think that Taiwan's security needs to be based not just on love but on a strong national defense. Yet Tzu Chi represents to them a vision of Taiwan at its best—a nation whose true strength rests in the generosity of its caring rather than in the power of its economy and military.

This is a popular vision among certain segments of Taiwan's emerging middle classes. Their prosperity has arisen from a number of different sources: globalized technology, heavily dependent on research and development; small scale, entrepreneurial manufacturing, networked with counterparts throughout "greater China"; government patronage (especially connected with the KMT); and local service industries. People whose path to success stems from different sources usually acquire different ways of thinking and feeling which lead them toward different religious affiliations.[51]

In popular discourse, Tzu Chi represents a particular place, a particular point of aspiration, on this map of middle-class status positions within Taiwan. Although, as suggested by survey data, its actual membership is more diverse, by reputation Tzu Chi is associated with managerial and professional workers, particularly in the service sector.

The Tzu Chi way of life is adapted to the sensibilities of urban people with college educations, or to those who would like to emulate such people. (Its popular magazine, *Rhythms,* contains ads for brands like BMW.) Many of such urban managers and professionals in Taiwan are only a generation removed from the folk religious customs of village life. They have left behind their village homes—and not infrequently gone to study and live abroad—and to a high degree their path to success depends on individual achievement certified through modern educational credentials, rather than the personal connections of rural communities. Nonetheless, they often retain strong feelings of connection to their parents and siblings, even when it is difficult to maintain regular contact with them. Thus the sometimes anguished testimonial discussions in books like *Rebirth* about how to practice filial piety in the modern world.

They are in practical professions, people who like to achieve results in an efficient and orderly way. They are people who feel they need spiritual cultivation, but are skeptical of the claims of Taiwanese folk religions to bring automatic benefit simply on the basis of performing proper rituals or paying the proper amount of money to a priest. They believe rather that the benefits of religion only come to people who properly cultivate their hearts and minds in the spirit of the religion. Though working with their minds, these are not really intellectuals fond of complicated philosophical discourse, and they like the notion of cultivating their hearts through practical service to the poor. Many of them are in professions that depend on exchanging techniques and information with colleagues around the globe. They are condescending toward people who do not share this openness.

TZU CHI AND TAIWANESE CIVIC VIRTUE

Few scholars at the beginning of the 1980s would have predicted that Tzu Chi would grow so rapidly and achieve such influence over the next two decades. Buddhism did not seem open to modernization. Buddhist nuns had not been a major creative force in Taiwan. An organization of housewives did not seem likely to have a transformative influence on a patriarchal society. Tzu Chi grew because Cheng Yen and her followers managed to adapt Buddhism and Confucianism in such a way as to resonate with the aspirations of Taiwan's emerging middle-class citizens.

Similarly, few scholars at the beginning of the 1980s could have predicted that Taiwan would make a successful transition to democracy. It was threatened by mainland China and had lost almost all political recognition within the international community. It was troubled by ethnic tensions between Mainlanders and Taiwanese, and by legacies of suppressed resentment that came from three decades under a harshly authoritarian regime. Its political culture had been formed by a Confucian cultural tradition that many experts have considered incompatible with democratic values. These handicaps were not illusory. If anything, they have become more apparent over time and to this day threaten to push Taiwan's political society to the brink of chaos. Nonetheless, Taiwan has managed a successful if shaky transition to a stable democracy, and it is not a coincidence that groups like Tzu Chi have become increasingly prominent as this transition has gone forward.

The surprising success of Tzu Chi is partly interconnected with the surprising success of Taiwanese democracy. I am not claiming that Taiwan's religious renaissance was a cause of Taiwan's democracy. I am arguing that under circumstances in which Taiwan's fledgling democracy needed all the help it could get, the country was fortunate to have religious organizations like Tzu Chi that provided a net positive contribution to a democratic political culture rather than religious organizations, as in other societies, that fan the flames of ethnic and class conflict and embroil society in discord.

Tzu Chi's most important contribution to Taiwanese democracy is in its production of what Western theorists call civic virtue—those habits of the heart that embody a disciplined sense of responsibility for the public good. Tzu Chi members do not usually talk about civic virtue—they talk about cultivating the heart to properly care for one's family and to have universal compassion and love. But, whether intentionally or not, Tzu Chi has cultivated a functional equivalent of civic virtue, even though its recipe for civic virtue is not what most Western theorists would use.

For most Western political philosophers, civic virtue is not just any kind of other-regarding moral self-discipline. It is a kind that is compatible with the individual freedoms protected by liberal democracy. In the thinking of classic Western political theorists, real civic virtue is based on a distinction between public and private life. Private life is par excellence the domain of the family, the relations within which depend on particularistic love and loyalty. Public life is the domain of citizens, relations among which depend on universal principles of fairness and justice. Civic virtue is that assemblage of habits of mind and heart that leads a citizen to treat fellow citizens differently from the way one would treat family members—according to reason-based norms of universal fairness and justice rather than emotion-based commitments to particular love and loyalty.

For Western philosophers, to gain civic virtue, one must leave home. Civic virtue is cultivated in voluntary associations, outside of the family but independent of the state. By being sustained by the free choice of their members, such associations nurture both the sense of personal autonomy and social responsibility that is necessary for the exercise of democratic citizenship.

Confucianism has not generally been regarded as a good source of civic virtue, because it blurs the distinction between private and public, between familial loyalties and loyalties to the state. It does not really encourage leaving home. Traditionally, Confucian societies have been built around large extended families and groups (like guilds and native place associations) based on familistic principles with particularistic, hierarchical relationships. Because of this, many political theorists, Chinese as well as Western, have argued that if they want to achieve democratic modernization, Asian societies will have to abandon their Confucian traditions in favor of Western moral values. Tzu Chi seems to prove otherwise.

In line with the Confucian tradition, Tzu Chi blurs the boundaries between private and public. It encourages its members to see public life not as different from family life, but as an expanded version of family life. The relationships it envisions in the public sphere are not those of impersonal fairness and justice but of expansive caring—caring directed not at broad categories of persons (for example, "the poor") but at particular suffering individuals, who receive gifts given face-to-face and hand-to-hand from Tzu Chi members. It sees itself as a large extended family under the absolute authority of a powerful matriarch.

Yet by mixing Buddhist benevolence with a Confucian moral framework, and by bringing these virtues out of the monastery and into the world, Tzu Chi pushes its members to widen the circle of familial care to include distant strangers, even enemies, throughout the whole world.

It thus cultivates habits of universal public concern, along with respect for people with whom one might disagree—a functional equivalent to the principles of universal equity that Western civic virtue is supposed to sustain.

Most of the people who belong to Tzu Chi are mobile professionals and entrepreneurs who have in fact left behind the restrictive ties to extended family and particular locality that once characterized rural Taiwan. That family-centered world indeed barely exists in modern Taiwan. Tzu Chi is one of many voluntary associations that fill the gap between the modern state and the individual citizen. As in the West, voluntary participation in such associations nurtures a sense of individual autonomy as well as collective responsibility. The same is true of participation in Tzu Chi. Although Tzu Chi members submit to the absolute spiritual authority of their Master, they are in practice encouraged to exercise a great deal of personal initiative. And although its members think of Tzu Chi as like a family, it is in fact a voluntary family, which one can leave if one disagrees with its policies. Thus in practice Tzu Chi members experience a great deal of personal agency even as they are being taught to exercise that agency in response to the needs of an interdependent moral community.

That community is envisioned as a family writ large rather than as a nation of equal citizens. By envisioning the nation and even the world as a family, Tzu Chi enables its Taiwanese members to feel at home, in continuity with the best of their traditional values, even as they experience the typical material and spiritual dislocations of a globalized modernity. This sense of continuity with the best of Taiwan's traditional culture sustains the sense of national consciousness that encourages civic participation in Taiwan's democracy. Thus Tzu Chi makes an important positive contribution to Taiwan's political life even though it does not engage in partisan politics.

PASSING ON THE LIGHT

Many of the themes discussed in this chapter were on display in a ceremony to "pass on the light" carried out with volunteers who had participated in the earthquake rebuilding efforts in 1999. The ceremony was held in a large auditorium in the Taipei branch office, filled to its seven-hundred person capacity. As one approached the branch headquarters, a large contingent of men from the Tzu Chi faith corps directed traffic while women clad in the navy blue dress of the Tzu Chi commissioner ushered participants into the auditorium. Most of the participants wore ordinary street clothes, which distinguished them from the core Tzu Chi members who were organizing the ceremony. The core members had already participated in a ceremony just for them. Video cameras recorded the event to broadcast on Tzu Chi's cable television program.

The ceremony was extremely solemn. It started out with opening hymns—not Buddhist chants, but Tzu Chi songs praising the virtues of generosity with lilting melodies—sung by a choir of commissioners, who, also in accord with Tzu Chi tradition, performed the hymns in a very graceful, ballet-like international sign language. Participants then went up two-by-two, hands folded as in a Christian Communion service, to receive a New Year's gift from Master Cheng Yen. The Master stood underneath a large wooden Guanyin, the bodhisattva of compassion. The effect was to make the Master seem like an extension of Guanyin herself.

As we went forward, some of the women in the line began to cry softly, and were given tissues to wipe their tears by the ever-prepared commissioners. The sacred gift handed out by Cheng Yen was the typical New Year's present given by Chinese parents to their children, a red envelope containing money—in this case one shiny, new Taiwanese dollar (the equivalent of about three cents). Cheng Yen was not only acting out the role of Guanyin, but also the role of mother of the Tzu Chi family. After receiving the gift, participants returned to their places and listened to a sermon by the Master (in Taiwanese) in which she told them that even investments as small as a penny could with the right spirit someday accumulate into great good. Finally candles (made by the nuns in the Abode of Still Thoughts) were passed out. Cheng Yen lit the first candle and the flame was passed through the room. At the end, participants linked arms and swayed back and forth as they sang closing hymns—a form of ritual practice much more similar to Christian church ceremonies than traditional Buddhist ceremonies.

The central metaphor of the ritual was that of the family, the extended family of Confucian imagination, embracing ever-widening circles of affiliation under the leadership of a benevolent parent. The circle of familial love could extend so far because it cultivated the compassion of Guanyin and was infused with the wisdom of Buddhism. But the ceremony was not held in a temple and the only nun present was Cheng Yen herself. The ceremony was basically the ritual celebration of a lay congregation, for which there are not richly developed models in the Buddhist tradition. So Christian-inspired ritual forms were used for expressing human love and solidarity.

The people receiving the gift had volunteered their time to help fellow citizens in a time of crisis. (Members who only contributed money were not invited to these ceremonies with Cheng Yen. They attended ceremonies in which they were given a red envelope by other nuns from the Abode of Still Thoughts.) They were being encouraged by Cheng Yen to expand the habits of generosity still further, to care for the poor and sick not only in Taiwan but around the world.

At the same time, there was something profoundly nationalistic about the ceremony. Cheng Yen spoke not in the Mandarin Chinese of public officials, but in the Taiwanese language spoken by the majority of the population. Yet the ceremony was translated into universal sign language—an attempt to be as inclusive as possible, even of the deaf (who have been aided by a number of Tzu Chi projects). The ceremony as a whole was a symbolic representation of the Taiwanese people at their best: generous, energetic, and devoted to the past while embracing the future—a people with unique moral lessons to offer to the rest of the world.

Perhaps the reason the ceremony inspired so much emotion was because of the way it offered a representation of national identity, which in other times and places would be provided by the government. In every society, the state is expected to do more than simply administer a society. It is expected to symbolize the nation's noblest aspirations and hopes. This burden of moral representation is even more important for Asian governments than for liberal Western governments. Yet the Taiwanese state cannot easily fulfill this representative function. Although Taiwanese society has been developing a strong sense of national distinctiveness since the late 1970s, Taiwan is not a member of the United Nations and it is not officially recognized by any important nation in the world. To avoid a war with the PRC, the Taiwanese state has to refrain from declaring its sovereign independence. Most Taiwanese accept the need for such compromise, but as long as the state makes this compromise, it can only represent the Taiwanese nation's resignation and fear, not its pride and hope. At the Passing on the Light ceremony—and at similar ceremonies throughout the year—Tzu Chi was representing the Taiwanese nation's pride and hope.

CHAPTER 3

Buddha's Light Mountain

*The Buddhist Contribution
to Democratic Civil Religion*

Though deeply moving, the Tzu Chi Passing on the Light ceremony seemed pale in comparison with the rituals of Buddha's Light Mountain (Foguangshan). Buddha's Light Mountain is a monastery and temple complex located near Kaohsiung in southern Taiwan. But as Master Hsing Yun, its founder and leader, says, "Buddha's Light Mountain is not just this monastery. It is a spirit that brings light and truth to the whole world."[1] Concretely, it is a large network of branch monasteries and education and social service institutions on at least four continents. It encompasses a lay organization, the Buddha's Light International Association, with over a million members, which its members claim is one of the largest voluntary organizations in the world. And it includes a vision of Buddhist practice carried on through its founder's many publications, in print and in multimedia.[2]

In size, influence, and fame, Buddha's Light Mountain shines at least as brightly as Tzu Chi, and maybe even brighter. But it is not so much a competitor as an occupier of a different social niche. If Tzu Chi has a popular image of an organization for managerial and professional segments of the Taiwanese middle classes, Buddha's Light Mountain is associated with business owners, small and large, and government officials and politicians.

According to the now classic theory of anthropologist Mary Douglas, people like educated professionals, whose way of life requires the mastery of an "elaborated code" of abstract language (which enables them

Figure 7. Master Hsing Yun. Permission courtesy of Buddha's Light Mountain.

to work together with many different people in an elaborate division of labor), tend to prefer forms of religion that devalue elaborate rituals in favor of interior religious experience and "humanist philanthropy." In contrast, people whose way of life requires mastery of a "restricted code" that affirms the emotional power of strong personal solidarities (and sustains cooperation based on respect for authority and mutual trust within relatively small groups) tend to believe in the efficacious power of rituals performed by religious authorities.[3] If we follow Douglas's theory (which we shall elaborate more fully in the conclusion to this book), we would expect that organizations like Buddha's Light Mountain, with relatively high identification with community-based business owners and local officials, would emphasize ritual and authority somewhat more than Tzu Chi. This is, in fact, the case.

Buddha's Light Mountain emphasizes a rich liturgical practice, like the solemn morning chanting that I attended one autumn morning at the main temple complex in 1999. As in other monasteries, including the Abode of Still Thoughts, my wife and I were awakened about four in the morning to get ready for the ritual, which started before five. We approached the Hall of Great Compassion, climbing a fifteen-foot-wide set of stairs. Outlined in small white lights, the temple was shaped like a building in the Forbidden City in Beijing. Muffled sounds of drums and chimes came from within. In front of the door was a long, wide portico, supported by massive, three-foot-thick pillars. We took off our shoes and entered the thirty-foot-high doorway. Inside the cavernous hall there were about eight hundred monks, nuns, and laypeople arrayed in two facing sets of precisely ordered rows. The monks and nuns wore robes of brown and orange, in patterns that indicated their ranks. The lay devotees stood in back, dressed in black robes. Towering over the chanters were three gilded statues: Sakyamuni Buddha in the middle, and Guanyin and the Medicine Buddha on either side. In front of the statues was an altar with huge bouquets of flowers, mounds of fruit, and incense burners. The walls of the temple, ablaze with light, were filled with more than a thousand small alcoves, each containing a statue of the Buddha and a small white light. On either side of the altar were two tall cones of votive lights.

The chanting was loud and sonorous, punctuated by the resonant beating of the "fish drum" (a wooden fish-shaped drum that is a standard accompaniment to Mahayana chanting) and a gong. Engulfed in the immensity of the buildings and overwhelmed by the sounds and smells, an individual felt at one with something deep and powerful. After about thirty minutes, everyone turned toward the altar and made a deep bow.

Then they turned toward one another and row-by-row filed out the door, down the stairs, and into a huge plaza in front of the temple. Chanting all the while, everyone walked back and forth throughout this plaza in a stately procession. The combination of fluid order and rhythmic sound, carried out in front of the twinkling lights of the temple and under a gradually lightening sky, was almost hypnotic. One was transported into an otherworldly time and space. Finally the procession reentered the temple where the chanting continued for another fifteen minutes. At the end, everyone turned toward the altar and prostrated three times. The chanting stopped and everyone proceeded out in silence.

The sacred envelope enclosing the ceremony was not necessarily seamless, however. The otherworldly space was punctured by a camera crew filming the event. Glaring beams from klieg lights penetrated the gentler radiance from the ambient votive lights. Video cameras were pressed closed to the solemn faces of chanting monks. The director was a woman with short, spiky hair who wore a T-shirt that read, "New York—Must Dance."

This surreal scene was not at all uncommon at Buddha's Light Mountain. Buddha's Light Mountain is not simply about reviving (and perhaps partly reinventing) traditional Buddhist ritual practices. It is also about publicizing those practices in ways that will teach and inspire people around the modern world. This requires not simply performing the rituals, but staging them—giving them a dramatic order and shape (the color-coordinated robes, the precisely arranged positions of the chanters, the almost-choreographed procession) that will convey spiritual meaning through modern media. As with Tzu Chi, video cameras are present for every major event. Meeting the technical demands of high-quality media may require cooperation with people rather far removed from the lifestyle of the monastic community.

An earlier version of the spectacular chanting ceremony that I have described was portrayed in the opening segment of the two-hour video Buddha's Light Mountain produced to advertise itself on its thirtieth anniversary in 1997. Tzu Chi would not have opened a similar promotional video with a ritual—its videos usually open with dramatically framed images of the works of charity the organization is devoted to. Tzu Chi's rituals are meant to energize the faithful rather than to convey the Tzu Chi message to the world. The morning chanting at the Abode of Still Thoughts uses the same sutras and the same rhythms, and it goes on even longer than the one at Buddha's Light Mountain, but it is not as telegenic. The wooden hall where it takes place is small and arranged so that it can double as a conference room. The nuns wear identical gray robes. There is only one elegantly carved Buddha statue and no votive lights. For Tzu Chi, ritual devotions are private supports for its public work of spreading Buddhist compassion in a suffering world. For Buddha's Light Mountain, rituals are its public work, meant to spread knowledge of the dharma around the world.

In an age of mass-mediated production, publicizing rituals brings changes to them. Buddha's Light Mountain draws on rich resources from the Mahayana Buddhist tradition to give its ceremonies a depth that might appeal to a mass audience, but its presentation of these rituals is more orderly and colorful than it might have been in the past. The framing of its videos emphasizes the visually dramatic elements of Buddhism—elements that might help attract new practitioners—rather than the mind-numbing monotony that actually helps the practitioner lose attachment to the independent self.

Besides presenting old rituals in new ways, Buddha's Light Mountain also develops new rituals, with creative use of special visual effects. An example is the presentation of "dharma functions" *(fahui)*, such as Master Hsing Yun's public lectures. I attended one of these in December 1999 at the packed three-thousand-seat Sun Yat-sen Memorial Auditorium in Taipei. (This was a moderately sized event for Buddha's Light Mountain. Hsing Yun sometimes speaks in Asian sports stadiums to audiences in the tens of thousands.) Entering the auditorium, one passed long rows of female lay devotees dressed identically in red *qipao* (a traditional Chinese-style dress), wearing white gloves, and handing out literature and gifts. As the event began (precisely at 7:30 P.M.), an elegant uniformed choral group sang a Buddhist hymn. Then a big red stage curtain opened. Billowing artificial smoke arose from the stage, in the middle of which was Master Hsing Yun, seated on a throne-like chair in front of an ornate mahogany table. Seated on the floor on either side were rows of monastics (monks on one side, nuns on the other), dressed in their orange and brown robes. Behind the nuns was a row of laywomen in rose-colored blouses and long black skirts. Behind the monks, a row of laymen in blue suits. A long row of devotees filed up to the Master, to present gifts of flowers and to receive Buddhist books. Then the talk began, an hour-long lecture (delivered without notes) on the concept of Nothingness, not so much an academic-style discussion, but a folksy one, interlaced with stories and anecdotes. After the lecture, the Master got up and walked off stage, and the audience quietly filed out, past the women in white gloves who waved goodbye and finally past rows of monks and nuns with identical alms bowls. The form of the ritual was more similar to a Billy Graham rally than a traditional Buddhist ceremony. But there were many distinctive signs—from the women in red *qipao* to the artificial smoke that wreathed the speaker in mystery—that made it clear that this was an expression of Chinese religion and Chinese values.

Through such widely publicized religious events, Buddha's Light Mountain has created a vocabulary for public ceremony in Taiwan. When there seems to be a need for some public religious response to a national tragedy or triumph, the Master or monks of Buddha's Light Mountain are on hand with a dharma function. In response to public consternation when the United States severed diplomatic relations with Taiwan in 1979, Buddha's Light Mountain carried out a great chanting ceremony. When there was a major airline crash at Taiwan Taoyuan International Airport, Buddha's Light Mountain carried out another large ceremony in Taipei. Another was held several days after the 1999 earthquake. Although, like Tzu Chi, Buddha's Light Mountain carried out deliveries of food, clothing, and medicine to earthquake victims, its video on its response to the earthquake disaster begins not with its provisions of material relief, but with its provision of free funeral services for the dead.

Buddha's Light Mountain is on hand for joyous public celebrations as well. In 1998, Master Hsing Yun managed to secure the donation of a precious Buddhist relic, a "Buddha's tooth" from Tibetan Buddhist monks in India. The tooth was brought to Taiwan via Thailand. In Taipei, it was welcomed with a huge celebration consisting of tens of thousands of people. It is now held in a reliquary at Buddha's Light Mountain, but the monastery is raising money to keep the relic in a huge stupa constructed in Ilan (on the northeastern coast of Taiwan)—to show that the tooth is not just for the glory of Buddha's Light Mountain, but is a gift to the people of Taiwan as a whole. All such events receive wide attention in the commercial media as well as in Buddha's Light Mountain's own publications.

Beyond this, Buddha's Light Mountain is lobbying to get the Buddha's birthday made into a national public holiday. As a secular state, Taiwan does not recognize religious holidays. But it does make December 25 a national holiday, officially a secular holiday that has nothing to do with Christmas, but obviously an accommodation to the Western calendar. Even if it were given an equivalent secular rationale, a national holiday on the Buddha's birthday (celebrated in May) would give public status to Buddhist strands of Taiwanese culture. It would further the ability of Buddhism to shape the rituals of Taiwan's civil religion.

BUDDHA'S LIGHT MOUNTAIN AND
THE MORAL BASIS OF TAIWANESE DEMOCRACY

By civil religion, I refer to the common sacred symbols, myths, and rituals that form the public basis of a society's moral order and a focus for its public debates about how it can become better.[4] In modern, secular liberal democracies, which Taiwan is striving to become, religion is officially relegated to private life. The state is not supposed to give a privileged position to any particular religious tradition. But even secular states depend for legitimacy on their capacity to represent a shared moral order. When they need to give symbolic expression to that order, they often draw upon symbols from their society's predominant religious traditions, while modifying those symbols in such a way as to demonstrate the government's independence from the religious communities that were the origins of those symbols. Thus, when the American president needed to lead a nation in public mourning following the terrorist attacks of September 11, 2001, and rally the nation for a "war against terrorism," he gave a major speech at the Episcopalian National Cathedral, all the while trying not to identify the American government with any particular expression of Christianity. Evocation of the civil religion requires a difficult balancing act for any government, because public authorities draw on religiously resonant symbols that are inevitably based on mainstream religious traditions, but at the same time have to refuse to publicly privilege any particular religion—even as public religious leaders try to get their version of faith insinuated into the civil religion. The ability of any government to pull off this difficult balancing act is dependent on an ever-changing configuration of social and cultural forces. For a new democracy in a divided society like Taiwan, the difficulty of pulling off this balancing act becomes even more challenging.

It is in this context that rapidly growing Buddhist religious organizations like Tzu Chi and Buddha's Light Mountain are trying to get their particular expressions of Taiwan's moral order transformed into part of the public representation of the nation as a whole. Tzu Chi is emphasizing its vision of family-rooted compassion supposedly held by most people within the Chinese moral tradition. Buddha's Light Mountain is placing more emphasis on its version of beliefs and rituals supposedly common to most people within the Chinese religious tradition.

To do this, Buddha's Light Mountain emphasizes what might be called the catholicity of its symbols. While Tzu Chi religious meeting halls are almost starkly simple—plain wooden rooms with one Buddha image in front—the spaces at Buddha's Light Mountain are packed with images. One's first impression upon entering the Buddha's Light Temple complex was of a vast clutter of Buddhas—thousands and thousands of Buddha statues of all sizes and styles, from the huge welcoming Buddha (one of the largest in Asia) on a hill near the entrance, to the thousand small Buddha that cover the inner marble walls of the cavernous central temple, and from the exquisite ancient Buddha in the museum to the kitschy statues in the "Buddhaland" cave (like a somewhat cheap imitation of a Disneyland exhibit).[5] Master Hsing Yun says that Buddha's Light Temple is like a "department store that sells many things."[6] There are four different temples on four hills within the temple complex, each representing one of the sacred pilgrimage mountains in China. Buddha's Light Mountain also intends to unify the eight major lineages of Chinese Buddhism. Almost any kind of Buddhist practice can be engaged in at the temple—from the austere practices of Chan (Zen) meditation to colorful folk Buddhist devotions.

Since most people in Taiwan engage in some form of Buddhist practice at some phase of their lives, the complex of symbols offered by Buddha's Light Mountain contains something that can speak to almost everyone. Its symbolic net is wide enough to be able to represent much of the diversity of the society as a whole. It is wide enough even to include nonbelievers. "This isn't a religion," said one of the nuns I met at Buddha's Light Mountain. "It is our cultural tradition." At this level, Buddha's Light Mountain simply claims to represent part of Taiwan's common cultural identity.

For those who do want religion, Buddha's Light Mountain will provide it, at different levels. For monastics, it provides an all-encompassing way of life. For many laypeople, however, it is, in the words of Master Hsing Yun, "like a gas station," a place where people come for brief periods when they are depleted of energy.[7] When one turns off a noisy, overcrowded Kaohsiung area road and enters the huge front gate of Buddha's Light Mountain, the first impression is one of marvelous order and serenity. There is a wide range of options for people wishing to draw some of that serenity into their own lives.

There is, first of all, what one might call a retail option, in which they might spend a few hours visiting the Buddha's Cave, where they can deposit money in slot machines to see dioramas of Buddhist legends, or deposit money to get a slip of paper that tells their fortune, or deposit some more money before a Buddha image that brings special merit; or they can pay the equivalent of about thirty dollars to have an electric votive

Figure 8. Welcoming Buddha, Buddha's Light Mountain. Photograph
by Ho Hua-chin.

light illuminated for a year to produce merit for a deceased family member; or they can just go to one of the several gift shops to buy Buddhist literature or trinkets.[8]

There are moderately demanding options, such as talking part in one of the many retreats at the monastery. There is a one-thousand-room guest house to accommodate retreat goers. On such retreats devotees spend one to several days following monastic rules. In processions with other devotees, they try to walk ("like the wind") in the graceful steps of a monk. They wear black robes, with brown sashes if they have reached the stage of taking the bodhisattva vows, take part in morning and evening chanting, and attend regular dharma talks.[9] They attend meals in the one-thousand-seat monastic dining room, where they eat in accordance with Buddha's Light Mountain's version of the complicated rules of monastic etiquette.

There are also highly demanding options, like spending hours in meditation. No matter what the option, however, the laypeople must exit the huge front gate and return to the boisterous bustle of Taiwanese society. The monks at Buddha's Light Mountain encourage their lay devotees to adapt to the pressures and contradictions of work and family. As a monk counseled devotees during a dharma talk directed to people who had just taken their bodhisattva vows, "Don't try to force others to act as you do. It will have the opposite effect. For instance, don't start banging the fish drum in your house when you return. [Laughter.] Your kids will just turn the television louder to drown it out. . . . As for vegetarianism, don't try to force it on your family or use it to break off relations with other people. The main thing is the heart, not the outward practice. . . . If your family wants it, don't stop serving meat. For yourself, avoid eating the meat if possible. But it's more important that you have the right attitude than be a strict vegetarian."

For those who want to develop their Buddhist practice while living in the world, Buddha's Light Mountain has since 1992 offered membership in the Buddha's Light International Association (BLIA)—a worldwide lay organization with as many as one million members that carries out educational, charitable, and cultural work.[10] The BLIA's philanthropic work is similar in kind to Tzu Chi's, but smaller in scale. Nor does the BLIA have a core of especially commissioned lay devotees that would be the equivalent of Tzu Chi's commissioners. While making important contributions to helping the poor and sick—and thereby smoothing over some of the rough edges of Taiwan and other market-driven societies—the BLIA's social service work does not define the mes-

Figure 9. Hall of Great Compassion. Photograph by Ho Hua-chin.

sage of Buddha's Light Mountain as thoroughly as such work defines the message of Tzu Chi.

The primary contribution of Buddha's Light Mountain to Taiwanese society and to the world remains its popularization of Buddhist symbols, rituals, and myth—to the point where they can contribute publicly to a broad civic cultural identity in Taiwan, as well as meet the private personal needs of citizens facing the stresses of the modern world.

While making these contributions, it has amassed considerable wealth and influence. A quasi-official biography of Master Hsing Yun estimated the assets of Buddha's Light Mountain at about US$5 billion.[11] Politicians of every political party need to come to pay their respects to Hsing Yun, as they do to Cheng Yen. In an exhibition hall at the center of Buddha's Light Mountain, there are pictures of Master Hsing Yun not only with Taiwan's major political leaders, but with world religious leaders, including the Pope and the Dalai Lama, and international political leaders, including a picture of former Vice President Al Gore, taken at the Hsi Lai Temple, the Los Angeles affiliate of Buddha's Light Mountain.

The Al Gore visit led to controversy after the Hsi Lai community presented Gore with what were later determined to be illegal political contributions. The money was given by members of the Taiwanese-American community in California and channeled through monks and nuns at the temple. The illegality perhaps stemmed as much from Buddha's Light Mountain's ignorance about the proper way to make political contributions as from any intent to circumvent the law. But the Gore incident illustrated the influence of Buddha's Light Mountain, even in the United States. It was an important enough voice in the Taiwanese-American community to warrant a visit from the vice president and it had access to enough resources to enable the Taiwanese community to think that they could use the temple to influence American politics.[12]

Buddha's Light Mountain grew to such influence at roughly the same time as Tzu Chi. The same cultural and social forces enabled both organizations to expand, but the different organizations interacted with these social forces in somewhat different ways, and came to occupy different positions in Taiwan's cultural landscape. To understand more fully the place of Buddha's Light Mountain in that landscape, we need now to discuss how Buddha's Light Mountain developed in the course of Taiwan's modernization.

THE GROWTH OF BUDDHA'S LIGHT MOUNTAIN

Buddha's Light Mountain's founder, Hsing Yun, was born Li Kuo-shen in 1927 in a small town in Zhejiang Province. Soon after the Japanese invaded China in 1937, his father disappeared while away on business. It was not uncommon for families under such distress to give one of their children to the care of a monastery. When the young Li was twelve, he was taken in by the monks of Qixia Temple, located near Nanjing. The master of the monastery, named Qi Kai, was the forty-eighth generation of the Linji lineage of the Chan school. Hsing Yun was ordained in 1941 at the age of fourteen. In 1945, after the War of Resistance against Japan ended, he was admitted to Qiaoshan Buddhist College—one of the best Buddhist educational institutions in China.[13]

Many of the teachers at Qiaoshan had been influenced by the reformist monk Tai Xu (1889–1947), and the young Hsing Yun became committed to Tai Xu's vision of a socially engaged, humanistic Buddhism. At a time when most Chinese social institutions, including the Buddhist sangha, were crumbling under the pressure of foreign imperialism and domestic revolution, Tai Xu was the most energetic and eloquent of a cohort of early-twentieth-century Buddhist monks and laypeople who sought to renew Buddhism by modernizing it. Modernization was in part conceived of as Westernization. For Tai Xu this entailed adaptation of some of the social gospel approach of contemporary Protestant missionaries, and a purge of "superstitious," folk religious practices, together with an emphasis on the systematic philosophical articulation of religious beliefs sought by European scholars of religion.

As summarized by Raoul Birnbaum:

> [Tai Xu] wanted to get rid of the buddhas and bodhisattvas, and eliminate the funerary rites that were a principal source of income for some clerics and their monasteries. The buddhas and bodhisattvas in their guise as celestial benefactors are illusions, as is the Western Paradise of Amita Buddha, to which so many Chinese Buddhist devotees seek rebirth. He proposed that superstition-free Buddhists turn this place right here into a pure land, by bright mental training and compassionate activity. The training would be achieved in *foxue yuan,* Buddhist studies academies, with a carefully constructed curriculum that emphasized advanced studies in Yogacara and Madhyamika treatises, highly philosophical traditions whose study had been neglected for some centuries in China but were especially appreciated by European academics at that time. Compassionate activity would most particularly take the form of charitable action, as was seen in the work of Christian missionaries in China.[14]

Another follower of Tai Xu was Yin-shun, who, as we recounted in the previous chapter, almost two decades later would become the mentor of Cheng Yen, Tzu Chi's founder. But Hsing Yun had a much more solid grounding in the intellectual basis of Tai Xu's vision than Cheng Yen could have had.

Hsing Yun graduated from the Qiaoshan academy in 1947 and became the principal of a Buddhist primary school. After the Chinese Communist Party took control of mainland China in 1949, Hsing Yun managed to flee to Taiwan. When he arrived, he was a penniless, twenty-three-year-old Buddhist monk with no source of support. Because he had no clear affiliations, in fact, the KMT military authorities suspected him of being a spy and put him in jail for several weeks. To find a meaningful position within the Buddhist world of Taiwan, a monk like Hsing Yun needed to exert enormous entrepreneurial initiative. This he had in abundance.[15]

After two years, he found a place as the monk in charge of a small temple in Ilan County, at the time an impoverished backwater in northeastern Taiwan. Buddhist devotees in Ilan, and for that matter in most of the rest of Taiwan, did not expect much from their monks, most of whom were poorly educated. Monks chanted sutras for the dead and carried out other routine rituals, but were neither willing nor able to teach courses on Buddhism.[16] The relatively well-educated Hsing Yun organized dharma lectures for various groups of people, but with special em-

phasis on outreach to young people. He also established a youth choir—
a first for Buddhists in Taiwan—and organized a variety of cultural activities that attracted people to his temple. He pioneered the use of au-
diovisual materials in these lectures. At the same time, he established a
Buddhist magazine and wrote books on Buddhist history and doctrine
aimed at a popular audience.

He did not confine himself to preaching at the temple, but went on
preaching missions further and further from Ilan, including Kaohsiung,
where he would eventually establish Buddha's Light Mountain. The emphasis on itinerant preaching was in part stimulated by the need to compete with the methods of Christian missionaries, who came to Taiwan
in large numbers after their expulsion from the PRC and had relatively
abundant resources. Monks like Hsing Yun feared that the Christian missionaries, with their relatively high education and sophisticated preaching methods, would dominate the religious culture of Taiwan. At least
once, Hsing Yun's own dharma lectures were disrupted by Christian ag-
itators, perhaps a sign of his own effectiveness in attracting a new generation of Taiwanese.[17]

The attitudes of mainland monks like Hsing Yun toward Taiwanese
culture were sometimes condescending. They saw native Taiwanese
monks as poorly educated and Taiwanese Buddhism as corrupted by the
influence of the Japanese. In the words of Hsing Yun's quasi-official biographer, "The occupying Japanese brought along a version of Buddhism
that was light on precepts and discipline. This subsequently produced
a glut of monastics who went to the extent of abandoning celibacy and
vegetarianism. Worse, some would wear their cassocks within the temple but not otherwise . . . they formed a picture so blurred that there was
no telling who were the monastics and who were not."[18]

Mainlander attitudes of cultural superiority often sowed deep resent-
ments among native Taiwanese, especially when combined with the bru-
tal suppression of native Taiwanese elites by the KMT military and police
forces. Hsing Yun was in a place, Ilan County, that had suffered some of
the harshest treatment during the white terror, and where Taiwanese resistance toward Mainlanders was especially strong. If he was to expand
commitment to the dharma as he wished, he realized he would have to be
sensitive to the needs and aspirations of local people. Hsing Yun could
claim to have been subjected to KMT oppression himself—he had been
jailed for twenty-three days and, he claims, came close to being executed.
But besides sharing with native Taiwanese an experience of victimization
at the hands of the Mainlander government, he had more positive means

of building connections with ordinary people. He has an extremely gregarious, outgoing personality that seems to put people at ease, even while telling them that they need to improve themselves.

This personality, or as the Buddhists say, "capacity for affinities," also enabled Hsing Yun to cultivate influential friends among Taiwan's emerging elites. He was a religious entrepreneur who shared similarities with upwardly mobile economic and political entrepreneurs. His version of humanistic Buddhism offered such people a more sophisticated version of the religion of their parents, but not one so sophisticated as to seem arcane. It was a version that provided social respectability without making too stringent demands on its lay followers. He also relaxed the somewhat puritanical teachings of Tai Xu with regard to restricting devotion to Buddhist images and to eliminating performing of rituals for profit.[19] As we have seen, Hsing Yun offered followers plenty of Buddhist images, even as he insisted that such images are only an aid in helping followers to realize their own Buddha-nature through practice. And in addition to funerals, he has added other revenue-producing rituals, like weddings and repentance ceremonies. The result has been to widen the circle of people to whom humanistic Buddhism might become attractive.

One set of affinities that Hsing Yun did not have in abundance was with members of the Buddhist establishment. As an instrument of the KMT for control and supervision of Buddhism, the Buddhist Association of the Republic of China (BAROC) was not hospitable to his entrepreneurial style. As Hsing Yun writes, "When the Chinese Buddhist Association set up office in Taipei in 1949, I had just arrived from the mainland. I wrote articles suggesting how the Association could strengthen Buddhist organizations and train followers. These were not well received."[20] Although in 1952 he was invited to sit on BAROC's leadership group, he "declined the invitation, and thereby unintentionally offended many people in the Association. This brought me a lot of trouble from them in later years."[21]

Hsing Yun's rise in stature followed the same trajectory as Taiwan's rise in prosperity. By the late 1960s, he had accumulated a wide enough reputation and an extensive enough network of supporters to plan to build a monastery of his own. To become abbot of one of Taiwan's established monasteries, a young monk like Hsing Yun would have had to work for years under the authority of an existing abbot and then wait for the abbot to pass away. In the fluid environment of 1960s Taiwan, there was an opportunity to rise quickly to the top by building his own institution.

The construction of Buddha's Light Mountain was a much larger un-
dertaking than anything that Cheng Yen would have been capable of at
the time. It was to be a full-scale monastery, not just the modest "Abode"
that Cheng Yen was establishing. It did indeed become a monastery on a
grand scale, with big temple buildings and residence and training schools
for a large number of monastics. Even in the beginning it was intended
to have a monumental style that would attract attention around Taiwan.

Hsing Yun had already built a Buddhist Cultural Center in Kaohsiung
in the early 1960s, and he commuted back and forth between Kaohsiung
and his temple in Ilan (one of the most inconvenient commutes one can
have in Taiwan, because Ilan and Kaohsiung are at opposite ends of
the island). He also established a Buddhist college, the kind of institution that had been advocated by Tai Xu to upgrade the sangha, which
graduated its first class in 1964. In 1966, he met a Vietnamese-Chinese
couple who were desperate to sell a large tract of mountainous land outside of Kaohsiung. In 1967 he built the first buildings of the monastery—
including the Hall of Great Compassion and a Buddhist college—and a
reception center for visitors. The rest of it was built in five phases over
a twenty-five-year period.[22] Buddha's Light Mountain attracted many
visitors by virtue of its style, both monumental and inviting. According
to his biography, "Monasteries used to be a picture of gloom and doom.
The many-splendored [Buddha's Light Mountain] has turned that all
around. It is the expression of its leader's disposition and traits, and projection of his reason and concepts."[23]

Just as building a hospital in Hualien gave Cheng Yen the reputation
needed to promote her vision, Hsing Yun's monastery gave him the reputation necessary to expand the Buddha's Light Mountain vision of Buddhism far and wide. Even before Cheng Yen became widely known, Hsing
Yun propagated his vision through radio and television programs, magazines and books, and public lectures. In 1985, he stepped down as abbot of Buddha's Light Mountain Monastery, in order, he said, to ensure
an orderly succession to the institution and to concentrate on spreading
the dharma around the world.[24]

The timing was fortuitous—an example of the shrewd grasp of
"causes and conditions" that Hsing Yun has demonstrated from the beginning. Taiwan's old authoritarian order was breaking down, and there
would be new freedom to expand the size and scope of religious and social organizations. The rising prosperity of Taiwan would also provide
the resources for that expansion. Resignation as abbot actually allowed
Hsing Yun to increase his influence. Besides giving lectures around the

world, he helped build many new branches of Buddha's Light Mountain. In the United States, the best-known is the Hsi Lai Temple in Los Angeles. Established in 1989, it is the largest Mahayana Buddhist temple in the United States. Altogether, there are now more than 120 Buddha's Light Mountain branches around the world.[25]

More important than the physical buildings are the organizations and innovative programs based in all of these branches. According to Hsing Yun's biography, "The global setup of [Buddha's Light Mountain] is unprecedented in the history of Buddhism. Similar to the Vatican but not quite, it is especially unique in the training and delegation of its forces."[26] It is perhaps similar to the Vatican in its attempt to subject all of Buddha's Light Mountain's worldwide affiliates to a central control, and perhaps dissimilar in the relatively high degree of efficiency and professionalism of its functionaries.

Hsing Yun, in fact, would like to expand beyond the creation of a centralized organization for Buddha's Light Mountain to the creation of a centralized system for all Buddhism in Taiwan. He is concerned that even poorly trained monastics can establish their own temples and gather groups of devotees. He would like to establish a unified system, administered by leading monks like himself, for training and certifying monks and for managing monasteries. So far, however, this has not happened.[27]

An important new addition to the Buddha's Light Mountain organization was the Buddha's Light International Association (BLIA), the Taiwan branch of which was established by Hsing Yun in 1991 and the international branch (headquartered in Los Angeles) in 1992. This is a lay organization, somewhat similar to Tzu Chi (and perhaps established in imitation of Tzu Chi). When the BLIA was established, Hsing Yun said,

> People used to think that Buddhism was for monastics, not for laypeople. The coming of BLIA, Republic of China, shall presage a transition from Buddhism for the sangha alone to Buddhism for everyone, a shift from the temple to society, to every household. The inertia, monotony, and solitary cultivation associated with Buddhism shall no longer be. . . . In the past, people used to think that there were many Buddhists in Taiwan only. However, because of the establishment of the BLIA, Republic of China, it's possible to spread Buddhist teachings to every corner of the world. . . . The coming of BLIA, Republic of China, shall enable qualified devotees to join the sangha to preach the dharma and to purify minds, correct social trends, and contribute to the happiness and prosperity of society and the nation.[28]

The establishment of a large lay organization like the BLIA was only possible after the lifting of martial law in 1987. As it was for Tzu Chi, the enormous growth of that organization was a response to the need for affiliation unleashed by Taiwan's transition to democracy. It was also a response to a need for Taiwan to expand its influence abroad. Hsing Yun's biographer notes that there are more branches of Buddha's Light Mountain abroad than there are Taiwanese embassies. The expansion of Buddha's Light Mountain, like the expansion of Tzu Chi, not only stimulates national pride by showing the global reach of cultural forms nurtured in Taiwan, but it provides a channel for informal economic and political diplomacy.

It provides a closer connection with Taiwan's political initiatives than Tzu Chi. Buddha's Light Mountain has no equivalent of Tzu Chi's strict rule forbidding its members from getting involved in partisan politics. Indeed, Hsing Yun has a widespread reputation as a "political monk"— not a laudatory term and one that Buddha's Light Mountain claims is unwarranted, but one that has some basis in Hsing Yun's career.[29] Unlike Cheng Yen, who could get her start because she was located in such a remote place, Hsing Yun's rise to prominence depended on a high level of visibility from the beginning. Without acquiescence by the ruling KMT, there would have been no way for him to develop such a visible reputation needed to build such a conspicuous monastery as Buddha's Light Mountain in 1967.

Hsing Yun gained such acquiescence by cultivating good personal relationships with members of the KMT. He used his skills as a mediator to settle political disputes in a way that maintained the stability of KMT rule. For instance, he says,

> In 1967, I recall, Mrs. Yu-chan Chien-yu was reelected to the Ilan County Assembly by forty-two votes over Mr. Hsueh-ya Chang. But because the KMT . . . did not want a woman in the assembly, the day after the ballots were counted Mr. Chang was declared the winner. Mrs. Yu was very discontent and would not rest until the court heard her suit. Since she was also a Buddhist, the KMT Ilan chapter approached me to get her to drop it. For the sake of local and national stability, I said I would try. Having just taken over the management of the Lanyang Charity House . . . I had planned to name Mr. Chueh-ho Lee, a devoted Buddhist layman, as director. To resolve the election controversy, I asked Mr. Lee to give the post to Mrs. Yu, thereby avoiding an ugly confrontation.[30]

Even if, for pragmatic reasons, Western politicians sometimes handle sensitive political negotiations in this way, it is so far removed from Western norms protecting individual rights and mandating procedural fairness that they would never openly talk about it in their autobiographies.

But Hsing Yun seems very proud of his role in this incident. It is an excellent example of a traditionally Confucian approach to handling political conflict. In the Confucian tradition, a proper moral education leads to the cultivation of virtues *(de)*. Good rulership is based on virtues, which are capacities to act flexibly in ways sensitive to one's total context to realize certain goods. Among the most important of the political goods are harmony *(he)* and righteousness *(yi)*. Harmony is to be achieved not by obliterating opposition, but by making the compromises necessary to maintain the relationships expressed through ritual. Righteousness is not the justice that gives every individual his or her due, but a principle that places everyone in a proper position within a web of relationships.[31]

By virtue of his political efforts, Hsing Yun was made a member of the central committee of the KMT. Hsing Yun sees precedents for such political engagement throughout the history of Buddhism: "The Buddha, who frequented the imperial court to lecture on the dharma; . . . Venerable Master Hsuan Tsang, who gave advice to the emperor; . . . great masters of various dynasties who helped rule the country. In the history of China, Buddhism has suffered persecution several times, but each revival of Buddhism has come with the support of high-ranking officials."[32]

Pursuant to his conviction that Buddhists must help those in power to rule in a humane, harmonious way, Hsing Yun has been willing to intervene in electoral politics at the national level. In the election for Taiwan's provincial governorship in 1994, the first popular election in Taiwan's (or China's) history, Hsing Yun persuaded the independent candidate Wu Po-hsiung to step aside, leaving the way for a direct contest between the KMT and the DPP (which, since it kept the KMT vote from being split, helped them to win). In the 1997 presidential elections, he backed his own Buddhist candidate, Chen Lu-an. Chen came in last, but according to André Laliberté, "it would be wrong to consider his bid a failure," because it indicated that an organized Buddhist constituency had at least a significant amount of potential power.[33]

Hsing Yun has also been involved in international politics. He tries to act as an informal go-between between mainland China and Taiwan, and, as in the ill-fated meeting with Al Gore at the Hsi Lai Temple, he has tried to facilitate stronger ties between the United States and Taiwan.

For all his efforts to promote harmony, Hsing Yun has also provoked his share of controversy and conflict. He has been accused of trying to aggrandize himself by taking control of Taiwanese Buddhism and of using religion to gain political influence. From the beginning, many of his efforts have been rejected by the BAROC. Citizens have objected to his political activities. He responds to all such accusations by claiming that he is acting not on his own behalf, but, like a good Buddhist, on behalf of higher principles. The higher principles are described not in terms of an unyielding defense of universal rights, but of basic Buddhist and Confucian principles:

> In solving problems and mediating disputes, changing violence to harmony, one establishes good conditions and accumulates blessing and merit. Such actions put oneself in another's position, and thus benefit all the people of the world. They also promote virtue and wisdom, so that one receives benefit from benefiting others. If everyone is willing to take on the responsibility of mediating and resolving disagreements, dissention among the human race will gradually disappear, and world peace will be within our reach.[34]

Hsing Yun's is a politics of persuasion and flexible compromise, smoothed by close personal relations. If in the Confucian tradition Cheng Yen plays the role of compassionate matriarch, then it is Hsing Yun who takes on the role of a responsible official.

ENTREPRENEURIAL BUDDHISM
FOR THE ENTREPRENEURIAL CLASSES

Among the new middle classes, both Tzu Chi and Buddha's Light Mountain propagate what Max Weber would have called the "spirit of capitalism": a spiritually driven quest to ceaselessly expand one's enterprise, and to use material success as an indicator of spiritual success. Both are constantly developing bigger and more expensive programs, and building new, expensive buildings. In both cases, material wealth is not supposed to be used for the gratification of individual members, but for the benefit of the poor or for the glory of the sangha as a whole. Hsing Yun tries to correct the view that Buddhism denies wealth.

> Many Buddhists absolutely refuse to discuss the subject, stigmatizing "gold as a viper," and certainly do not recognize *gold* as a sustenance of practice and necessary in the spread of the dharma for the benefit of all living beings. The truth is, however, that the wise cherish wealth and know the correct way to acquire it. For when wealth comes in a proper way, the more the better. No Buddhist should have any cause for resistance against wealth. . . . Neither one who devalues wealth or a miser is called wise. *Possessing* wealth is a pleasure, but to be able to utilize wealth for the benefit of others is truly *enjoying* wealth.[35]

In the end, such a vision gives a religious justification and inspiration for the restless expansion of the Taiwan economy, an expansion built on the "inner-worldly asceticism" of hard work and self-discipline. It is the spirit of Taiwan's new middle classes. Weber thought that this ascetic ethic of the capitalist middle classes arose from a Western Protestant worldview and was incompatible with Confucianism and Buddhism.[36] The developments of Buddhism and Confucianism represented by Tzu Chi and Buddha's Light Mountain prove him wrong.

Another characteristic of such middle classes is upward mobility based upon one's own efforts, and both Tzu Chi and Buddha's Light Mountain present themselves as models of such virtuous upward mobility—of starting from nothing and building something great through heroic effort. This has appeal to Taiwan's mobile middle classes, but the two groups tend to appeal to different segments of those middle classes: Tzu Chi to managers and professionals and Buddha's Light Mountain to entrepreneurs.

Hsing Yun's way of building Buddha's Light Mountain has similarities to the paths followed by thousands of successful Taiwanese business entrepreneurs in developing Taiwan's modern economy: identifying a new market created by advances in science and technology; finding and training workers with the skills necessary to meet the new needs; and developing good connections with flexible networks of financiers and suppliers, both within Taiwan and in the global Taiwanese diaspora.[37] Technology-based economic development has created a Taiwanese middle class which wants modernized religion, the kind of religion that the humanistic Buddhist Tai Xu advocated, which emphasizes philosophy and ethics rather than supernatural intervention through the practice of folk rituals. Hsing Yun helped meet these needs, not only through his own preaching, but through training a new generation of monks and nuns who could exemplify and propagate a modernized Buddhism. He also has been a master at making connections with a wide, global network of sponsors and supporters.

Unlike Tzu Chi, which is financially based on the systematic development of a wide circle of supporters who pledge to give a certain amount of money every month, Buddha's Light Mountain receives its funding from cultivation through personal relationships with flexible networks of supporters who contribute for special purposes. There are some wealthy business people who have donated large sums of money to gain good karma. There are other wealthy entrepreneurs who have undoubtedly contributed money to display piety and to gain status within their communities. And a great deal of money comes in response to services rendered. Contributions are expected for weddings (modeled after Western wedding ceremonies, with the bride wearing a white dress), funerals, and retreats. In the temple in Kaohsiung there are thousands of votive lights lit by families (for a fee of ten U.S. dollars a month) to gain merit for their deceased relatives. In the main exhibition hall, the shrine holding the Buddha's tooth is lined with thousands of small tiles, each bearing up to six names, each name inscribed after a contribution of two thousand U.S. dollars. There are little contribution boxes at each of the many small shrines to receive gifts to accompany prayers for the Buddha's assistance. A contribution of about thirty U.S. dollars is expected for a night in the Buddha's Light Mountain guesthouse. At each of Master Hsing Yun's dharma talks, monks line up with bowls to collect donations. Although the talks are officially free of charge, most attendees feel obligated to contribute. The same is true of the large dharma functions sponsored by Buddha's Light Mountain, like the Chinese New Year Lantern of Peace ceremony.

According to his biographer, "though assailed for 'multifaceted commercialism,' Hsing Yun is at peace with his own intentions." "It is for us to trade our labor for our livelihood," he says. "Most of all, Buddhism, having received donations from society, must give in return. This basically explains the business ventures of Buddha's Light Mountain."[38] Religious work thus becomes a business venture similar to that of the small-scale entrepreneur, who provides specific services for specific fees. In the Taiwanese context, such entrepreneurs also attempt to encourage clients to return by establishing warm personal relationships with them—as does Buddha's Light Mountain with its devotees. Since the Buddha's Light Mountain "business model" models the experience of Taiwanese entrepreneurs, it is no surprise that Buddha's Light Mountain is particularly adept at attracting members from this segment of Taiwan's middle class.

The identification is reinforced by Buddha's Light Mountain's contrast with Tzu Chi. Tzu Chi's way of development does not depend on directly trading religious labor for livelihood. The nuns at the Abode of Still Thoughts do not ask for money in return for performing religious services (and they therefore have no incentive to multiply religious services). They do not even ask for money from visitors who stay at the Abode (in much more spartan accommodations than at Buddha's Light Mountain). In the nuns' interpretation, trading labor for livelihood entails making useful products, like candles, and selling them. Donations to Tzu Chi are given for charity work, without any expectation of a specific religious favor, only of the kind of general blessing that comes to people who live a life of care for others. The difference between the Tzu Chi and Buddha's Light Mountain forms of development is the difference between salaried professional work and independent entrepreneurial work. The differences between the two organizations' self-presentations reflects this as well—Tzu Chi's activities are marked by the understated elegance that comes from relatively high ratio of "cultural capital" to economic capital, while Buddha's Light Mountain's are marked by the flashiness that comes with the reverse ratio.

BUDDHA'S LIGHT MOUNTAIN
AND TAIWANESE NATIONALISM

As a publicly prominent religious organization, Buddha's Light Mountain, like Tzu Chi, has at least an important, even if indirect, part to play in the public conversation about Taiwan's meaning and destiny. As mentioned in chapter 1, a strong sense of Taiwanese cultural nationalism has been evolving over the past decade. Before the end of martial law, there was a dedicated core of native Taiwanese nationalists who secretly advocated that Taiwan become an independent nation. The freedom of speech made possible after the end of martial law made open advocacy of independence possible. But a majority of people, even of native Taiwanese, remained cool to the idea of independence. Part of the reason was political, based on the fear that any formal declaration of independence would provoke a military attack from the PRC. But there was also a widely shared sense that Taiwanese culture was part of a wider Chinese culture. That sense has been changing in the past ten years. Even though a large majority still opposes a formal declaration of independence, an ever-larger majority now seems to think that Taiwan has a distinctive culture that makes its citizens different from those in China, and that Taiwan *ought* to be independent. When I returned to Taiwan after a ten-year absence in 1999 to do research for this book, I was in the habit of referring to the PRC as "mainland China." A friend corrected me: "They are China, we are Taiwan." Not everyone in Taiwan would talk like that, but in popular discourse the evolution is toward a China/Taiwan distinction.

It would seem that Buddha's Light Mountain would inhibit this development. Its founder is a Mainlander who has said that "all conscientious Chinese people want a unified China." Buddha's Light Mountain represents a continuation of Buddhist lineages based in China. Its temples are based on classical Chinese styles. Its museums are filled with classical Chinese art—not just Buddhist art, but art representing the whole Chinese tradition. At the front of the Buddhist museum at the Kaohsiung monastery is a replica of one of the terra-cotta warriors that guards the tomb of China's first emperor—reportedly purchased for US$6 million dollars, I was told. Buddha's Light Mountain, in short, presents itself as a local version of a Chinese tradition.

Although Buddha's Light Mountain is indeed more China-oriented than Tzu Chi, Buddha's Light Mountain itself is becoming Taiwanized. It is geared toward steady expansion, which could not have happened if Buddha's Light Mountain had confined itself to Mainlanders. Although Hsing Yun himself does not lecture in Taiwanese, most of the monks who gave lectures at Buddha's Light Mountain retreats speak half in Mandarin, half in Taiwanese. The congregations at various dharma functions that I attended seem well mixed between Taiwanese and Mainlanders. Insofar as Taiwanese members of Buddha's Light Mountain begin to absorb general cultural currents in Taiwan, they may shift toward feelings of Taiwanese nationalism.

Although there obviously are features of the ethos of Buddha's Light Mountain that may inhibit this shift, there are other features that might actually encourage it. There is, first of all, a strong competitive element in Buddha's Light Mountain's missionary efforts. As will be recalled, part of Hsing Yun's sense of urgency came from the fear that Christianity would become the dominant religion of Taiwan, because it was well funded and during the cold war enjoyed the support of Taiwan's rulers. Although it learned from certain aspects of Christianity, Hsing Yun's humanistic Buddhism saw itself as a competitor of Christianity and a competitor of Western culture in general. The building of the Hsi Lai Temple is described as gaining a foothold in a Christian country.[39] Buddha's Light Mountain is about spreading *Buddhism,* with its books, teachings, and rituals, not simply about spreading humanitarian "great love." There is a bit of the clash-of-civilizations rhetoric embedded in the vision of Buddha's Light Mountain.[40] Even when developed in support of a supposedly universal Chinese civilization, the spirit of competition can become detached from its original aims and be used to deepen a competitive Taiwanese nationalism.

The sense of working to enhance Taiwan's own culture, not just some universal Buddhist culture, is deepened by the use of Buddha's Light Mountain branches to promote Taiwan's national interests abroad. In the absence of formal diplomatic relations with most other nations, the Taiwanese government uses informal channels, including Buddha's Light Mountain. Because of his political connections with the KMT, Hsing Yun was perhaps more willing to let his organization be used for these purposes than other Buddhist leaders might have been. But the local Taiwanese business people who support branches like the Hsi Lai Temple in Los Angeles are also interested in using the temple as a base for extending Taiwan's influence—which is what they were trying to do, clumsily, in their meeting with Al Gore.[41] In the 1980s, the Taiwanese influence that Hsing Yun and his congregants were trying to promote was the influence of the Republic of China on Taiwan, which was still at least formally committed to eventual reunification with mainland China. However, as the government and citizens of Taiwan become more committed to a sense of a distinctive national identity, the Buddha's Light Mountain network has begun to promote this identity.

The national identity that Buddha's Light Mountain would help create is less ethnic than situational. That is, instead of being based on any supposedly primordial characteristics of the Taiwanese language or any deep roots in Taiwanese traditions, it is based on transcendent values that have been given particular shape by the circumstances of Taiwan over the past half century. Buddha's Light Mountain has helped shape a new modern Buddhism by taking advantage of Taiwan's unique political circumstances. Even though the original impulse to modernize Buddhism came from Tai Xu on the Chinese mainland, Hsing Yun extended and institutionalized this modernization in a way that would have been impossible in the PRC. Even though this modern Buddhism is seen to have relevance to the whole world (there are African and European monks in residence at Buddha's Light Mountain, and the Buddha's Light International Association has members from all nationalities), its source of inspiration is clearly Taiwan.

Buddha's Light Mountain moreover acts upon its universalism in ways that separate it from the PRC. For example, in the name of unifying all schools of Buddhism, Hsing Yun has reached out to the Dalai Lama and even hosted him on his trip to Taiwan—a move that the PRC considers aiding and abetting separatism. Hsing Yun also builds relationships with Theravada Buddhists in Thailand and other parts of Southeast Asia— work that encourages Southeast Asian Buddhists to see Taiwan, not the PRC, as the real center of Mahayana Buddhism at the beginning of the twenty-first century.

Members of Buddha's Light Mountain are proud that it was made in

Taiwan, and proud that Taiwan has become the center of the Mahayana Buddhist world. This is part and parcel of a generalized pride in the creative spirit of the Taiwanese people. Pushed on by this pride, the relationship between Taiwanese culture and Chinese culture becomes something like the relationship between American culture and English culture, different transformations of a common heritage. It is a less radical version of national difference than that advocated by the most ardent Taiwanese nationalists, but it is a powerful vision nonetheless, and one closer to mainstream sentiment than the radical nationalist vision.

This vision was on display in December of 2000, when Hsing Yun hosted Ye Xiaowen, the director of the PRC's State Agency for Religious Affairs. Hsing Yun urged mainland China to "peacefully co-exist" with Taiwan in a "rational and gentle" manner and insisted that Beijing should never resort to the use of force against Taiwan. "Chinese do not fight Chinese," he stressed. He was conceding that people on both sides of the Taiwan straits are Chinese, but also implying that they were different sorts of Chinese who needed to maintain their separateness in a cordial and peaceful manner.[42]

On other occasions, Hsing Yun has made his position more explicit. He wants a "peaceful, equal form of unification. Prior to unification, attainment of the following must be complete: first, mutual strengthening of the economy; second, cultural dialogue; third, respect for religion; and fourth, political democracy. China isn't the exclusive property of a few. The country is the convergence of the majority."[43]

It is a position midway between the radical separatists who form part of the pan-green coalition and those who espouse unification among the pan-blues—an ambivalent middle ground that corresponds closely with majority public opinion on Taiwan. Even though public opinion is shaped by pragmatic considerations (the need for good economic ties, fears of an attack) such considerations are given a moral weight by the support of Buddha's Light Mountain.

The moral weight also comes from a resonance with a larger Confucian political heritage. It is a vision of autonomy that is not based on an assertion of an inalienable, sovereign right to be independent—the kinds of rights posited by Western liberalism. Rather it is based on a Confucian method of solving conflict "in a rational and gentle manner" through persuasion and mediation. It is a method that assumes that leaders on both sides of the conflict have cultivated their hearts in the Confucian virtues and have achieved a modicum of wisdom. Perhaps an unrealistic expectation in this day and age, but one that still has some hold on traditionally educated people across the Taiwan Strait. Insofar as Buddha's Light Mountain promotes a classic taste for persuasion and compromise (and claims for this a nationalist dignity), it gives some small hope for an Asian-style political resolution of Taiwan's political crisis.

A BASIS FOR CIVIC MORALITY

The political vision of Buddha's Light Mountain does not come in the form of a comprehensive political philosophy. In takes the shape of specific moral counsels aimed at giving to a broad, diverse public Buddhist and Confucian answers to practical moral questions. Sometimes this advice seems contradictory, with no attempt to systematize it or to supply the casuistry that would enable general principles to fit specific cases. Yet, taken as a whole, these teachings provide a vision of civic order that is supportive of modern democracy, but with different strengths and weaknesses than Western liberal visions.

There are three qualities that are usually associated with a democratic civic culture. The first is solidarity—in the words of Robert Putnam, citizens have to be "alive to the interests of others." The second is equality—citizens have to be willing to treat one another as equals, and not defer to natural hierarchies. The third is tolerance—people have to be willing to accommodate a wide variety of views and to resolve most differences on the basis of persuasion and compromise rather than winner-take-all conflict.[44]

The moral teachings of humanistic Buddhists are obviously strong on social solidarity. The Buddhist belief is that the independent self is an illusion; the reality of our existence is found in our interdependence. When Hsing Yun gives speeches at college commencements, he tells the graduates, "Think of all the people who gave you your education—parents, teachers, fellow students, and others. It is an illusion to think you did it yourself."[45] Ridding oneself of such illusions does not simply yield a satisfying psychological insight, it leads to action on behalf of others. Like Cheng Yen and the other Chinese Buddhists we discuss in this book, Hsing Yun stresses cooperative behavior and is partial to institutions that enhance such behavior. In line with the Confucian tradition, he thinks that the family is the most important of such institutions, but in line with Buddhist wisdom, he believes that the interdependence learned in the family should be extended to society as a whole. The humanistic Buddhist vision is much more conducive to a generalized social solidarity than the individualistic vision of classic Western liberalism.

Classic Western liberals might argue that it is *too* conducive to solidarity and does not develop the sense of personal autonomy that is necessary to resist authoritarian rule. Yet, in a way that may not be totally consistent with his teaching about the illusion of the independent self and the ultimate reality of interdependence, Hsing Yun tells his followers to be self-reliant: "Many people tend to seek help outside themselves . . . relatives, friends, society. When a person relies completely on the support of others, he or she may become short on inner strength and may lose the ability to continue on with life once the external support is withdrawn. . . . Therefore we all must learn to depend on ourselves—the most reliable friend of all."[46] Perhaps in keeping with his religious appeal to upwardly mobile entrepreneurs, Hsing Yun emphasizes material self-reliance (rather than taking responsibility for one's own spiritual cultivation) more than Cheng Yen. "One cannot rely solely on others, nor can one rely just on heaven to provide progress. Progress can only be attained by one's own labor, perseverance, and striving. Therefore, we must be independent . . . before we can become strong. A proverb says, 'Heavenly help or help from others is no match for self-help.'"[47] This independence is based on self-respect: "A person must first have self-respect before he or she can gain others' respect. To earn the respect of others, our speech should be meaningful and our actions should be beneficial toward others."[48]

The self-respecting, but mutually regarding people who make up the world are fundamentally equal: "Equality means to realize that we are not more important, more knowledgeable, wealthier, or better than others. We are ultimately the same as others. Once we have the mindset that all people are equal, we can then respect others, help others, abide by laws, and cooperate with others."[49] In context, this is not a counsel to submissive humility but to the self-respect that would resist the formation of any arbitrary authority.

This affirmation of self-reliance and equality is not based on a notion of inalienable rights under the law. It is rather based on an insight into ultimate reality that comes only with proper cultivation of one's heart and mind. However, it is not incompatible with a political system based on a modern conception of rights. And it helps to overcome some of the deficiencies of a rights-based political system.

Inviolable individual rights place a boundary around persons, which protects them from interference by others, but also allows them to lead an isolated private life and avoid the civic engagement on which a viable democracy depends. The kind of Buddhism preached by Hsing Yun affirms the need for the individual dignity of persons to be protected, but it also exhorts those individuals to move beyond their rights-based shell to offer one another material and moral support. It thus has somewhat the same effect as some Christian and Jewish religious teachings in the United States to overcome the competitive social atomization that comes with a liberal rights-based political system.

A problem with using such religious supplements to rights-based liberalism in the United States, however, is that religious communities are sometimes intolerant, prone to demonize citizens who do not share their religious and moral beliefs. Too often, such intolerance leads to politically troubling "culture wars." Yet, for all of the problems that Taiwanese society faces, it has not been afflicted with passionate conflicts over issues of religious doctrine, sexual morality, or life-and-death issues such as abortion and capital punishment. (There is support in the Taiwanese legislature for legalizing gay civil unions. If proposed legislation is passed, Taiwan would be the first government in Asia to do so.) The teachings of Buddha's Light Mountain help support civic harmony by emphasizing tolerance, even while affirming universal moral values.

"Evil is always wrong and improper," says Hsing Yun. "To endure evil out of love is to err grossly. . . . We must be kind and compassionate towards one another. However, we must take care to give of ourselves only to righteous people and for legitimate matters. The meaning of kindness and compassion are lost when we tolerate lawlessness in the name of kindness and compassion."[50] Yet Hsing Yun goes on to say that one must give up the notion of "I'm good and you're bad." "Now suppose that I insist that I am indeed always good, while others are always bad. Would others want to befriend me or forgive my mistakes? Sometimes letting others be good guys while I play the bad guy, on the contrary, will enhance sympathy and good feelings between us."[51] He illustrates this approach with stories in which people are willing to be self-critical and to see reality from another's point of view. It is an exhortation to righteousness without self-righteousness, to the acquisition of wisdom through being open to learning from different points of view. Hsing Yun quotes Confucius, "When we see the virtuous, we should learn from them; when we see the unrespectable, we should reflect on ourselves."[52]

This way of approaching social life looks for wisdom not by heightening competition in a marketplace of ideas, but by creatively developing practices that enable people to get along harmoniously. An example of such practice is the fine art of saying "No." According to Hsing Yun, "How to say 'No' and how to refuse others tactfully is a skillful art."[53]

He counsels against declining quickly, recklessly, angrily, callously, cold-heartedly, or arrogantly. He gives advice about how instead to decline tactfully, with a smile, an alternative, or a helpful solution.[54] Such ethical practice was turned into a fine art by scholar-officials in Chinese imperial history. Through his spectacular public lectures, his homely speeches, and his output of easy-to-read publications, Hsing Yun is helping to popularize this once elite ethical practice and make it available to the upwardly mobile middle classes. This is obviously not enough to eliminate the confrontational spirit that is common in contemporary Taiwanese discourse. But to the millions of people who associate themselves with organizations like Buddha's Light Mountain and Tzu Chi, it perhaps smoothes some of the rough edges in civic life. No small contribution to a nascent democracy.

This Buddhist-Confucian vision of civic harmony presumes that members of society can achieve a basic consensus about the good life, that they can "purify their minds" so as to see the folly of "greed, violence, false views, and chaos," and that they can develop the magnanimous habits of the heart necessary to achieve compromise in difficult situations. In imperial China, Confucian scholars held that it was possible to achieve such a consensus, but only among a social elite—the scholar-officials who led the society. In a modern democracy, the burdens of consensus are much greater—it would have to be disseminated among the broad mass of citizens. In their different ways, Buddha's Light Mountain and Tzu Chi are both trying to do this—with impressive, though inevitably limited, success.

It is inevitably limited, because, as Hsing Yun puts it, "Our modern society is replete with polluting influences."[55] Buddha's Light Mountain's main method of overcoming such influences is to invite laypeople to spend some time away from the world in retreat in the monastery. But once they leave the monastery, they are in a world in which they are not only exposed to greed, violence, false views, and chaos, but also in which economic, political, and cultural survival requires them to contribute to such pollutants.

Hsing Yun has many friends among the business class, the military, and the popular culture circles. In line with the teaching of Chan masters, he tells all such people to play their roles as best they can: to be honest, valiant, and creative. He does not necessarily confront the difficulties of doing this in a globalized world. For example, success in a global economy requires participating in competition that is much more intense than what was found in the premodern economies in which traditional Buddhist teaching was formulated. One secret to Taiwan's strong economic growth is its ability to exploit cheap labor in the PRC. (Indeed, the Taiwanese have a reputation for running some of the harshest sweatshops in China.)[56] Success in global politics—especially the high-stakes politics of PRC-Taiwan relations—requires amassing military assets. Success in a commercialized global culture requires producing slick entertainment. Hsing Yun's popularity is based on not placing impossible (or even extremely inconvenient) demands on people enmeshed in modern worldly systems of wealth and power. He only asks that people act with good intentions and try to lessen the greed, violence, and beguilement that are part and parcel of their work.

Although Hsing Yun's views about moral ideals are both clear and conservative, he does not make firm pronouncements about how followers should balance ideals with the demands of reality. For example, he and all other Buddhists think that abortion is wrong—it violates the precept against taking of life. But he would not tell a follower to never terminate a pregnancy. Abortion would bring bad karma, but in particular circumstances it might be necessary to avoid bringing even greater harm to others.[57] (Tzu Chi takes the same stance. As the head of one of the Tzu Chi hospitals says, "We are not in favor of abortion, but we will not interfere with a clinical decision between a doctor and patient.")[58]

The result of all this is that the kind of social consensus that Hsing Yun promotes is a fuzzy, ambiguous social consensus that allows for a great plurality of interpretation among people in different circumstances. Under these circumstances, it may be possible to promote a quite broad set of common understandings about the desirability of improving social life without provoking sectarian civil strife.

THE LIGHTNESS AND THICKNESS OF BEING

It might be tempting to see the moral consensus facilitated by Buddha's Light Mountain as nothing more than a tissue of socially ineffectual platitudes. However, such a view would ignore the depths of earnestness generated by Hsing Yun's lectures and the dharma functions of Buddha's Light Mountain. The moral consensus cultivated by these may be light, but it is thick.

To explain what I mean with such adjectives, let me describe how such a consensus was cultivated in a Taking Refuge ceremony at Buddha's Light Mountain in the fall of 1999. Taking refuge in the Buddha, the dharma, and the sangha is the basic rite of initiation into the community centered on a particular temple. The ceremony was held at 7:00 A.M. in the chill of dawn on the huge plaza in front of the Hall of Great Compassion. There were one thousand participants, although about two-thirds of them were accepting the five precepts (a higher level of initiation) instead of simply taking refuge. Those who were accepting the precepts had spent the previous three days on retreat. They wore black robes, while those taking refuge wore street clothes. On the next morning, another large group would accept their bodhisattva vows, a higher level of initiation. In all, about three thousand people would go through various levels of Buddhist initiation that weekend. Such ceremonies are held not only at Buddha's Light Mountain itself, but in its branches around the world every three months.

People of all ages were participating, including young children, although most participants appeared to be middle aged. Marching in procession, the participants took their places in front of long rows of kneeling pads. At the end of each row stood a nun, who guided the participants on when to stand, kneel, and prostrate themselves. The sounds of beautifully harmonic, rhythmic chanting were broadcast through loudspeakers placed alongside the plaza. Positioned behind an altar in front of the congregation was Hsing Ting, the abbot of the monastery, resplendent in orange robes and assisted by several monks. He led the participants in chanting, praying, and finally in making their professions of faith. When those who were accepting the five precepts made their vows, they draped a brown sash over their black robes.

At the end of the ceremony, the abbot came down through each row and sprinkled each participant with sacred water. Then red envelopes were distributed so that each participant could contribute money, and each participant received a certificate of declaration stating that he or she had taken refuge or accepted the precepts at Buddha's Light Mountain. To my surprise, I received a certificate, with my new "dharma name" (Zhen Hui—True Wisdom). I was surprised because I had attended the ceremony as a participant observer, standing in the back, bowing and kneeling at the proper times, but with no intention of being initiated as a Buddhist. I had told my hosts that I respected their beliefs and was interested in knowing more about them, but I had never said that I wanted to be initiated into Buddhism. Yet they seemed to assume that as long as I took part in all aspects of the ceremony, I was now a Buddhist, professed intention or not.

They were willing to accept someone who had been only weakly

Figure 10. Taking refuge at Buddha's Light Mountain. Photograph
by Ho Hua-chin.

formed in Buddhist teaching. If they considered me part of their religious
and moral consensus, it was indeed one that did not impose heavy moral
and cognitive burdens—a light consensus. But there were many others
at that ceremony who had spent a considerable amount of time preparing for it and were indeed very serious about their commitment. After
the ceremony, we listened to a lecture by one of the monks instructing
us on how to reconcile our Buddhism with the demands of family life
and how to steadily deepen our commitment. If the weight of the Buddhist practice that I had taken on that day seemed light, it was part of a
thick, complicated discourse and practice engaged in by a great many
people, which could pull one in deeper and deeper as one encountered
the inevitable sorrows and impermanence of existence.

Because of its "lightness"—the vagueness of its strictures and their
lack of ability to constrain any given individual's behavior at any given
time—it is difficult to measure the influence that Buddha's Light Mountain's humanistic Buddhist teachings may have on public opinion. But
because of its "thickness"—its capacity to enfold a great many people
and to mold their thinking over a long period of time—we may assume
that the influence of Buddha's Light Mountain is significant. It is an

influence that is conducive to a democratic civic life. The millions of Buddha's Light Mountain devotees agree that they should help the poor and the weak, and they do not distinguish between deserving and undeserving poor. Devotees also listen sincerely to Hsing Yun's teaching that they should maintain the ecological balance of nature and that "ultimately, when we harm others, we are harming ourselves." However imperfect, their efforts to put such teachings into practice help provide the discipline and the sense of responsibility that make democracy possible.

CHAPTER 4

Dharma Drum Mountain

Transcendent Meaning in a Broken World

Within days of the earthquake, a black-and-white picture of a thin, bespectacled monk, with thick prayer beads around his neck and head bowed deeply in prayer, started to appear in every sort of media, including full-page ads in the major newspapers and huge billboards along central thoroughfares. The image bore the caption "Get Going Taiwan." The monk was Sheng Yen, the master of Dharma Drum Mountain, who, along with Cheng Yen of Tzu Chi and Hsing Yun of Buddha's Light Mountain, is one of the best-known Buddhist leaders in Asia.

Dharma Drum Mountain has a narrower popular appeal than either Tzu Chi or Buddha's Light Mountain. Its lay membership is nonetheless significant (about three hundred thousand regular followers), its influence is deep, and in crucial ways it pushes Taiwanese political culture further than Tzu Chi and Buddha's Light Mountain toward a global vision of universal significance.

On the second Sunday after the 1999 earthquake, I attended a sutra-preaching session at the Nung Chan Monastery, the center of Dharma Drum Mountain's activities in Taipei. Regular prayer and meditation sessions are held every Sunday at Nung Chan—an adaptation to the day of rest provided in a workweek structured according to the Western calendar. All of the middle-class Buddhist groups that we have studied have adapted the styles of their rituals to Western-structured space and time, but Dharma Drum Mountain seems to have gone even farther than the others, which do not have regular Sunday services.

Figure 11. Master Sheng Yen. Photograph courtesy of the Dharma Drum Mountain Buddhist Association.

In its arrangement of space and style of presentation, the event I attended that Sunday seemed more similar to a Protestant service than the other Buddhist ceremonies that I participated in. The worship space was a large, simply furnished room, with sliding glass doors on all sides. There were neat rows of about three hundred steel folding chairs for the congregation. In the front was a simple altar table with large vases of flowers; behind this was a large statue of the Buddha. The ceremonies centered on an exposition of Buddhist scriptures by Sheng Yen.

Each congregant was given a hymn book and a book of sutras. The service began with an a cappella hymn sung by the whole congregation. Then a stately procession of lay devotees in black robes and monks and nuns in grey robes filed in, followed by Master Sheng Yen in a saffron robe. Tall, thin, and wearing large glasses, the Master both looked and talked like a scholar.

When Sheng Yen reached the front of the hall, he bowed deeply to the statue of the Buddha and was helped into a lotus position atop a raised platform facing the congregation. Those who accompanied him in the procession took seats on either side of the sanctuary at the front of the hall. Then he began his exposition of the scriptures.

He had an informal style of preaching, which aimed to engage the congregation as much as possible. He had the congregation open their sutra books to a particular page. "Where did I leave off last time? I think

it was here. It's been a number of weeks since I last preached on the sutras. Something happened during that time. What was it?" Everybody
answered, "Earthquake." "Yes, the earthquake. Did you read about
Dharma Drum Mountain in the newspapers? How many saw the articles about what Dharma Drum Mountain is doing to respond?" A large
show of hands. "We don't have as many resources as other Buddhist organizations. So we're concentrating our resources on what we're best at:
cultural work, healing the spirit, counseling, psychological work."

GIVING MEANING TO AN UNSETTLED WORLD

Although Dharma Drum Mountain does indeed have fewer material resources than Tzu Chi and Buddha's Light Mountain, it has a propor-
tionately higher level of cultural capital. It is especially attractive to
knowledge workers, scholars, teachers, and creative artists—or to those
who want to emulate such intellectuals. According to the theory of Mary
Douglas, highly intellectual members of the middle classes tend to emphasize a religion of inner experience and "humanist philanthropy" over
elaborate rituals. Dharma Drum Mountain exceeds both Tzu Chi and
Buddha's Light Mountain in the simplicity of its rituals and the single-
mindedness of its quest for individual enlightenment.

Sheng Yen seemed to see his role primarily in terms of alleviating the
psychological trauma of the earthquake by providing meaning to a shaken
population. "Did you see me on TV?" he asked the congregation. He
had been giving television interviews making a case for a positive Buddhist understanding of the disaster. Why had such a terrible thing happened? One explanation from a Buddhist perspective was that the earthquake was the result of bad karma, a consequence of accumulated
misdeeds of the Taiwanese people. But that was not the right way to think
about it, said Sheng Yen. The earthquake was an opportunity for Taiwanese people to acquire good karma by responding generously to the
needs created by this tragedy, and by warning other people in the world
about the need to undertake ecologically friendly development that would
minimize future earthquake damage. The people who had been killed or
injured were not suffering retribution for past sins—they were bodhi-
sattvas whose suffering would warn people about the need to be better
prepared for natural disasters in the future. He pressed further his optimistic view of the human condition. He asked the congregation how many
bad people they thought there were in the world. One in ten? One in one

hundred? One in one thousand? "I think," he said, "it's no more than one in a thousand."

"Did you see the posters 'Get Going Taiwan'?" Sheng Yen continued. The message of this exhortation, he explained, was that Taiwan would emerge from this terrible crisis strengthened in spirit.

After about forty-five minutes of back-and-forth dialogue about how to respond with a Buddhist spirit to the earthquake, Sheng Yen turned to his exegesis of the day's sutra verses. It was about transformation of light into darkness and vice versa. This led into a fairly abstract and complicated discussion about Buddhist epistemology. Our perceptions about the world were illusions. But there was a distinction between perceptions of "hard realities," like buildings falling down in earthquakes—these were not illusions—and interpretations of the meaning of these realities. The understanding of this earthquake as a disaster was an illusion. One needed spiritual healing to understand this event in a positive light, an understanding that would comfort the afflicted and produce good karma for generations to come.

At the end of his exposition, Sheng Yen announced that this would be his last session of the year. He spends only about a half year in Taiwan. The remainder of the time he is based in New York, either at a Chan (Zen) meditation center in Queens or a retreat center in upstate New York. He also travels frequently around the world. Among other places, he has recently given dharma lectures in Vancouver, Tel Aviv, and Moscow.

Both Tzu Chi and Buddha's Light Mountain have affiliates around the world, yet the roots of these institutions remain deeply embedded in Taiwan. Members of Tzu Chi centers in the United States, for example, often talk about their desire to return to their "spiritual home" at the Abode of Still Thoughts in Hualien. Monks and nuns at the Buddha's Light Mountain temples also look to the main temple in Kaohsiung for guidance. But followers of Sheng Yen in New York do not necessarily look to the temple complex in Taiwan as their spiritual home. The master, after all, spends half of his time in New York. Dharma Drum Mountain represents a cosmopolitan Buddhist space that has broken free from its geographical origins.

It also represents a form of Buddhist practice that pushes beyond its cultural environment. As we have seen, the social ethics of both Tzu Chi and Buddha's Light Mountain are heavily grounded in the Confucian tradition. Tzu Chi members constantly speak of themselves in familistic terms. The pure land that they want to create on earth is like an idealized big family in which the familial relationships that are at the heart of Confucianism will be purified and expanded to embrace the entire world. The principles for social and political life promulgated by Buddha's Light Mountain are also Confucian, although a Confucianism expanded and enriched by a Buddhist religious vision. As we will see, there are indeed Confucian elements in the teaching and practice of Dharma Drum Mountain. But the prime focus of Dharma Drum Mountain is on Chan practice, which pushes the practitioner beyond conscious thought, beyond distinctions between self and other, and beyond commitment to bounded social institutions. Compared with the other two Buddhist associations we have studied, Dharma Drum Mountain is much more Buddhist than Confucian. It seeks to free the self from illusions of autonomy. But in doing so it paradoxically deepens the practitioner's self-consciousness. It creates an individuated self, separated from traditional attachments to family, ethnic group, or even nation—and then it strives to reintegrate that self with others on the basis of universalistic principles. It provides Taiwan's emerging civil religion with an important thrust toward transcendence.

To more fully understand why and how these qualities of Dharma Drum Mountain have been generated, we need, once again, to look more closely at how they developed.

THE CREATION OF DHARMA DRUM MOUNTAIN

The early career of Sheng Yen, the founder of Dharma Drum Mountain, parallels that of Hsing Yun of Buddha's Light Mountain. He was born near Shanghai in 1930 (about four years after Hsing Yun) and sent by his parents, who were too poor to support him, to a monastery at the age of thirteen. The monastic training was similar to Hsing Yun's experience, a harsh routine of strict rules with little attempt to explain the meaning of spiritual practice to the young monks. After two years, he ran away to a Buddhist academy in Shanghai founded by a student of the humanist Buddhist reformer Tai Xu. About three years after that, when the Communists occupied Shanghai, he fled to Taiwan, where he was conscripted into the KMT army.[1]

Here his career path diverged from that of Hsing Yun. He served in the army for about ten years—outside of the framework of Buddhist institutions inhabited by Hsing Yun, who was steadily developing his career as a monastic teacher. Nonetheless, Sheng Yen continued reading the Buddhist scriptures and practicing meditation. In his autobiographical writing, he describes himself as a "big ball of doubt." Since his time in the monastery on the Chinese mainland, he had felt a strong desire to follow a Buddhist path, but he had no idea how to do so. "There were many contradictions in Buddhist teaching that I could not resolve. This was very disturbing since I had deep faith in the Buddha's teachings and believed that the sutras could not be wrong. I was burdened with such questions as 'What is enlightenment?' 'What is Buddhahood?' Questions like these were very numerous in my mind and I desperately needed to know the answers."[2]

Finally, in 1959, at the age of twenty-eight, he achieved "the deepest spiritual experience in his life." In his own words,

> I was visiting a monastery in southern Taiwan, where I sometimes lectured. I learned that a famous monk, Ling Yuan, was also visiting. That night we happened to share the same sleeping platform. Seeing that he was meditating instead of sleeping, I sat with him. I was still burdened by my questions and was desperate to have them resolved. He seemed to be quite at ease, with no problems in the world, so I decided to approach him.
>
> He listened patiently as I spoke of my many doubts and problems. In reply, he would just ask, 'Any more?' I continued like this for two or three hours. I was extremely agitated and anxious for answers. Finally he sighed and said, 'Put down!' He slapped suddenly on the bed, and shouted 'Put down!' These words struck me like lightning. My body poured sweat; I felt like I had been instantly cured of a bad cold. I felt a great weight being suddenly lifted from me. It was a very comfortable and soothing feeling. We just sat there, not speaking a word. I was extremely happy. It was one of the most pleasant nights of my life. The next day I continued to experience great happiness. The whole world was fresh, as though I was seeing it for the first time.[3]

For all of its drama, this passage fits a common pattern of Chan enlightenment experiences: years of painful doubt in spite of constant efforts at meditation, and then a sudden insight triggered by an unexpected remark from a master. In itself, having a deep experience of enlightenment does not make one a Buddhist master. The experience must be personally certified by other masters, who then agree to make one a member of their line of dharma transmission. This certification and dharma transmission would not be given until sixteen years later.

First, Sheng Yen had to leave the army and "take on the monk's robes again." He undertook training at the Buddhist Culture Center in Peitou, a suburb of Taipei, under Tung-Ch'u, a master who, though "seeking neither fame nor followers," was "widely known and respected." As was common with traditional Chan masters, Tung-Ch'u was a harsh taskmaster.

> My stay with him turned out to be one of the most difficult periods of my life. He constantly harassed me . . . . For example, after telling me to move my things into one room, he would later tell me to move to another room. Then he would tell me to move back in again. Once, he told me to seal off a door and to open a new one in another wall. I had to haul the bricks by foot from a distant kiln up to the monastery. We normally used a gas stove, but my master often sent me to the mountains to gather a special kind of firewood that he liked to brew his tea over. I would constantly be scolded for cutting the wood too small or too large. I had many experiences of this kind.
>
> In my practice it was much the same. When I asked him how to practice, he would tell me to meditate. But after a few days he would quote a famous master, saying, "You can't make a mirror by polishing a brick, and you can't become a Buddha by sitting." So he ordered me to do prostrations. Then, after several days, he would say, "This is nothing but a dog eating shit off the ground. Read the sutras!" After I read for a couple of weeks, he would scold me again, saying that the patriarchs thought the sutras were good only for cleaning sores. He would say, "You're smart. Write an essay." When I showed him an essay he would tear it up saying, "These are all stolen ideas." Then he would challenge me to use my own wisdom and say original things.[4]

This kind of arbitrary, almost sadistic treatment toward disciples was indeed common among traditional Chan masters. According to Sheng Yen, "Although it was hard to think of his treatment as compassionate, it really was. If I hadn't been trained with this kind of discipline, I would not have accomplished much. I also realized from him that learning the Buddha dharma was a very vigorous activity, and that one should be self-reliant in practice."[5]

Only a religious virtuoso could have endured such harsh treatment and found it meaningful. However, in the atmosphere of Taiwan during the late 1950s and early 1960s, such discipline might not have seemed abnormal. This was still a period of heavy-handed military dictatorship, resented by many Taiwanese, but at least partially legitimated by the need to fight the cold war. People—especially low-ranking troops in the army—were used to the experience of submitting to capricious authorities. As Taiwan's authoritarianism became more routinized in the late 1960s, as an entrepreneurial urban middle class began to form in the 1970s, and as Taiwanese began to absorb messages of individualism through their interaction with the West, such arbitrary discipline would have increasingly come to be seen as pathological. When he became an established master himself, Sheng Yen would continue to emphasize the need for hard work and self-reliance that he had learned from Tung-ch'u—this, after all, fit the emergent ethos of a cosmopolitan, middle-class society. But he would not impose on others the harsh treatment he had endured from his master. He would rather emphasize the necessity for the hard work of focused study and the discipline of consistent meditation.

After two years with Tung-ch'u, Sheng Yen embarked on a solitary retreat. He lived as a hermit in a hut in the mountains of southern Taiwan. He ate one meal a day, consisting of sweet potato leaves that he cultivated himself. He spent his days reciting sutras, prostrating (going from upright to facedown for hours on end), and meditating. He says that he had originally planned to stay for three years, but he liked it so much that he continued on for six.[6] His time in the wilderness parallels that of Cheng Yen—it was a part of establishing one's credentials as an authentic Buddhist master at that time. But unlike Cheng Yen, who traveled with a companion and later gathered a small band of lay followers, Sheng Yen emphasized self-reliance. Before he embarked on his retreat, his Master Tung-ch'u had told him, "The Master cannot worry over his disciple like a mother. The master just leads the disciple onto the Path; the disciple must walk the Path himself."[7]

After six years, Sheng Yen returned to Taipei, but there wasn't a place for him within the Buddhist establishment there. Thus, he concluded that "to teach Buddha dharma in this age, I needed a modern education and degree. So I made plans to study in Japan." A year later, at the age of thirty-eight, he began doctoral studies in Buddhist literature at Rissho University in Japan and received his LLD in 1975.[8] He has more formal academic education than any other major Buddhist leader in Taiwan.

In 1975, he received formal dharma transmission in the Tsao Tung (Caodong or Soto in Japanese) Chan tradition from his former master Tung-ch'u. In 1978 he received transmission in the other major Chan school, the Lin Chi (Linji or Rinzai in Japanese) tradition, from Ling Yuan, the monk who had inspired his first enlightenment. But in the mid-1970s, there wasn't yet an opportunity for him to become a master of a large temple in Taiwan. The only such opportunity was in the United States, at the Temple of Enlightenment in New York. Even though he couldn't speak English, he became abbot there in 1977. When he expressed misgivings to his Zen teacher in Japan about going to America— "But Master, I don't know English"—his master replied, "Zen doesn't rely on words. Why worry about words?"[9]

In 1978, however, he was back in Taiwan as a professor in the Chinese Culture College (at the time not a fully accredited university) and as president of the Chinese Institute of Buddhist Culture in Taipei, an institute for publishing Buddhist books and magazines that had been founded by his old master, Tung-ch'u, who had died in December 1977.[10] Connected with the Institute of Buddhist Culture was the Nung Chan Monastery, which Tung-ch'u had established in 1975. Like Tung-ch'u himself, the monastery was well respected but somewhat marginal to religious life in Taiwan. It was originally a simple two-story farmhouse, built on land that was not zoned for religious buildings. This was eventually expanded into a six-thousand-square-foot compound.[11] The main worship space was constructed with sliding glass doors on all sides and with a partition that can shut off the Buddhist altar from the rest of the building—so that it could be classified as a shed rather than a temple. The local authorities were willing to tolerate the existence of the monastery partly because it was located in a marginally inhabited district on the outskirts of Taipei.[12] However, new roads (and by the late 1990s, a subway line) provided convenient transportation to the temple. With charismatic leadership under Sheng Yen it was poised to grow.

A major thrust of Sheng Yen's work was to provide advanced education in Buddhist scholarship. He began a graduate program in Buddhist studies at the Chinese Culture College. In 1984, the college received formal accreditation as a university—but because laws discouraging Buddhist activity were still in force at the time, the price of becoming an accredited university was the termination of Sheng Yen's program, which was not purely academic but aimed at training students for advanced religious practice. This led Sheng Yen to reestablish the program in advanced Buddhist studies at the Chinese Institute of Buddhist Culture.[13] At the same time, he expanded the Nung Chan Monastery. His reputation as a highly cultivated Buddhist educator was increasing. This led to a rapid growth in participation in the Nung Chan Monastery's activities after the end of martial law in 1987.

Sheng Yen was also developing Chan practice in New York and gaining an international reputation. A Chan meditation group was established in the late 1970s at the Temple of Enlightenment in New York. As this grew, Sheng Yen moved it to a Chan meditation center in Queens. In the 1980s, he also established the Chan Retreat Center in upstate New York.[14]

After martial law ended in Taiwan, the political restrictions on publicity were abolished; at the same time, advances in information technology provided multiple vehicles for mass communication. Like the other Buddhist masters discussed in this book, Sheng Yen steadily expanded his reputation through multimedia publicity—books, pamphlets, audio and video tapes, CDs, a regular television program, and multilingual websites. The era of reticent masters like Sheng Yen's mentor, Tung-ch'u, who gained powerful influence while "seeking neither fame nor followers," was over. The future seemed to belong to masters who could ride the tidal wave of the new media.

As Taipei's building boom continued in the 1980s, the marginal land on which the Nung Chan Monastery was located became expensive real estate, and the city government grew less willing to tolerate the presence of an illegally zoned building. To begin to provide a more permanent home for his growing Buddhist community, Sheng Yen acquired a declining temple in 1989 in the mountain valley now called Dharma Drum Mountain, and began efforts to acquire more land for building a major Buddhist center there. It was at this time that all of the institutions directed by Sheng Yen, in both Taiwan and the United States, received the common name Dharma Drum Mountain.

It was also at this time that Sheng Yen began systematically to organize lay volunteers to aid in the development of the organization. Tzu Chi, with its organized commissioners and its networks of supporters throughout Taiwanese society, had shown how effective such lay groups could be in fund-raising and outreach. Under the leadership of Sheng Yen, Dharma Drum Mountain established the Dharmapala Organization to help raise the funds that would be necessary to build a monastic and educational complex at the Dharma Drum Mountain site.

This organization carried out fund-raising meetings. As with Tzu Chi, core supporters were each urged to recruit ten other supporters. They developed a computerized system to identify and keep track of this network of donors and volunteers—by 1999 there were three hundred computers available for this purpose. Volunteers were organized into sixteen groups with specialized functions ranging from hospitality, publicity, security, construction, and environmental cleanup. These groups provide support for the large retreats and other events carried out by Dharma Drum Mountain. The basis for this interlocking set of lay organizations was the large network of followers who attended Sheng Yen's lectures, retreats, and meditation sessions. Now such people were being transformed from disciples into partners and given the resources to shape the future of Dharma Drum Mountain.

Dharma Drum Mountain expanded steadily in Taiwan during the 1990s. By the end of the millennium, it had about three hundred thou-

Figure 12. Dharma Drum Mountain. Photograph courtesy of the Dharma Drum Mountain Buddhist Association.

sand lay members, in addition to about one hundred monks and nuns at the Nung Chan Monastery. In the mid-1990s, construction began on the monastery complex on the 120-acre site on Dharma Drum Mountain. The cost of building this complex was about US$30 million. It now includes a Buddha Hall, a Chan meditation hall, a lecture auditorium, retreat facilities, and a Buddhist university. It was officially opened with a solemn ceremony in October 2005. Meanwhile, the study courses, retreats, books (Sheng Yen himself has published ninety books), magazines, and videos (all of Sheng Yen's dharma talks are televised) of Dharma Drum Mountain have extended its influence well beyond its formal membership.[15]

RELIGIOUS VISION

Sheng Yen would say that the primary purpose of all of this building and organizing is education. Cheng Yen and Hsing Yun would say the same of their organizations. But Dharma Drum's education is more academic in emphasis—more about thinking than acting. Although Sheng Yen would insist that the ultimate aim of this education is to produce right attitudes and to lead to an enlightenment that transcends words, he still emphasizes a thoughtful study of Buddhist doctrines, the kind of study that goes beyond learning the content of the doctrines, and enables the student to extend them creatively to new situations. The Chinese Institute of Buddhist Studies has an international faculty and has educated about two hundred graduate students in advanced Buddhist studies. The monks and nuns in Sheng Yen's monastery tend to enter with higher levels of education than those of Cheng Yen's Abode of Still Thoughts and Hsing Yun's Buddha's Light Mountain. The nun who arranged my visits to Dharma Drum Mountain had a PhD in economics from a top-tier American university. Sheng Yen, like Hsing Yun, has arranged for many of his monastics to study for higher degrees abroad. Several were studying at Yale University at the time I did my research. By encouraging this higher education, Sheng Yen encourages the monastics to think for themselves, even to question the master. Lay followers I interviewed also seemed more willing and able to think originally about the religious basis of their commitments—not just (as in the case of many Tzu Chi volunteers) to think creatively about the practical means of carrying out their work.

Nonetheless, the speeches and writings of Sheng Yen remain the primary source of Dharma Drum Mountain's vision. At the heart of the vision is the practice of Chan. According to Sheng Yen:

> Chan is often referred to as the "gateless gate." The gate is both a method of practice and a path to liberation; this gate is "gateless," however, in that Chan does not rely on any specific method to help a practitioner achieve liberation. The methodless method is the highest method. So long as the practitioner can drop the self-centered mind, the gateway into Chan will open naturally.
>
> The primary obstacle to attaining wisdom is attachment to the self. When you face people, things, and situations, the notion of "I" arises immediately within you. When you attach to this "I," you categorize and judge everything else accordingly: "This is mine; that is not. This is good for me; that is not. I like this; I hate that." Attachment to the idea of self makes true clarity impossible.
>
> But how might we define non-attachment? According to Chan, non-attachment means that when you face circumstances and deal with other people, there is no "I" in relation to whatever may appear in front of you. Things are as they are, vivid and clear. You can respond appropriately and give whatever is needed. Clear awareness of things as they are, in this state of selflessness, is what Chan calls wisdom. Giving what others may need with no thought of the self is what Chan calls compassion. Wisdom and compassion describe the awareness and function of the enlightened mind. In Chan, these two cannot be separated, and both depend on putting down the attachment to the self.[16]

The way to shedding oneself of such attachments is to practice meditation, achieved with the help of exercises to concentrate the attention and to control one's breathing. Beyond this, one tries to transcend one's thoughts.

> Transcending your thoughts . . . is a method that consists of maintaining the attitude of non-involvement with yourself or others. The goal of this method is roughly described as a phrase that translates as, "Be separate,

or free, from the mind, from thoughts, and from consciousness." To be free from all of this is to be in a state of enlightenment. In such freedom of mind it might be said that we see the world.

No matter what method you choose, you must remember that when we practice in the Chan tradition, we refrain from using words and speech. . . . Nonetheless, you will notice that Chan masters talk a lot. They sometimes write a lot too. But the import of what we talk or write about is to convey that whatever you think or say is wrong. That is the content of all my talks. No words or description will suffice to describe a state of realization. Anyone who attempted to describe such a state would be considered by a Chan master to be a smart devil, not an awakened being.[17]

Sheng Yen does indeed write a lot, but at the core of his teaching is a demand that his followers transcend his words. Each individual must follow his or her own path. This helps to create an open, evolving community of individuals who think freely yet are committed to connecting compassionately with one another—a community with at least the beginnings of a democratic ethos.

This outlook drives Sheng Yen toward quite radical pronouncements about current cultural and political problems. To worries about the "clash of civilizations" he proposes a basis for tolerance and cooperation between opposing faiths.

When people maintain what they believe is the best religion in the world, they should not forget that others also have the right to say that their faith is the best. . . . Therefore, I would like to make a sincere proposal: if you find that the doctrines of your faith contain something that is intolerant of the other groups, or in contradiction with the promotion of world peace, then you should make new interpretations of these relevant doctrines. Why? Because every wholesome religion should get along peacefully with other groups so that it can, step by step, influence humankind on earth to stay far away from the causes of war.[18]

In a speech delivered nine days after the terrorist attacks of September 11, 2001, Sheng Yen pushed further his insistence on simultaneously respecting and relativizing all religions.

Once on an airplane, I was sitting right next to a Christian missionary who was piously reading the Bible and praying. Seeing that I had nothing to do, he gave me a Bible and showed me how to read it. I praised his good intentions and enthusiasm, and agreed with his statement that Christianity is the only religion through which one can attain salvation. He immediately asked me, "If this is the case, why are you a Buddhist monk? Isn't that a pity?" I said, "I'm sorry, but for me, Buddhism is most suitable. So I would say that Buddhism is the best religion."[19]

Sheng Yen's position is that all religions are part of a single ultimate reality that is expressed in different ways in different religions, a position that will not be acceptable for a fundamentalist monotheist, but which has a strong foundation in the Chan tradition.

Adding a touch of sociology to a classical Buddhist analysis, he distinguishes between a culturally relative "sacred" and the ultimate truth.[20]

> The definition of the "sacred" varies according to time, place, and individual. This is something we must be aware of in a modern, pluralistic, and globalized society. . . . The supreme truth revered by every religion should be absolute and flawless. It is definitely sacred. But once secular elements and outside agendas are incorporated into the interpretation, it becomes a subjective notion and thus generates diversity. For example, the theory of causes and conditions is the utmost sacred in Buddhism. But we do not deny the value of monotheism. While we neither identify with nor accept monotheism, we can understand and respect it. We acknowledge that all virtuous religions have room for continuous development and also have the right to proclaim themselves to be the world's best religion. Likewise, I myself would say that Buddhism is the best religion.[21]

Such thinking makes sense from a Chan perspective that holds that mere words and concepts can never express the ultimate truth.

> The days of monocultural societies are long gone and will not return again; and fortunately so, otherwise the destiny of humanity would be a very tragic one! Therefore, I would like to make this appeal here for all humanity: humankind must understand that the notion of *sacred* is interpreted differently in a multicultural pluralistic world, and that we should strive to seek for harmony. Such harmony is not to be found in dogmatic homogenization or elimination of difference. It can only come through a grassroots discovery of commonality within difference, and difference within commonality.[22]

For Sheng Yen, this leads to a strongly held conviction that all divisions between nations, ethnic groups, and even families must be transcended. "In an open society, one may find several different faiths even within a family. We must respect, even support, each other's choices with an attitude of appreciation, and should never criticize other faiths based on our own subjective standpoint. We should cooperate to create a harmonious, peaceful, happy, and warm community in which to live."[23]

When applying this vision to the practical problems of global conflict, Sheng Yen combines pacifist idealism with a resigned realism. In an interview given soon after the attacks of September 11, 2001, he stressed that the best response would be nonviolent. Yet he notes that "it is well recognized that under such attack the U.S. could not possibly just endure without retribution." Nor is he against all use of force. "The nonviolent approach Buddhists take is not weakness without the backing of strong force. We are in favor of deterring the rogues with strong military backup and then steering them to the right path."[24]

In general, however, he is in favor of positive measures to alleviate the poverty that breeds international resentment and to build bridges of cross-cultural understanding. Moreover, he calls on "all people of love and wisdom, to employ all means and approaches to actively interact with, understand, and empathize with every ethnic group, region and individual who is prone to terrorism." And he advises "all religious and spiritual leaders that while they should pay attention to politics, they should not harbor ambitions in politics. Furthermore, they should warn their followers not to be provoked, manipulated, and controlled by politicians and become their tools."[25]

After the United States invaded Iraq, Sheng Yen declared "As a religious teacher, I do not support any kind of war." He prayed that the war end soon with minimal death and destruction, and he pledged to use the resources of Dharma Drum Mountain to help reconstruct Iraq. Like their response to the Taiwan earthquake, Dharma Drum Mountain's aid to Iraq mostly took the form of "calming and easing the minds of the people."[26]

The other Buddhist leaders we have studied in this book have not engaged as much as Sheng Yen in global dialogues about issues of terrorism and war, and their statements are not as directly challenging to hegemonic ideologies. Cheng Yen is focused more on the practical means to relieve the suffering caused by wars. Hsing Yun said that "all religions endorse peace but sometimes peace is attained through force. War is a means of last resort and can be transformed into a force for compassion. In fact there are other means that can be employed besides war. For example, compassionate persuasion, wise guidance, the censure of public opinion, and restrictions on travel. . . . Only by overcoming violence with compassion can permanent peace be achieved."[27] It is not that these other two Buddhist leaders would have major substantive disagreements with Sheng Yen, but the style of their responses is more practical or diplomatic than intellectual.

As such, their approaches embed them more deeply in the Confucian ethic of compromise than does the intellectualism of Sheng Yen. The practical concerns of Hsing Yun and Cheng Yen work hard not to offend anyone. The intellectualism of Sheng Yen pushes him toward a vision that is somewhat more challenging to the Confucian ethics or the nationalist sentiments that shape Taiwan's political culture.

THE EXPERIENCE OF PRACTITIONERS

But how deeply does Sheng Yen's vision affect his lay followers? Besides having a number of casual conversations with participants on a daylong bus excursion to the Dharma Drum Mountain site outside of Taipei, I interviewed five active volunteers, including the head of the Dharmapala Organization. Although most of them had read or listened to many of Sheng Yen's teachings, they did not cite these teachings very much, and they did not attempt to apply the teachings directly to practical life circumstances. They talked instead about the experience of being a part of Dharma Drum Mountain.

They talked first and foremost about the effects of the experience on their personal lives and then on its effects on their social relationships. According to those I interviewed, they joined Dharma Drum Mountain to resolve personal difficulties, not to propagate Sheng Yen's broader pronouncements on social morality and world peace. Their personal difficulties were not of the dramatic kind that one sees in Tzu Chi testimonials; most of them had stable families and successful professional careers: radio broadcaster, dentist, teacher, lawyer. They had not encountered major life crises but had felt harried by the pressures of life and dissatisfied by the superficiality of consumer culture. Dharma Drum Mountain had attracted them because of its emphasis on Chan meditation. Some said that they had started practicing Chan because they thought it would be good for their health. They also saw their involvement with Dharma Drum Mountain as a good education, and they had been impressed with the quality of Sheng Yen's books. As they participated in Chan sessions and in educational sessions, they were gradually recruited into one of Dharma Drum Mountain's volunteer groups, eventually participated in its retreats, and then took refuge at the monastery. They spoke of their embrace of Buddhism as a slow process rather than a dramatic conversion. "Before I became involved with Dharma Drum Mountain," one of them said, "I started every day by looking at the newspapers about where to go for entertainment and shopping." She was encouraged by a monk to volunteer for one of Dharma Drum Mountain's service groups and her life slowly became more meaningful and happy. "What I learned, I slowly gave to other people."

Many of them then developed what a Westerner might call an evangelical attitude. "My main goal is to share this harmony and happiness." But it was not a kind of proselytizing that put them in sharp conflict with the world. It was based on a desire to improve the lives of others, not rescue them from damnation. Although the lay followers claimed that their outlook on life had changed, they did not want to disrupt their primary social relationships. "After I took the bodhisattva vows," said one woman, "my husband took a look at a copy of them—and he wouldn't speak to me for a week. But then he saw that I didn't neglect to cook for him and take care of him. I would go out to practice meditation after he left for work in the morning and be back before he returned home. Then he accepted me." She thought that her Chan practice made her a better wife. The lay followers in Taiwan thus were more inclined to transform themselves so as to better adapt to the world, rather than to attempt to change the world.

The world was first of all a Confucian social sphere based on idealized families. Indeed, like Tzu Chi and Buddha's Light Mountain, Dharma Drum Mountain begins its pedagogy by stressing traditional Confucian conceptions of mutual responsibility within the family. At a day of retreat for parents and adolescent children that I attended in 2005, the emphasis was on getting children to appreciate and express gratitude for the sacrifices that their parents had made for them. But then they were told to appreciate the importance of this interdependence in all realms of life. After a string quartet played a piece of classical Western music, there was a sermon by a young layman, who explained that "Buddhism is like music." It requires that different people work together to produce harmony. Even though the people in this string quarter weren't from the same family, they came together to make beautiful music.

The Dharma Drum Mountain way of understanding such social interdependence, however, also pushes them to cultivate a deeper sense of their individuality. Although his followers had enormous respect for Sheng Yen—attributing to him an almost supernatural wisdom—they seemed to rely on their own informed consciences when presented with problems rather than rigidly seeking to apply the Master's teachings. When I asked doctors at the Tzu Chi medical center if they allowed animal experimentation, they replied that their Master had told them that it was acceptable. When presented with a question at Dharma Drum Mountain, a dentist said that the problem was very complicated, there were many angles to the dharma, and since he wasn't a fully enlightened Buddhist he could not be sure of the right answer.

Thus, participation in Dharma Drum Mountain's activities brings with it a certain kind of powerful experience: the experience of a slow, steady cultivation of the self through Chan practice; an experience of developing a deep sense of self, even as it stresses that the self is an illusion. This emphasis on self-consciousness was apparent in a dialogue session attended by fifteen hundred people in Taipei between Sheng Yen and one of his celebrity disciples, the martial arts movie star Jet Li. Jet Li credited Buddhism for giving him the "wisdom and strength to break the bond of fame that has tied him down for many years." Asked by Sheng Yen to give advice to the audience, Jet Li said, "The one big problem with human beings is that we blame everybody and everything else for our problems, but never reflect upon ourselves."[28]

Such self-consciousness could isolate practitioners in narcissistic self-absorption, but Dharma Drum tries to avoid this by linking self-cultivation with participation in a well-ordered group life within Dharma Drum Mountain's web of voluntary associations, which pull the practitioner out of the matrix of familial and national bonds and into an international community of practitioners.

In the end, Dharma Drum Mountain cultivates a kind of disciplined detachment coupled with a sense of impersonal connection with everything. Such a state of being was symbolized in the walking meditation I participated in at the Nung Chan Monastery in December 1999.

About two hundred of us dressed in black robes stood in a large simple room lit only by dim natural light. We began by prostrating ourselves a hundred times (which was like doing calisthenics) while reciting the name of Buddha. Then a procession formed in which we walked two-by-two back and forth within the room, while continuing to recite the Buddha's name. We began at a normal walking pace, but gradually the person leading the procession began to slow down, until finally we were walking no faster than a snail. The mind, though wishing to move forward, was gradually focused into the present. The procession finally ended with everyone back at their original places. Sitting in the lotus position in near darkness, we began chanting faster and faster. The effect was hypnotic. Everything melded together, and we seemed to become one extended self.

It was a powerful lesson on Buddhist emptiness—the individual self as an illusion, the true reality of the world subsisting in our interconnection. At the same time, such practices lead the individual's consciousness to become intensely focused. It is perhaps a consciousness particularly suited to modern middle-class life in Taiwan's knowledge-intensive industries, in which individuals have to take initiative for thinking through problems while being acutely aware that they are part of a collective enterprise.

Although Sheng Yen is from mainland China, his followers in Taiwan reflect the ethnic composition of the island as a whole; that is, they are mostly Taiwanese. Yet like cosmopolitan knowledge workers everywhere, they see themselves as global citizens as much as Chinese or Taiwanese nationals. Sheng Yen takes no formal position on cross-straits relations, and Dharma Drum Mountain, like Tzu Chi, resolutely stays out of partisan politics. Yet the practice cultivated there among influential professional elites may contribute an important measure of calm objectivity into Taiwan's raucous political debates.

CHAPTER 5

The Enacting Heaven Temple

Hybrid Modernity

A week after the earthquake, I went to the Enacting Heaven Temple (Hsing Tien Kung) in central Taipei to be cleansed of the bad energy caused by the disaster. The ritual to cleanse this energy is called *shoujing*. It is based on Daoist cosmology, which sees the universe as constituted of interlocking permutations of primordial matter or energy known as *qi*. The cleansing I underwent was a commonly practiced Daoist ritual to pull out *(shou)* fright *(jing)*, which causes a loss of vital energy resulting in anxiety and confusion. Every day a steady stream of people enters Enacting Heaven Temple—or one of the thousands of other Daoist temples in Taiwan—to undergo this ritual, but in the wake of the earthquake their numbers had vastly increased. The Enacting Heaven Temple is known as an especially good place for *shoujing*. In fact, in its reporting on earthquake responses, one Taipei newspaper featured a picture of people receiving *shoujing* at this temple—it was the natural place a photographer might look for a stereotypical image of Daoist responses to disaster.

In the ritual, a person empowered by the temple passes a bundle of burning incense sticks around the recipient's body. The Enacting Heaven Temple is considered a good place to receive *shoujing* because it is done quickly and efficiently there. On the afternoon when I arrived, there were three long lines of people from all walks of life awaiting the rite, which was done almost in assembly-line style. The people performing the ritual were late-middle-aged women, dressed in light blue smocks. When I

Figure 13. Enacting Heaven Temple, incense burner.

reached the head of the line, the woman asked my name, then quickly passed the smoky incense around me. The whole procedure took less than a minute.

This was all done in front of an ornate sanctuary dominated by three huge dark-faced, bearded statues—and in the midst of the bustle of hundreds of people variously offering incense, placing offerings of food and

flowers on a huge table, milling about, chatting with friends, and gawk-
ing at the spectacle. It is a familiar sight to anyone who has traveled
among the Chinese communities of Asia. The popular religion practiced
in such temples is usually a syncretistic mix of traditions, but the predominant tradition is religious Daoism. The religious Daoism practiced
in these temples should be distinguished from the Daoist philosophy de-
riving from Laozi (Lao-tzu) and Zhuangzi (Chuang-tzu) between the sixth
and fourth centuries B.C.E. Though it has connections with philosophical Daoism *(Daojia)*, religious Daoism *(Daojiao)* derives from the second century C.E., supposedly from a revelation by Laozi to a man named
Zhang Daoling. Philosophical Daoism was extremely skeptical of ritual
and institutions, but religious Daoism developed elaborate rituals and
social institutions. There are thousands of such temples in Taiwan[1] and
many thousands more are being rebuilt or are springing up anew throughout rural areas of mainland China.[2]

From the point of view of secularized Westerners, it might be tempting to imagine such temples as remnants of a disappearing past. They
bear a passing resemblance to those magnificently ornate, aesthetically
enchanting, and emotionally comforting old Catholic cathedrals of Europe, which tourists love to visit but which attract fewer and fewer real
worshippers. And there would be some truth to the notion that they belong to Asia's agrarian past rather than its high-tech urban future. The
humanistic Buddhist organizations we have introduced in previous
chapters are an alternative to the Daoist temple worship represented by
the Enacting Heaven Temple, and they attract large numbers of urban
middle-class people who no longer find the folk religion of their rural
past meaningful.

But the practices of worship and forms of community life connected
with Daoist temples are, at the very least, not going to disappear any-
time soon. Unlike old Catholic churches in Western Europe, they are still
full of people, even in the cities. And some, like the Enacting Heaven Temple, are with some success adapting their teaching and practice to fit the
experience of the urban middle classes. To show how they are doing this
and to counter the impression that only humanistic Buddhism can meet
the modern needs of the new middle classes of Taiwan, let us take a closer
look at how the Enacting Heaven Temple is undergoing reform. Like the
Buddhist reforms we have discussed earlier, this Daoist reform does not
leave behind the religion's basic spiritual traditions, but rather gives new
vitality to the dynamic, transcendent elements of those traditions and en-

ables these elements to go beyond the more "primitive" and "archaic" elements within those traditions.

FROM LOCAL TEMPLE TO UNIVERSAL COMMUNITY

One sign of its modernization is the way the temple organizes and trains laypeople to help carry out its rituals. The women performing the *shoujing* ritual are called "attendants" *(xiaolaosheng)* and are a unique feature of the Enacting Heaven Temple. Almost all Taiwanese Daoist temples have a wide variety of functionaries, ranging from the community leaders, who manage the temple, and the priests, who are masters of the central rituals, to spirit mediums, shamans, puppet masters (who direct the theatrical performances that are a central part of Daoist liturgy), and musicians. The Enacting Heaven Temple is distinctive for having dispensed with many of these. There are no spirit mediums or shamans there, and none of the puppet shows or other theatrical performances that accompany most Daoist liturgy are ever performed. Instead, the temple has institutionalized the role of the attendant. These are volunteers (mostly women, but also some men) who are supposed to undertake a regime of moral cultivation and are systematically organized to carry out temple affairs, including the chanting of scriptures, performance of personal rituals like the *shoujing*, counseling visitors on what type of ritual they may need, distributing incense to visitors, and arranging and cleaning the temple's ritual implements.[3]

Reliance on these attendants is a response to a changing relationship between the temple and Taiwanese community. As Kristofer Schipper has put it,

> Before modern iconoclasm held sway, religion was in evidence everywhere in China: each house had its altar, each district and village its temple. They were numerous and easy to spot, for as a rule, the local temple was the most beautiful building, the pride of the area. . . . On the whole, the majority of temples were—and, where they still exist, continue to be—part of Daoism, the religion of the people. They were always built by an association or a local community. In the cities, they were often the work of a merchants' or artisans' guild, or even that of the inhabitants of a given district. In the countryside, they were erected by all the members of a village community or regional association.[4]

Religion is still everywhere in Taiwan and it is, just as Schipper says, mostly community-based and mostly Daoist.[5] But since its economic boom in the late 1970s, Taiwan has generated a large urban middle class whose members have different forms of community than their rural forebears. In particular, they find it difficult to maintain the kind of long-term, fixed social relationships that came with many generations of family residence in farming villages. They increasingly move around a great deal and seek fellowship and mutual support through voluntarily chosen associations. The Enacting Heaven Temple is for such mobile people. It does not belong to a local community. It was not built by a guild or a community association, but by a wealthy individual who made a fortune in coal mining. It is a resource for the people of Taipei, a resource for a large impersonal metropolis. People come to it not because they, their neighbors, or their ancestors built it, but because it efficiently and effectively offers a convenient, albeit somewhat impersonal, service. Because many of the visitors come infrequently and are unfamiliar with temple worship, the temple has posted a chart next to its front entrance explaining how to carry out the rituals.

In traditional Taiwanese Daoist temples, a rite like the *shoujing* would be performed by someone who lived in one's own community. The efficacy of the ritual depended not simply on a mechanical performance of the actions but on the quality of one's relationship with the person who performed the ritual. The practitioner who performed it would have been recruited because of special spiritual abilities, including the capacity to become possessed by the gods. The rite would have been more like an exorcism—the bad energy would have been personified as a demon—than a therapeutic exercise.

But for most of the people who flocked to the Enacting Heaven Temple, the rite is performed by an attendant with whom they had no prior relationship, someone who had to ask for their name. How was one to know that this stranger really had the power to relieve the forces causing inner turmoil? Because the temple claimed that it had chosen these attendants not because of their ability to become possessed by some outside spiritual force, but for their willingness to cultivate high moral qualities. A central theme in the teaching of the temple's founder was that rituals like *shoujing* were efficacious because of the moral qualities of the giver and the recipient. The efficacy of personal relationships, grounded in a particular community in a particular place, was being replaced by the efficacy of universal moral qualifications possessed by the individual carrying out the rite.

The Enacting Heaven Temple was thus the center not of an actually experienced community, but of an imagined community, a metropolis of strangers seeking common moral values and common solace in a time of trial. To individuals in such an imagined community, it offered a partially disembedded Daoism.

As with religion in the West before the modern era, Daoism in China was integrated with and embedded in the full spectrum of social and cultural life. Before the twentieth century, the Chinese did not have a concept of religion, conceived as a set of beliefs and practices separate from scientific, economic, social, and cultural institutions. Daoism was a teaching that provided a comprehensive theory of how the physical world was structured, a theory that assumed reality is constituted of an intricate matrix of energy nodes—interplays between yin and yang *qi* within the phases of a complexly conceived time. Daoist temples were centers of economic, social, and cultural life for the community. Daoist practices attempted to manipulate cosmic energies through combinations of technological intervention (such as traditional Chinese medicine in all its forms), as well as prayer, moral cultivation, and ritual.[6] Modernization in the West disembedded religion from science, art, politics, and the market economy. (Until the eighteenth century, the word *religion* did not refer to an institution separate from other spheres of life.) The same has been happening in Asia. The result is a fragmentation of social life.

As in the West, this fragmentation can be both liberating and painfully disheartening. Individuals are released from closed cognitive horizons and fixed social roles. They are free to think for themselves, to reconcile the competing demands of faith and reason within the privacy of their own consciences. Individuals are free also to seek their own paths to personal fulfillment, without being bound to the expectations of sacrosanct social roles. But with this freedom come painful existential dilemmas, as people are forced to reconcile in their own ways the competing demands of faith, family, work, and citizenship. All the while, the apparent freedom of these disembedded individuals is being undermined by globalized economic and political forces.

It is hard to imagine a completely disembedded Daoism. Popular Daoist ritual assumes a primordial oneness underneath all things and Daoist practices assume that this oneness is manifested in the interplay of yin and yang. If one were thoroughly to disenchant this world, to purge it of magical forces and spiritual powers, it is hard to imagine what would be left of popular Daoism.

Moreover, all of the imagery in Daoist art and literature assumes that this world is full of invisible, personal beings: the gods and demons who must be invoked, propitiated, or defended against through prayer and ritual. These spirits (who once were living human beings themselves) are members of one's community and in the end they can only be adequately addressed in and through one's community, which is centered on a local temple. As Kristofer Schipper puts it,

> [The temple] is a place open to all beings, divine and human. A community as well as truly communal house, it is a place for casual and formal meetings. The elders go there daily to discuss village affairs. Grandmothers, the family delegates in religious matters, go there every day with offerings of incense and to fill the lamps with oil. Music and theater associations, along with clubs for boxing, reading, chess, charity, pilgrimages, automatic writing, medical research, kite flying, and cultural associations of all kinds create their headquarters in the temple and find here as well a place of worship for their particular patron saint.[7]

It is hard to imagine a popular Daoism disconnected from such a community life. Indeed, a completely disembedded Daoism could probably not exist.

As we shall see, the Enacting Heaven Temple is by no means an example of a completely disembedded Daoism. But the Enacting Heaven Temple has achieved enough of a partial disembedding that it can reach out to a modern, mobile urban middle class. It does this through a strategy that is more compatible with the Chinese cultural tradition than with Western tradition—syncretism. In traditions dominated by monotheistic religions, there is relatively little basis for a principled coexistence between the religion of the one true God and other deities, and when syncretism does occur, it has often been vulnerable to purification movements. But especially since the Ming dynasty (1368–1644), people have resolved inconsistencies between popular Daoism, Buddhism, and Confucianism by believing in all of them at once, while emphasizing the practice of one tradition over another at different points of the life cycle. Thus, they may educate their children in Confucian values, call upon Daoist deities to bring about good fortune, and bring in Buddhist monks to chant sutras for the dead. The Enacting Heaven Temple confronts modernity by deemphasizing (though not rejecting) Daoist cosmology and reemphasizing the expansive aspects of the Confucian morality that had been connected with popular Daoist religion, all the while grafting the methods of secular science onto its organization.

The Enacting Heaven Temple encompasses differences. At any given time of the day, the temple is busy with well-dressed people of all ages, about two-thirds women, and half under forty. There are hip adolescents and young adults sporting fashionable clothing and dyed blond hair; studious young women with ponytails; clean-cut young men carrying book-laden backpacks; trim men and women in dark suits who look as if they work in some executive position; and others, wearing the neat but more casual clothing of office workers. Some men, who look to be retired, walk around in Bermuda shorts and tennis shoes, while their counterparts, late-middle-aged and elderly women, have frizzy perms. They seem to represent almost the full range of urban occupations—office workers, store clerks, and students, as well as small business owners and housewives.

At least some of the people who come to the temple are university educated, immersed in scientific, analytic, and critical discourse, and cosmopolitan in outlook. My research assistant, who had a degree in anthropology from National Taiwan University, Taiwan's best university, said that many of her classmates came to Enacting Heaven Temple to pray for success in exams. Among university students, she claimed, the temple has a reputation of being especially powerful *(ling)*. They thought of the nature of that power in somewhat different terms, however, than their rural forebears. Secular education makes it difficult to imagine the real presence of the gods in the temple. My research assistant told me that she did indeed believe in the existence of Lord Guan (Guan Gong)—the principal deity worshipped at Enacting Heaven Temple—"but he exists in my mind."

And the official pamphlets issued by the temple agree with people like her. "Faith is the only emphasis of the ritual," they read. The rituals are symbols of a person's intention to practice the virtues exemplified by the gods, not techniques for eliciting the gods' favor. The deities represented by the statues in the front of the temple are historical exemplars of right virtue, but they do not exist as active agents in the world. A typical sermon delivered at the temple declared,

> Worship should begin with a good heart. Right morality is better than right [ritual] techniques. We need to practice filial piety and have a heart of mercy. . . . Every day we say a good word, every day we pick up a bag of garbage [the temple urges followers to help clean up the environment], we continue the spirit of our temple. We hope we can renew the spirit of our society. We hope our society can do good things together. Happiness comes from a (morally) good heart.

These are sentiments that would be completely acceptable to a sophisticated, secular university student. But they offer a faded, pale version of the vivid cosmology embedded in popular Daoist practice in Taiwan.

At the same time, the Enacting Heaven Temple partially disconnects its religious functions from the community associational life that was once embedded in rural temples. People do not come to the Enacting Heaven Temple for "boxing, reading, chess, charity" and so forth. They come for religion. But the temple has not abandoned its social functions. It has spun them off into a foundation, staffed by professionals, which runs libraries, social service organizations, and a hospital, and eventually plans to open a university. The library contains a good multimedia collection of general interest literature, as well as reputable scholarly works on world religions. Its auditorium and meeting rooms are used for modern cultural events: Western and Chinese classical music, lectures on art, even pop psychology workshops on how to cope with the stresses of modern family life. Some of its posters are adorned with the "happy face" symbol common in Western popular culture. The Enacting Heaven Temple also organizes teams of volunteers to visit the sick and to help with environmental cleanup. Through its foundation, the Temple contributed over US$6 million to help earthquake victims. But these works of community service are physically separated from the temple and managed by professionals chosen for their expertise rather than their religious devotion.

A HYBRID MODERNITY

Yet the Enacting Heaven Temple has by no means fully extricated itself from the richly imagined cosmos of traditional Daoist teaching or the densely intertwined social activities of local temples. This is clear from even a superficial observation of temple activities. The temple looks like a typical Taiwanese Daoist temple. At its center is a huge incense burner. Facing the burner, in an ornate building with the typical curved roof of Taiwanese temples, is a statue of red-faced, long-bearded Lord Guan (who in the temple is addressed by one of his alternate names, Enzhu Gong) flanked by lieutenant deities. Lord Guan was a legendary general in the period of the Three Kingdoms (220–265), known for his loyalty and courage, but treacherously murdered by an opponent. His exploits are recounted in *The Romance of the Three Kingdoms,* one of the most popular works of Chinese literature. Because of his financial skills and honesty, over time he became a patron of merchants. Most of those who come to the temple do not come simply to be reminded of his virtues. They come to intercede with him and gain his practical help.[8]

Devotees first take six sticks of incense (handed to them by an attendant), turn their backs to the gods, hold the incense up to their foreheads, and bow, offering it to heaven. Then they turn in the direction of the gods and bow again, offering the incense to earth. Then they put three of the sticks into the burner. Finally they proceed to the front of the temple, face-to-face with Lord Guan, and "report in," quietly telling him their name and where they are from, and placing one stick in an incense pot in front of his statue. Then they do the same for the lieutenant gods on the right and the left. Almost everyone does this. Their brains may be telling them that this is only symbolic, but from the seriousness of their expressions and the grace of their gestures, one gets a strong sense that in their bodies and hearts they believe that they are making a real connection with a spiritual presence.

Having reported in, they then usually pick up a pair of wooden oracular blocks, one side of which is rounded, the other flat. Standing before Lord Guan, they formulate a question for him and cast the blocks on the floor. If one rounded side (the yang side) and one flat side (the yin side) land up, the answer is affirmative. They then pick a numbered divining stick out of a bundle in front of Lord Guan and cast the blocks again. If the blocks fall in the yin and yang pattern, the stick is the correct one. The stick is then exchanged for a corresponding slip of paper on which are written some enigmatic stanzas, which are taken for interpretation to a priest sitting behind a counter off to the side of the temple. (When performing rituals, the priests put on ornate robes, but when interpreting fortunes on a hot day they simply wear dark pants and white T-shirts. They are employed by the temple, but do not manage it. Management is carried out by a board of businessmen.) The temple's official documents state that one's fate is in one's hands and depends on an individual's own efforts at moral cultivation. The popularity of the fate-divining ritual, however, suggests that many devotees do not fully believe this. Nor do they fully believe that the *shoujing* ritual, which they may next proceed to undertake, is just a reassuring symbol to calm psychological anxiety. If it were only such a symbol, it would probably be not worth the trip to the temple to undergo the ritual. At some level, they seem to believe that the ritual is really drawing some evil forces out of their bodies.

Undoubtedly, some visitors believe this more deeply than others. In fact, most worshippers at the temple seem to believe more deeply than the temple's founder in the literal reality signified by the rituals. At the beginning of each day, the temple regularly plays tape recorded sermons of Hsuan Kung, the temple's founder. The sermons stress the importance of morality over ritual: *Do not rely on the rituals to gain fortune. Work hard and do good deeds and good fortune will come. This is the lesson you get from Enzhu Gong.* Temple visitors sit quietly during the broadcast, but most of them do not seem to be listening. Some of them nod off to sleep. Then the tape is finished and they enthusiastically get back to their ritual work.

One of the most important rituals is offering food to the gods. The founder forbade animal sacrifices, so there are no offerings of meat. But in front of the statues of the gods are long tables piled high with every other kind of food—even cases of Coca-Cola. (The glossy magazine published by the temple has many beautiful pictures of the temple, but none of the offerings.) The temple does not officially support any of this. But, nonetheless, crowding against the sidewalk adjacent to the temple are dozens of peddlers (mostly women in typical peasant garb) selling materials for temple offerings. There is a red line painted along the edge of the sidewalk, and any peddlers who cross it are driven away by the temple's security guards. They continue to try to cross it so as to partake of the power that resides inside the temple precincts. But for the majority of the time, they have to stay on the opposite side of the red line. This, however, violates city laws, so every few hours, city police drive up and force the peddlers to retreat across the street. But after about ten minutes, the peddlers return. Business is brisk.

On the walls of the temple's reception room are photographs of diplomats and delegation leaders from around the world. (I myself first visited the temple in 1997 as part of an American delegation to study the development of civil society in China and Taiwan.) The Enacting Heaven Temple is something of a showcase of Taiwan's modern religious consciousness for foreign visitors, a consciousness supposedly purged of nonscientific ideas and devoted to universalistic moral values rather than to the socially embedded attachments of an agrarian society. Yet if the temple has made a partial move to modernity, as defined in these terms, the move has been additive rather than transformative. It has sponsored forms of professionalized social service to partially take the place of the informal social activities traditionally associated with temples and it has added an emphasis on universalistic morality (appealing to educated professionals) to a vivid ritual practice. It is like a hybrid modern flower with roots still firmly planted in a traditional soil.

Figure 14. Offerings for the gods.

To understand the significance (and the limitations) of this hybrid modernity for Taiwan's civic culture, let us first trace the development of the temple and then scrutinize more closely its various parts.

THE FOUNDING OF ENACTING HEAVEN TEMPLE

The Enacting Heaven Temple in central Taipei is actually one of three branches of a single temple organization founded by a wealthy coal mine owner. The other two branches are in the suburbs of Peitou and Sanhsia, the latter a mountainous community where the founder's coal mine was located. Hsuan Kung—"Mysterious Emptiness" (*mysterious* being a fundamental term in Daoist scriptures and *emptiness* a fundamental term in Buddhist ones)—is the founder's "Dao name," taken when he had already begun a process of intense spiritual cultivation in the early 1950s. He was born Huang Tsung in 1911, and grew up poor during the Japanese colonial era. According to the biography that appears in Enacting Heaven Temple's official publications, his story is one of rags to riches through hard work and a strong entrepreneurial spirit—and then of transcending material entrepreneurship by engaging in the religious entrepreneurship of temple building.[9]

He was so poor as a youth that he sometimes did not have enough to eat and had to walk barefoot to school, carrying a pair of shoes to put on in the classroom. After finishing middle school, he made a living by peddling ice cream and sugarcane at temple fairs. In the early 1930s he and his brothers went to work in a Japanese-owned hardware shop in Taipei, where they saved up enough money to buy a truck and establish a shipping business. Some of his business was with coal mine owners. In 1939 he and his brothers opened a hardware shop of their own and in the early 1940s used some of their profits to invest in a coal mine on White Chicken Mountain in Sanhsia. So far, this was a story of achieving modest success by working hard and making shrewd investments based on what he and his family had learned in their various jobs. He married in 1935 and had several children.[10]

Huang Tsung and his brothers only expected to make modest profits, even though they put a lot of effort into improving the mine's infrastructure. But then he struck it rich. According to the official story, the good fortune was made possible by miraculous intervention. He had been praying at a temple in Taipei for success, when one day, "while sleeping under a Banyan tree," he had a dream in which a bearded man told him to dig in a particular place. He dug and discovered a huge vein of coal. He originally thought that the man he had seen in his dream was the Earth God. Then he saw an image of Lord Guan in a Taipei temple and was flabbergasted to recognize it as the person in his dream. Thereafter he decided to build a temple to propagate the cult of Lord Guan.[11]

He built his first small shrine on White Chicken Mountain in Sanhsia in 1945, just as Taiwan was being returned from Japanese to Chinese rule. The timing was fortuitous. The Japanese had discouraged the expression of traditional Taiwanese folk religion. (They tried instead to propagate Buddhism as a "tool to unify their pan-Asian empire.")[12] After Taiwan's return to China, repression of folk religion was lifted—so long as such religion did not seem to foster rebellion against the state.

The kind of Lord Guan cult that Huang Tsung was fostering would have been acceptable to the Nationalist Party. In Chinese mythology, the figure of Lord Guan is a multivalent one, called upon by state and society for different purposes. As a man of legendary loyalty, Lord Guan was historically used by the state as a model of Confucian virtues. According to Robert Weller, "temples to Guan Gong were sometimes considered Confucian and made part of the state cult."[13] Because of his legendary shrewdness, Lord Guan also came to be seen as the patron saint of merchants. But Guan Gong was also a violent, somewhat rash warrior, who after his death took his revenge against the king who betrayed him. Ordinary people were often more impressed with this reckless, rebellious power than with Lord Guan's Confucian virtue.[14]

Huang Tsung emphasized the Confucian side of Lord Guan. Whether intentionally or not, this fit well with the aspirations of a successful businessman in 1945, as the ruling Nationalist Party was legitimating itself partly through its claim to represent the best in China's Confucian heritage. A Confucianized Lord Guan fit well with the party's preferred interpretation of that heritage—a model of loyalty to his ruler and a fierce fighter against enemies of the state. As the patron of merchants, Lord Guan also represented the ambitions of Taiwanese businessmen who would make money while giving due respect to the state.

The specific reason for building the first shrine to Lord Guan was to seek protection from an epidemic that had broken out in Sanhsia in 1945. Some people then attributed the ending of the epidemic to the power of Lord Guan, and the shrine became popular. In 1949, Huang Tsung replaced it with a larger temple.[15] In the process, he developed distinctive features of what would become Enacting Heaven Temple. When Huang first began to expand upon the Lord Guan cult in 1943, he relied on the full traditional apparatus of Daoist liturgy, including spirit mediums and automatic writing (in which the gods communicate via writing traced in beds of sand by people who have gone into trance), to help him choose key associates and make important decisions. But by 1949, he had concluded that "because of impure hearts" these methods did not work.[16] With a successful businessman's sense of rational procedure, he made decisions through careful study and cultivated new disciples through systematic moral training, establishing the forerunners of his attendants. His "purified" cult of Lord Guan abjured mysticism, emphasized a Confucian loyalty to the state, celebrated pragmatic entrepreneurial work, and even included a touch of Buddhist asceticism. Permanent celibacy had very little role in the Daoist tradition, but in 1952, Huang assumed the Daoist name Hsuan Kung and supposedly "gave up relations with his wife."[17] This was a Buddhist gesture, in keeping with Hsuan Kung's aspiration to "save all living beings."

In 1956, he began to build the large temple that now stands in Sanhsia, on property owned by his coal mine. He also planned to build a new temple in Taipei, but the government wanted to build a school on his preferred site, so he acquired land in Peitou and began building a temple there. This was all happening during the "golden age of the mining industry" when Hsuan Kung had plenty of money for new ventures. In the end, Hsuan Kung financed his temples with a US$29 million loan. Some of his followers wanted him to solicit donations to repay the loan, but he refused. This was his own charitable enterprise.[18]

The construction of temples on this scale by a single individual was something new for Taiwan. Temples were usually seen as the work of a whole community. In practice this might mean that a group of wealthy businesspeople from a community would come together to finance the temple, but in the name of the community as a whole. Hsuan Kung, however, was a businessman whose wealth was more than any local community could absorb. He used it to build temples that did not so much represent a community as create a regional and even national community by attracting devotees from far and wide.

Work on the Sanhsia and Peitou temples took nine years, and it included building new roads and even a railroad spur to Peitou to provide convenient access to the sites. In 1963, as work on the Sanhsia and Peitou temples was nearing completion, Hsuan Kung decided to build another temple in central Taipei, in a convenient location that could attract the maximum number of worshippers. The Sanhsia and Peitou temples were dedicated in 1965 and the Taipei temple in 1968.

As the temples were completed, Hsuan Kung took another innovative step. He drew up a formal constitution for the temples (which, among other things, adopted rationalized management practices and formally rejected "superstitions" like spirit writing) and applied for official incorporation. In 1969, the temples were given "legal person" status as the Taipei City Enacting Heaven Temple: legally one temple with three branches.[19]

Hsuan Kung died in 1970 at the age of fifty-nine, and after death he became a god. There is a shrine to him at the Sanhsia temple where followers pray to him and burn incense in front of his statue. After his death, a committee of businessmen led by his son, Huang Chung-chen, took over management of the temple. There were two major elements to Hsuan Kung's legacy. First, a body of teachings pointing toward a modernized and Confucianized understanding of popular religion, and, second, a corporate structure that would allow the temple to expand beyond the confines of popular religion. Together, these would enable the temple to play an important role in the development of Taiwan's civic culture after the end of martial law in 1987.

HSUAN KUNG'S CONFUCIANISM

The religious Daoist tradition is much more of a liturgical than doctrinal tradition. It has been carried on through the centuries by a rich body of ritual practices, which are explained by esoteric texts. There are no institutions within the Daoist tradition for giving an authoritative interpretation of these enigmatic texts. Thus the meaning of Daoist practices is subject to ceaseless social interpretation.[20] Agents of the state and of society, local elites and ordinary people all contribute different interpretations as to what Daoist icons and Daoist practices are supposed to mean. Lord Guan, as we have seen, can be understood from an elitist or a populist perspective. He can be understood as a model of Confucian rectitude, an upholder of the order of a bureaucratic state, or as a fierce fighter against injustice.

Hsuan Kung promoted Lord Guan's Confucian attributes. In the view of its founder, the Enacting Heaven Temple is perhaps as much a Confucian as a Daoist temple. In his ethnography of religion in Sanhsia, Robert Weller mentions the Enacting Heaven Temple only in passing, but he describes it in this way:

> In the past, temples to Guan Gong were sometimes considered Confucian and made part of the state cult. While the state religion no longer exists (except in a token annual ritual for Confucius), this temple apparently claims to inherit its prestige. Like a temple to Confucius, its doors have 108 raised yellow bumps on a red background instead of door gods. Furthermore, the birthday ritual is clearly modeled on the one that takes place each year in Taipei's temple to Confucius.[21]

Although he may have wanted the Enacting Heaven Temple to inherit the prestige of state Confucianism, Hsuan Kung's moral teaching was not exactly the same thing. State Confucianism tended to be authoritarian. A central focus was on the "three bonds," which emphasized obedience of son to father, wife to husband, and subject to ruler. According to Wm. Theodore de Bary, the three bonds "have no place in the Confucian classics, and were only codified later in Han texts [first century C.E., after Confucianism had become an official state ideology]."[22] Authoritarian regimes in East Asia, including that of Chiang Kai-shek in Taiwan, used this authoritarian version of Confucianism to justify their rule. Hsuan Kung, on the other hand, emphasized a more expansive version of the Confucian tradition, which does not deny the importance of obedience to rightful authority, but emphasizes mutual obligation and personal integrity. The classic formulation is from Mencius (ca. 371–289 B.C.E.), based on the "five relationships":

> Between parent and child there is to be affection
> Between ruler and minister, rightness
> Between husband and wife [gender] distinctions
> Between younger and older [siblings], an order of precedence
> Between friends, trustworthiness[23]

Emphasizing complementary reciprocity rather than submission to authority, this formulation is in fact being used today by intellectuals, like Harvard professor Tu Wei-ming, who want to lay the basis for a Confucian form of democratic modernity in Asia.[24] In the 1960s, however, when Hsuan Kung was giving his sermons about the five relationships, this relatively non-authoritarian version of Confucianism was not widespread, especially in Taiwan. It was solidly enough based on the classics, however, and its political implications were muted enough so as not to seem threatening to the Nationalist government.

Besides the five relationships, Hsuan Kung's teaching emphasizes the "eight virtues": filial piety, brotherliness, loyalty, trust, ritual propriety, righteousness, incorruptibility, and shame.[25] Hsuan Kung emphasizes that both the five relationships and eight virtues have to be interpreted in light of modern conditions. According to Hsuan Kung, modern society's problems include the lack of a proper balance between the individual and the public, family breakdown, generational discord, institutional rigidity, and the weakening of democracy. Confucianism, modeled by the life of Lord Guan, can provide answers to these problems, but only if its categories are made flexible. The five relationships mean a different thing in a traditional agrarian society, he says, than in a modern society. In an agrarian society, the primary need is for family members to stick together. In modern societies, we are tied to a wider circle of interdependence. Thus the relationships that tie the family together must be extended more widely, to the nation.[26]

Similarly, the virtues have to be enacted in new ways. Filial piety must mean more than simply providing for parents' material needs and protecting their reputations. We now have to be sensitive to their psychological needs. Brotherliness must be extended to classmates and neighbors. Loyalty includes loyalty to one's professional responsibilities. Trust must become the bedrock of all social relationships. Ritual propriety is about "beautifying relationships." Righteousness is acting legally and appropriately. Incorruptibility is about acting according to principles rather than personal advantage, and refers to people in all walks of life. And shame means to be guided by conscience.[27]

Hsuan Kung's interpretation of the classic virtue of shame *(chi)* is especially telling.[28] It is not about conforming to social expectations. It is about an interior knowledge of why things are right and wrong. It requires constant self-reflection *(fanxing)* to determine how one's principles should lead to action under changing circumstances. Hsuan Kung emphasizes the need for self-reflection over and again. It seems to be a call for constant revision of Confucian norms, in accordance with a well-cultivated conscience in the light of evolving circumstances. This leads to a steady evolution of interpretations of his teachings to take account of changes in Taiwan society in the decades after his death.

Hsuan Kung's Confucianism, then, is an interpretation that may have looked superficially compatible with the Nationalist Party's authoritarian Confucianism at the time when Hsuan Kung first formulated his teachings, but it was really not state Confucianism. It was an early formulation of what Tu Wei-ming has called "bourgeois Confucianism," which some have argued lay behind the economic success of the newly industrializing Asian countries in the 1980s.

One problem with the attempt to formulate a new Confucianism for the twentieth century, however, is that it has lacked a religious basis. According to Tu Wei-ming, "The difference between classical Confucianism and neo-Confucianism is arguably more pronounced than the difference between Catholicism and Protestantism and, mainly because of the impact of the West, the rupture between neo-Confucianism and the new Confucianism of the twentieth century is perhaps more radical than that between traditional Christology and the contemporary 'God is dead' theology."[29] The metaphysics that underpinned the Song dynasty's neo-Confucianism no longer seemed plausible to Chinese intellectuals in the early twentieth century. In the past two centuries, most of those who have tried to adapt Confucianism to modernity have tried to base Confucian notions of moral excellence on sociology and ecology. It is argued that the Confucian virtues are good because they promote social trust and facilitate the social transactions necessary for the harmonious functioning of an interdependent world. While this may be plausible to some intellectuals, such rationalizations are probably not compelling to ordinary people. In any case, the state-Confucian religious rituals that might have made Confucian ideas emotionally powerful and morally compelling to some ordinary people are no longer held.[30]

Hsuan Kung himself uses sociological arguments to bolster his understanding of Confucianism (e.g., he explains that trust is necessary for the smooth functioning of society). But it was his founding of a Daoist temple that gave him a platform to spread his teaching to broad masses. As Robert Weller noted in his 1979 ethnography, "to most people . . . [the Enacting Heaven Temple in rural Sanhsia] is just an ordinary temple with two unexplained restrictions: one never offers meat nor burns paper spirit money." But so long as they came to the temple they had to hear sermons by Hsuan Kung. Weller also notes that the temple attracts many outsiders "because of its association with its two sister temples and the fame of its cult, and partly because of its beautiful setting."[31] The complex of three Enacting Heaven temples had already become a magnet for people throughout the greater metropolitan Taipei area, people perhaps of divided consciousness, who were newly arrived into the urban middle classes, who still felt comforted by the ritual of traditional Daoist community temples but who wanted the more upscale association with Confucian teachings that the Enacting Heaven temples also provided.

Hsuan Kung's Confucian message was never fully integrated with the religious practice at his temples. Even though he wanted to purge religion of "superstition," he never really succeeded. Rather than rely simply on moral cultivation to achieve happiness, people at his temples continue to seek shortcuts to fulfillment. They entreat the gods for favors and discern from the gods their fate, activities that Hsuan Kung would have considered superstitious. Perhaps, though, Hsuan Kung's Confucianism gained power and even credibility from association with the earthy "religion of the people," practiced through offerings of food and the casting of oracle blocks amidst clouds of incense—all under the eyes of the formidable Lord Guan.

PROFESSIONAL ORGANIZATION

Hsuan Kung's organizational innovations may be an even more important part of his legacy than his ideas. By incorporating the temple as a legal entity, he established the foundation for a professionally organized outreach to Taiwanese society. In traditional temples, religious activities were inextricably intertwined with medical, philanthropic, and cultural activities on behalf of the local community. Such practices were managed through informal agreements among the local elites in charge of the temple. The legal incorporation of the Enacting Heaven Temple created a platform for turning these traditional community activities into professionally managed social services.

This transformation began after the ending of martial law in 1987. The temple was caught between two tendencies stemming from this event. In some ways the emerging multiparty system actually generated new incentives and opportunities for backdoor deals, influence peddling, and cronyism. Citizens bribed politicians and politicians sought to gain advantage by handing out special favors to key constituencies. But political opponents of those who had successfully gotten ahead by the "black gold" of illicit payoffs could use a muckraking press to expose the corruption. So there were increased public appeals for openness, transparency, and fairness—appeals that came mainly from the emerging professional middle classes.

Popular temples in Taiwan are often accused of corruption, which is partly a result of changing standards. Temples have traditionally been managed through a nexus of informal relationships among local elites. The informal allocation of money that was taken for granted in the past is no longer acceptable to modern advocates of transparent accounting based upon universalistic principles. Like many popular Taiwanese temples, the Enacting Heaven Temple was managed in an informal way by a board of directors consisting of people who had been personally connected with the founder and headed by his son. Such procedures were consistent with the Confucian principles preached at the temple: human affairs were best managed through the interpersonal interaction of virtuous men rather than through impersonal rules and procedures. As Enacting Heaven Temple's founder had been an extremely wealthy businessman, it had more assets than most temples. After death his assets were all at least indirectly connected with the temple. The coal mining industry itself had come to an end, but the temple controlled increasingly valuable pieces of land and a considerable amount of cash, which it invested in new profit-making ventures. These assets made the temple the object of scrutiny.

At least in legal form, the temple was a modern corporation, subject to laws for transparent management and open accounting, especially for assets that were not directly connected with the religious functions of the temple. The temple managers had incentives, therefore, to invest some of their money into professionally run, community service institutions. To gain good will and to assure the public that the temple's wealth was being used in an efficient, professional way, they had to disconnect its social services from the diffuse social life of the temple. The professionalized social services are neither very Daoist in outlook nor very Confucian in management. Their connection with religion and morality seems to consist simply of a general sense that they ought to be committed to helping others.

In 1995, an Enacting Heaven Temple Foundation was established for "education, culture, and social service." The foundation extends the reach of Enacting Heaven Temple throughout Taiwan. It is governed by a board that includes some of the directors of the temple, including the founder's son, Huang Chung-chen, and notable community members who are not directly connected with the temple. Situated in the fashionable shopping district, the foundation's brightly lit offices, sleek modern furniture, and fashionably dressed staff contrasts with the smoky, cluttered, bustling interior of the temple. There is a small meditation room in the foundation headquarters, but no religious images. When I asked whether the staff were required to be worshippers at the Enacting Heaven Temple, they responded with an emphatic "No!" They stated that they "have every kind of belief here. People are chosen on the basis of professional qualifications." By professional qualifications they seem to mean a mixture of expertise and moral earnestness. The staff projects an attitude of earnest concern for raising the cultural level of Taiwan, fostering values of respect and decency, and helping those in need.

"Our job is not necessary to promote religion," one staff member told me, "but good family values. A problem for Taiwan is the transformation of the big extended family into the small nuclear family. We have to adapt traditional values to this small family. How to do this? We rely on various experts." Not Confucian philosophers, but mostly psychologists and social workers. Connected with this effort is the provision of cultural enrichment through the Enacting Heaven Temple library, originally housed in a building next to the central Taipei temple, and later expanded to include a larger branch in another part of the city. The foundation also runs scholarship programs for needy children throughout Taiwan (about thirty-four thousand U.S. dollars per year), organizes "values education" programs in schools and universities, sponsors art exhibitions and cultural performances, and runs health and exercise programs for the elderly.

The foundation also organizes volunteers, mostly retired women, to carry out various social services. There are presently about five hundred such volunteers, who wear a distinctive yellow vest when doing their work. Members of the foundation claim that they were in a good position to mobilize such volunteers because the Enacting Heaven Temple had a tradition of organizing its attendants. However, they also stress that their volunteers *(yigong)* are different from the attendants. "The attendants take care of religious affairs. The volunteers are much more modern." Unlike the attendants, who often claim that they received a kind of vocation to be an attendant after being spared by Lord Guan from a serious illness or after receiving an auspicious dream, the volunteers describe their motivation in more general humanitarian terms.[32] It is the linguistic move that we talked about before—the shift from a condensed code of highly metaphorical language that sustains a religion of external rules and rituals to an elaborated code of abstract language and analytical concepts that leads toward a religion of inner experience and humanitarian philanthropy.

The Enacting Heaven Temple modernizes through an additive rather than an integrative process. It juxtaposes modern, professional forms of language and organization with traditional forms. It is an ill-fitting combination that appeals to a wide range of people, from different levels of the Taiwanese middle classes. In contrast, the humanistic Buddhist organizations we have discussed here have (to varying degrees) integrated their religious traditions with modern forms of life. They have not only created volunteer social service organizations, but also infused those organizations with their particular religious spirit.

The looseness of fit between Enacting Heaven Temple's religious practices and its social service organizations is clearest in the case of the Enacting Heaven Temple's hospital. The hospital is a general hospital located in Sanhsia, the place where Hsuan Kung had his coal mine and where he built his first temple. Once a rural town, it is now a bustling suburb, with modern roads and mass transportation making it only about a half hour from central Taipei.

The hospital was completed in 1997, partly in response to the temple's need to make public use of some suspiciously acquired assets. The temple had bought some land for a hospital in the 1980s. Some people claimed that they paid more than the land was worth at the time as a way of benefiting a business crony of the board members. It then took them a decade and a half for them to do anything with the land, which increased suspicions that the purchase had been done for underhanded reasons. (In the meantime, though, because of the development of Sanhsia, the land greatly appreciated in value.) In the mid-1990s, there was a well publicized lawsuit over allegations of impropriety in the original land deal. The temple won the lawsuit—and celebrated its victory with a major ritual. In the meantime, though, it built the hospital at a cost of about US$10 million.

Unlike the Tzu Chi hospital, which consciously tries to infuse a distinctively Buddhist version of "compassionate care" into all of its activities, the hospital is, as some of the senior staff put it, religion free, with no one "forced to believe anything or practice anything." The only clear signs of a connection to Enacting Heaven Temple are some of the temple's magazines and pamphlets in the waiting room and a small but apparently seldom-used altar with a statue of Lord Guan. Some members of the staff admitted that they had never even been to the Enacting Heaven Temple, even though they lived nearby. Some seem almost embarrassed by the hospital's connection with the temple and expressed continued suspicion of the land deal that had enabled the hospital to be completed in the first place. The hospital staff see themselves as well-educated modern professionals (some educated at medical schools in the United States) who are doing their best to provide good, quality care to their community. They are attracted to work in the hospital because it is an expanding new institution located in a metropolitan area. As they see it, the hospital's religious origins do not interfere with their work. Some of them nonetheless like to keep the religion at arms length because it does not fit their identity as modern professionals.

On the first floor of the temple is a chart depicting ambitious plans for future development: an Enacting Heaven Temple university and a second hospital devoted to psychiatric and long-term care. As a well-endowed corporation, the temple has the ability to differentiate its secular and religious activities and to allow the secular activities to develop in a specialized, rationalized way based on modern professional norms. But as a form of Daoist religious practice whose roots are still deeply embedded in the particular rhythms of local Taiwanese culture and intertwined in the relations of local Taiwanese community, the Enacting Heaven Temple becomes separated from the activities it has spun off. It cannot reintegrate them into a new ethical-religious vision. As a multifaceted corporation encompassing the three places of worship, the foundation, the libraries, and the hospital all within one legal entity, the temple is a syncretistic hybrid, whose parts are connected more symbiotically than organically. The parts need each other, at least for now, but they do not, as it were, share the same DNA: they are not animated by the same principles.

A HYBRID ETHIC FOR A HYBRID WORLD

It might be objected, of course, that the various parts of the temple-corporation are all animated at some level by Confucian principles, embodied in the mythical virtues of Lord Guan. But the difference in their interpretations of the Confucian heritage is so profound as to constitute fundamentally different ethics and ways of life.

The differences are not much based on the differences in philosophical interpretation. They are rooted in different practical values, which are a result of picking and choosing among the Confucian tradition by people who occupy different roles within a differentiated modern society.

The foundation of the Confucian project was the extension of family virtues beyond the confines of home. It was easier to do this when most people lived in rural extended families in contexts within which family, commerce, politics, and religion were closely intertwined. But what resources does the Confucian tradition have for a modern society, in which economy, society, polity, and culture are driven by different logics, pushed along by different kinds of specialists? Those most connected with these different dimensions of modern society use a loose Confucian language to articulate and justify values most congenial to that dimension. Business people extract a bourgeois Confucianism, politicians a political Confucianism, and so on. But these versions of Confucian ethics are becoming less and less compatible.

The values of the elderly temple attendants are perhaps akin to the idealized values of deference and care that were associated with women's roles in rural households. The temple has published a book of stories about the attendants. Unlike stories of Tzu Chi volunteers, which stress a conversion experience from troubled, aimless, or conflicted lives to a disciplined cultivation of virtue, the stories of the attendants stress the continuity with their lives as mothers. Most of those featured in the book are elderly women; the oldest is over ninety. The typical story sees a mother become an attendant after her children have left home, and perhaps after she has suffered a health crisis resolved through intercession with Lord Guan.[33]

The values of the temple board are perhaps an example of the business ethic of "*guanxi* capitalism," in which business deals are regulated by networks of relationships between relatives and friends rather than impersonally applied laws. Although the economic growth of East Asian Newly Industrializing Countries (NICs) shows that this bourgeois Confucianism can be quite conducive to market-driven economic development, the problems of the Enacting Heaven Temple board also show some of the problems that this ethic can create. In 2001, the temple became embroiled in another scandal involving the laundering of US$30 million of temple funds though a corporation in Malaysia.[34] A legal investigation continues and the temple may again be exonerated. But the suspicions were raised over the unclearly documented personal connections between the temple board's head, Huang Chung-chen, and Malaysian business contacts—hallmarks of the "crony" deviation of bourgeois Confucianism.

The values of the professional staffs of the foundation and hospital are perhaps an example of socially responsible expertise. There is a concern for education, for enhancing families, for maintaining personal integrity and for extending care to widening circles of people. These do affect the work of both the professional staffs of the foundation and its volunteers. As invoked by the professional staffs, however, these values seem bland and abstract, cut off from the myths and rituals that may have once given them their justification. Their understanding of values is perhaps like that of the educated American professionals described in *Habits of the Heart*, who may have learned virtues of honesty, integrity, and compassion from childhood immersion in a conservative Christian church, but have now left that faith behind. They may still profess their values and indeed put them into practice in their professional life, but because they have no way of explaining their source, they may have difficulty defending them against the pressures of the modern marketplace, and they may have difficulty passing these values on to the next generation.[35]

Hsuan Kung's teachings may have helped make classic Confucian values flexible enough to be relevant to a modern commercial, urban, and globalized society. By grounding those values in the myths of Lord Guan—whose exploits are known to virtually every Chinese youth through the classic story *Romance of the Three Kingdoms*—Hsuan Kung gave them a popular reach much greater than they would have received if based simply on philosophical discourse. By associating them with a somewhat purified version of folk Daoist worship, he gave them an emotional resonance. But the folk Daoist rituals remain too embedded in forms of local community that are being overwhelmed by the metropolis. They are "part of life," as one staff member at the Enacting Heaven Temple put it. I do not doubt that they will remain a part of Taiwanese life for some time to come. But they do not fit neatly together with the other pieces of a dynamic Taiwanese society.

The hybrid ethic of the Enacting Heaven Temple reflects the wonderfully jagged development of Taipei itself, where sleek modernist office buildings and innumerable McDonalds and Starbucks restaurants line the main thoroughfares, while a vibrant world of artisans, peddlers, folk healers, and traditional Taiwanese food vendors clog the side alleys. Postmodern intellectuals might revel in this kind of incoherent diversity. Yet many ordinary people may hope for a vision that could reconcile these various pieces and for spiritual practices that would enable them to lead more integrated lives. Those who most keenly desire such social and moral integration will not find it at Enacting Heaven Temple, but they might find it in the humanist Buddhist associations that we have discussed in previous chapters.

Conclusions

As noted in the preface, there are two main themes to this book. One concerns the relation between religion and democracy in Asia. The other explores the conditions for the growth of progressive forms of religion in the modern world. In this conclusion, I weave together the strands of each theme. The first section is grounded in theory and data, the second reaches toward vision and hope.

RELIGIOUS RENAISSANCE AND
THE CHALLENGES OF DEMOCRATIC MODERNITY

Taiwan has been a happy exception to many generalizations about Asian values and Asian politics. It negates the "Asian values consensus" that Confucian cultural legacies are not conducive to democracy, and it shows that there is no real basis for a clash of Asian and Western civilizations.

Over the past two decades of the twentieth century, Taiwan has made a successful transition from an authoritarian to a democratic society. If Western liberal values were essential to democracy, we would expect that this democratic transition would have been accompanied by a shift toward Western forms of moral discourse, manifested perhaps in an increasing importance of Christianity (as in South Korea) or in an increasing emphasis on secular forms of individualism. But, while embracing democracy, large parts of the Taiwanese public have, as we have seen, also been embracing Asian values. Adherence to Christianity has declined. Revivals of Buddhism and Daoism have taken place, both of which are heavily intermingled with Confucian moral discourse. These religious and moral revivals have not only seemed completely compatible with democracy, but they also have also facilitated the democratic transformation. These facts show that the Asian values consensus was based on incorrect assumptions either about the requirements of democracy or the nature of Asian values—or, as I will argue in this conclusion, about both.

By recapitulating the story of how the religious movements discussed here facilitated Taiwan's democratic transition, let us first discuss how the Taiwan case makes us rethink standard liberal theories about the requirements of democracy.

Religious Renaissance and Taiwanese Civil Society

In the Anglo-American liberal tradition, it is commonly assumed that the foundation of democracy is a vital civil society, which consists of a multiplicity of independent voluntary associations. As long as they are independent of the state, such associations block the formation of authoritarian rule and indeed, because they regulate themselves, minimize the need for state control. Insofar as a state is still required, the associations of civil society enable citizens to articulate their interests and to hold the state accountable for responding to them. It is usually held that such civil society is the product of a broad middle class of mobile individuals, which is developed in an expanding market economy.[1]

The groups studied here fit part of this picture, but not all. Like other East Asian Newly Industrializing Countries (NICs) in the 1970s, Taiwan's authoritarian government preserved social stability while opening itself to the global market.[2] A market economy led to a rising middle class which then generated an active civil society which played an important role in the transition to democracy. Drawing their members from the new middle classes, the religious associations studied here have made important contributions to Taiwan's civil society. Yet the civil society developed in Taiwan has been different from that envisioned by theorists of liberal democracy, and these religious associations demonstrate that difference.

First of all, Taiwan's civil society has not been as independent of the state as envisioned by Western theories of civil society. In the late 1970s and early 1980s, to be sure, there were important dissident groups who braved harsh repression to challenge the government and whose pressure eventually contributed to the ending of authoritarian rule. But these groups did not have the support of a large array of independently organized citizens. Apart from the dissident organizations, most voluntary organizations were only partially independent of the authoritarian government. The religious groups studied here illustrate this partial independence.

Though they are now widely popular among various segments of Taiwan's middle classes, the four organizations studied here did not attract wide attention when they began, and their religious practices were not fashioned with a view to achieving popularity, at least not quickly. In the 1970s, these groups gradually grew and developed their distinctive approaches to Buddhism, Daoism, and Confucianism, but even as economic development began to produce a sizeable middle class, their followings remained relatively small. A major obstacle was political. Religious organizations had to contend with government suspicion of any large groups not under government control.

From the beginning, the groups studied here contained important seeds of autonomy, the basis for which was religious. Their founders were primarily devoted to religious concerns and this devotion took precedence over pressures to meet the demands of economic and political powers. A characteristic shared by all of the founders was that they were nonconformists whose strength came not from the abandonment of their religious traditions, but from a search for the deepest insights of those traditions. Hsing Yun refused to take part in BAROC and for years was regarded with suspicion by the Buddhist and political establishments. In 1962, Cheng Yen took the very untraditional act of shaving her own head to become a Buddhist nun. When she applied for formal ordination in 1963, she was at first rejected because she had not received her tonsure at the hands of a recognized authority. Sheng Yen had to largely fund his own education in Japan (by chanting sutras for the dead) and, after years of religious training, could not find a monastery to lead in Taiwan. In spite of his wealth, even Hsuan Kung had to overcome many obstacles before he could take over the Enacting Heaven Temple. But theirs was a kind of autonomy that found its expression not in confrontation with authority, but in voluntary cooperation with it.

None of the religious leaders studied here achieved autonomy by directly challenging the government. Hsing Yun, of Buddha's Light Mountain, overcame some of the government's suspicion by cultivating favor with KMT politicians.[3] The other groups simply remained too small to pose a threat to the government. It might be tempting to see the explosion in popularity of such groups in 1987 as driven by citizens' desire to participate in organizations that were not controlled by the state. In fact, however, it was the state itself that helped these groups gain an important social role in the late 1970s and early 1980s, a role that prepared them for takeoff in 1987.

As noted in chapter 2, in 1976 the Taiwan provincial government instructed all temples to carry out charity work.[4] It fit a general strategy (common to East Asian NICs) of keeping government social welfare expenditures low by relying on the private sector to take care of the poor, sick, and weak.[5] In earlier stages of development, this had meant mostly relying on extended families to take care of their own. Because of the increasing complexity and mobility of Taiwanese society, however, families could no longer meet such needs. Christian churches had carried out many types of welfare work since the 1950s, but the Christian community remained tiny. If the government was to rely heavily on religious groups to provide welfare, these would have to be Buddhist and Daoist.

The difference between the current proposals in the United States to promote "faith based charities" and this Taiwanese approach was that the government commanded rather than encouraged, and it gave special support to groups it deemed to have followed its commands most effectively. Tzu Chi won an award for being the best provider of welfare services—an important milestone in its rise to prominence. Later in the early 1980s, it was Taiwan's provincial government that played a major role in the building of the Tzu Chi General Hospital. The initiative—the vow—to build the hospital came from Master Cheng Yen. But when she made her vow, she had no resources to carry it out. In particular, she had no land upon which to build a hospital. In October of 1980 Provincial Governor Lin Yang-kang visited the Abode of Still Thoughts, followed a few days later by President Chiang Ching-kuo. The government offered to help Tzu Chi obtain a site and the hospital was eventually built on public land donated by the Hualien County government. Prominent political leaders Lee Teng-hui (the future president of Taiwan) and Lin Yang-kang (then minister of the interior) attended groundbreaking ceremonies.[6]

In the late 1970s and early 1980s Buddha's Light Mountain similarly benefited from government support in obtaining land for its temples and for other ventures.[7] The Nung Chan Monastery (the foundation of Dharma Drum Mountain) benefited from government willingness to let it remain on illegal land, even as that land was becoming extremely valuable. Favorable connections with the government enabled Enacting Heaven Temple to benefit from its land deals. Even though the government may have been ambivalent about initially supporting such Buddhist and Daoist religious organizations and may have slowed their growth, the government actually helped build a solid foundation for their later expansion. Thus these religious organizations do not fit the image of a civil society that grows up independently of the state.

The religious organizations we have studied here were in no position to apply massive pressure on the KMT party-state to give up its authoritarian rule. Neither were most other organizations within Taiwan's slowly emerging civil society. The reasons that Chiang Ching-kuo accepted reforms that culminated with the ending of martial law in 1987 had as much to do with his need to keep the Western democracies from abandoning Taiwan in favor of the People's Republic of China as with his need to respond to the pressure of independently organized domestic political groups. In Taiwan, an extensive, vibrant civil society emerged *after* the end of martial law, not before it.

Even then, it was not as independent as the civil society envisioned by political theorists in the Anglo-American liberal tradition. Yet this lack of independence was not just a defect of Taiwanese civil society, an imperfection to overcome as the society developed. The relative lack of independence has in fact played a positive role in the development of Taiwanese democracy by mitigating the centrifugal forces that democracy can engender.

In the years following the end of martial law, when most restrictions on free association were swept away, there was an explosion in the size and complexity of civil society, but not all of the new groups flourished, and not all made a positive contribution to a stable, self-governing society.[8] The religious groups studied here grew quickly and steadily precisely because they had not grown up in opposition to the government. Participating in them was a respectable and safe way of taking initiative to help address Taiwan's social problems. Such organizations were by no means transmission belts from the government to the people; they were more like belt buckles joining private and public sectors in a tighter embrace than envisioned by liberal political theorists.

Though there is some necessary tension in this union, it is considerably more cooperative than any relationship between religious organizations and the state currently possible in the United States. Although Tzu Chi and other Buddhist organizations embarrassed the government in 1999 by responding more quickly and efficiently to the earthquake than the government itself, some of its most important reconstruction efforts have actually been aimed at rebuilding government schools. Tzu Chi has built fifty new public schools to replace ones destroyed in the earthquake. Though Tzu Chi raised the money, carried out the designs (with special concern for earthquake-resistant architecture and environmental friendliness), supervised construction and mobilized volunteers to help with landscaping and decoration, these schools are to be government-run public schools, with curriculum and teachers furnished by the government. Unlike faith-based organizations in the United States, which currently want public money to do their private work, Tzu Chi raises private money to do public work.

The other organizations we have described have similar cooperative relations with the government. Such political cooperation is an important value for the Confucian social ethic that we have argued is common to all of the groups studied here. It is difficult for Westerners, especially those brought up in the Anglo-American liberal tradition, to appreciate, because this tradition sees free and open competition between interest groups as the best guarantee for political outcomes that represent the common good. From the point of view of classic theories of liberal democracy, the willingness of organizations like Tzu Chi to act on behalf of the state may be a sign of an immature civil society. I would suggest that in Taiwan, at least, such "immaturity" has in fact been an important part of the consolidation of democracy.

During Taiwan's transition to democracy, these religious "belt buckles" have played a conservative, stabilizing role in a rapidly changing political situation. Even though their leaders and most committed members see them as religious rather than political enterprises, such religious organizations have non-intended, beneficent civic consequences. They help take some of the rough edges out of the conflicts between native Taiwanese and Mainlanders and between the relatively successful and relatively poor. They nurture a spirit of engagement with public affairs and encourage a cooperative (but not uncritical) attitude toward the government. By no means do I argue that such religious organizations are the solution to Taiwan's social and political problems (though some of their members, particularly those in Tzu Chi, believe this to be the case). As previously noted, Taiwanese political culture continues to have many rough edges and sometimes teeters on the brink of chaos. Yet despite all of its problems, Taiwan has nonetheless avoided this chaos and made a successful if still shaky transition to a stable democracy, and an analysis of its public-private belt buckle groups can help explain how this was possible.[9]

The Civil Religion of an Ecumenical Nationalism

Such groups challenge conventional democratic theory not only because they blur the boundaries between public and private in accordance with a Confucian ethic, but simply because they are religious. Forged in re- action to the European wars of religion, Western theories of liberal democracy see mostly danger in the close engagement of religious groups with the state. Although some have recognized the role of religion in con- tributing to a "civil religion" that helps legitimize the democratic state, many secular theorists today would fear that the potential benefits of this contribution are offset by the tendency of religion to foment sectarian division and to provoke "culture wars" by trying to use the government to advance their agendas. This may well be true for conservative Chris- tian groups in the United States, but it does not seem to be true for these Buddhist and Daoist groups in Taiwan. They help to ground the Tai- wanese state in an open and tolerant civil religion without provoking culture wars.

This is the civil religion of a nation, a beloved community of memory and hope. It is what one might call an "ecumenical nationalism," a sense of national community that respects both the pluralism of Taiwanese so- ciety and the pluralism of the international order. It encourages the Tai- wanese to affirm their distinctive identities in the world community through peaceful dialogue rather than violent confrontation. How do the groups I have studied build this ecumenical form of nationalism? They direct the public's attention to particular strands of the collective imag- ination that is part of Taiwan's emerging sense of nationhood.

The political and cultural ferment unleashed by the ending of marital law have led to a strong sense of Taiwanese nationalism. Taiwanese his- torians, linguists, and literary figures have been imagining a community that it is distinct from mainland China.[10] Politicians like Lee Teng-hui and Taiwan's current president, Chen Shui-bian, have fostered a sense of Taiwan's independence from China, even as they have refrained from any formal declaration of independence that would surely bring war with China. Public opinion largely supports this stance.[11] Nonetheless, while the public does not want war with the PRC, there is a strong sense— seemingly getting stronger every year—that Taiwan differs from China not only in its politics, but in its national culture as well.

Taiwan's religious renaissance both springs from and contributes to this sense of cultural nationhood. It is no accident that Taiwan's religious renaissance was based on the Asian values found in Confucianism, Bud-

dhism and Taoism rather than Christianity. Although the Taiwanese Presbyterian Church was for many decades a major source of support for
Taiwanese nationalism (and is still flourishing), most of the other Christian denominations neglected the aspirations of the native Taiwanese.
Their missionaries (many of whom came to Taiwan after having been
expelled from the PRC) did not speak Taiwanese, and most local church
leaders were Mainlanders. While not being especially identified with Taiwan, most of the Christian churches were identified with the West.[12] As
mentioned earlier, they benefited from government grants of special privileges to Christianity in order to maintain the favor of its American pa-
trons during the cold war. Buddhism and Daoism, on the other hand,
were seen as native religions, and Confucianism as a native ethical system, deeply rooted in Taiwan's soil, although they had of course all been
brought from mainland China along with almost every other part of Taiwanese culture. Thus, both at Tzu Chi's Abode of Still Thoughts and at
Dharma Drum Mountain I met nuns who had embraced their vocation
after studying in the West, because they thought, as one nun put it, that
Buddhism was the "religion of my race." Humanistic Buddhism and reformed Daoism were attempts to purify and modernize this indigenous
religion in a way that would have been impossible to accomplish on the
mainland—just as the Taiwanese have purified and modernized other aspects of traditional Chinese culture in a way that can claim to be pecu-
liarly Taiwanese.

Although Tzu Chi, Buddha's Light Mountain, and Dharma Drum
Mountain all emphasize that their practices transcend nationality, in fact
the world of religious connection that they create is centered on Taiwan.
Tzu Chi claims, for example, that it is making Taiwan an "Island of Great
Love." Although it tries to disseminate its love around the world and
wishes to respect all cultures, nationalities, and religions, its leaders always make it clear that the source of that love is on Taiwan. The huge
Hsi Lai Temple in Los Angeles, belonging to Buddha's Light Mountain,
means the "Coming to the West Temple." The Buddha's light shines from
Taiwan to illuminate the rest of the world. Dharma Drum Mountain also
takes pride in being a Taiwan-based organization even as it extends ecumenical cooperation toward the world.

It is not just that these organizations originated in Taiwan, but that
the political and economic system of Taiwan gives them the freedom and
economic resources needed to develop and disseminate their message. It
is clear that Beijing would never allow such large and independent religious organizations to flourish. Even if one has no other reasons to be

pro-Taiwan, a practitioner of humanistic Buddhism, or, for that matter, of reformed Daoism, would feel particular gratitude for the religious policy of the Taiwanese government and for people who helped develop and disseminate these modern spiritual movements.

The version of Taiwanese nationalism that gets the most attention in the West is the belligerent version that sharply differentiates Taiwan from China and lays the basis for a claim to Taiwan's independence. Although this certainly has its appeal within Taiwan, most Taiwanese are afraid of it. They want to be a distinctive nation, but they do not want to provoke a war with China. The ecumenical nationalism of the groups studied here resonates with this ambivalent mix of hope and fear.

Yet the religious organizations studied here all affirm (to varying degrees) the transcendence of their vision of ultimate reality. That is, they say that the interests of the individual, the family, the local community, and the nation must be subordinated to the universal good of the whole world. While encouraging a sense of Taiwanese nationhood, they say that neither nationalism nor any other kind of parochial attachment should be seen as the be-all and end-all of existence, especially if such attachments are promoted and maintained through violence. These groups loyally support the Taiwanese state, but the support is voluntary and based on moral principles that transcend any particular political interest.

Asian Values and Globalization

This ecumenically nationalistic version of Asian values also resonates with the Taiwanese experience of globalization. Taiwan's economy thrives on globalization. It is based on exporting goods and services and importing the knowledge and skills necessary to produce successful exports. Both economic and cultural exchange are absolutely central to the Taiwanese economy. The groups that I have studied here are religious representations of Taiwan's position in a system of globalized cultural exchange. They take in external religious influences, transform them by application of indigenous values, and export them to the rest of the world.

Although based on Chinese religious traditions, the organizations I have described on Taiwan have absorbed many influences from Japan and the West to create their new forms of religious practice. The most important influence has been from Japan, both from the Japanese colonial period (1895–1945) and from the more recent past.[13] Japanese Buddhism has been more focused on worldly service than traditional Chinese Buddhism. Master Cheng Yen's first Buddhist teacher, Master Hsiu

Tao, had gone to school in Japan and helped introduce to Cheng Yen the notion that monasteries should work in the world.[14] Japanese Buddhism had also pioneered the organization of educated laywomen for community service. (After the Meiji Restoration, Japanese women were able to pursue higher education, but could not work in most occupations. Thus their knowledge and energy could be mobilized for volunteer community service.) But the Japanese Buddhists had moved away from the strict practices of Chinese Buddhism—for instance, Japanese monks were allowed to marry. While adopting the social concerns of the Japanese Buddhists, Taiwanese Buddhists maintained the purity of Chinese monastic life, and thus helped maintain a distinctive cultural identity.

Taiwanese religions also borrowed from the West, sometimes in order to compete with it. Administrators at the Enacting Heaven Temple Foundation said that the idea of organizing volunteers to help the community was brought to Taiwan by the service clubs formed by American military wives. According to Tzu Chi's official history, Master Cheng Yen was inspired to take up social service work after being visited by three Catholic nuns who tried to show her that Catholicism was superior to Buddhism because it performed so many works of social service. Whatever the accuracy of this story, it suggests that competition with Christians was one force driving Tzu Chi's religious evolution. The theme of competition becomes even stronger with Buddha's Light Mountain. Master Hsing Yun saw the encroachment of Christianity in Taiwan as problematic. He thought that he had to adopt some of the effective religious marketing used by Western Christian organizations if he was to maintain Buddhism's place in Taiwan.[15] Other Buddhist and Daoist groups adopted his methods. By now, all of the religious organizations we have described in this book have more sophisticated magazines, television programs, and websites than most Christian organizations in Taiwan. Perhaps because the Taiwanese Buddhists and Daoists saw themselves in a relatively weak position with respect to their Christian competitors, they were motivated to learn from the competitors more than most Christians were motivated to learn from the Buddhists and Daoists. The learning seems to have led to genuine respect for the competitors. So now, all of the groups that I studied seem to talk more about dialogue than competition.

Like the rest of Taiwan's emerging national culture, these religious organizations achieve a distinctive reconfiguration of Chinese cultural traditions under the stimulus of influences from Japan and the United States—a distinctive blend of East and West that is made in Taiwan. With their visibility and global outreach, they can become vehicles for the collective representation of national identity, a role that looms especially large in Taiwan's peculiar geopolitical circumstances.

The crux of Taiwan's geopolitical predicament is that it is becoming a nation but it cannot have a fully legitimate state. Besides the obvious political problems this creates, there is also a moral problem, a crisis of moral representation. In all cultural traditions, the state is never seen just as an administrative apparatus. It is a vehicle for representing the moral aspirations that make its citizens into a national community. The state in Asian cultural traditions perhaps bears even more of this burden of moral representation than the state in the American tradition.

But the Taiwanese state cannot easily fill this function of representing the aspirations of the people. For one thing, the Taiwanese state is not officially recognized by any major government in the international community. For another, even under the administration of President Chen Shui-bian, whose Democratic Progressive Party (DPP) has since its founding propagated the ideal of Taiwan independence, the Taiwanese government has refrained from claiming that Taiwan is an independent nation in order to avoid unduly antagonizing the PRC. Indeed, most people in Taiwan want to do whatever it takes to avoid war, even though there is a widespread belief that they have created a unique culture and that they share a community of fate.[16] Under these circumstances, the government in Taiwan can represent only their compromises and fears, not their ideals and hopes. Locally grown religious organizations inevitably pick up the burden of symbolizing the aspirations of the Taiwanese people.

On the walls of the reception room in the Enacting Heaven Temple are pictures of foreign ministers, heads of state, and other international dignitaries that have come to see the good work that the temple is doing. Tzu Chi is known around the world for its relief work. Its yearbooks have pictures of numerous important visitors who have come to visit the Abode of Still Thoughts, including not only political leaders, but also cardinals sent by the Vatican, the head of the Nobel-prize winning Doctors Without Borders, and so on. Buddha's Light Mountain displays pictures of huge candlelit rallies staged by Hsing Yun in Hong Kong, Malaysia, and even South Africa, as well as pictures of Hsing Yun with the pope, the Dalai Lama, and world political leaders. Dharma Drum Mountain's Sheng Yen also has an international reputation. Through their international celebrity, our humanistic Buddhist and reformed Daoist organizations display Taiwan's national culture as a source of wisdom and generosity and solutions to the world's problems, a Buddha's light to the world.

Facing a serious challenge from the Chinese mainland, however, the Taiwanese can ill afford to assert their national identity in a way that would antagonize supporters in the United States, Europe, and Japan. There is a special incentive to portray Taiwanese cultural uniqueness in a way that emphasizes Taiwan's openness, tolerance, and flexibility, in contrast to mainland China's relative closed-mindedness, aggressiveness, and rigidity. This helps explain why middle-class Taiwanese are attracted to forms of religion that are different from mainstream religion in the West, but display an ecumenical openness that would be attractive to the West.

Globalization has influenced not just the content of Taiwanese Buddhism and Daoism, but its forms of organization as well. The religious organizations studied here have expanded so rapidly because of their mastery of global communication. In the past two decades, Taiwan has become one of the world's leading manufacturers of information technology. The expertise is available for local religious groups to make full use of this technology. Just as important as mastery of the hardware, however, is mastery of the software—the ability to use global icons and idioms to communicate via television, the internet, and image-laden magazines. Taiwan's emerging middle classes, many of whom travel widely throughout Asia, the United States, and Europe and who are immersed in an advertising-saturated consumer culture, have become very familiar with such images.

Thus, everything from the arrangement of rituals to the methods of dispensing charity have been influenced by demands of making them into internationally accessible representations. Under the hangings of classical calligraphy in front of the lecture hall at the Enacting Heaven Temple are the little heart symbols that now seem to be used around the world as expressions of sentiment. The notices for Enacting Heaven Temple's cultural events use the kinds of cheerful graphics that one might see on greeting cards in the United States. The graphic layouts of their magazines—plenty of sentimental color photographs of people of all ages expressing joy or sorrow—are similar to popular Christian magazines in the West. When Master Hsing Yun of Buddha's Light Mountain gives his public dharma lectures, he uses theatrical effects that one might find at a rock concert or a Las Vegas floor show. As the curtain slowly rises, artificial smoke pours from the stage, colored lights flash, and the music swells. Sometimes members of the audience are given candles, the auditorium is darkened, and flames are passed from candle to candle—an effect one sees often in Western church services, but not in traditional Buddhist ceremonies.

Sheng Yen of Dharma Drum Mountain gives his dharma lectures not

according to the traditional Buddhist calendar, but on Sunday, in a ritual that looks much like a Protestant church service. There are opening
hymns and common prayers. Then everyone opens a book of Buddhist
sutras to a passage indicated by Sheng Yen and he explains the meaning
of the passage in the light of current events. Finally, there are closing
prayers and a recessional. During some workshops at the temple, guests
are served vegetarian Italian spaghetti and cheese rather than Chinese
vegetarian food. As we have seen in chapter 2, Tzu Chi's most impressive ceremonies resemble Christian church services even more closely.

While adopting Western methods of disseminating their messages
through media, the four organizations studied here have utilized Taiwanese business methods for creating flexible forms of organization. Taiwanese businesses have pioneered flexible methods of organization
through networks. In the Taiwanese economy, relatively small, autonomous, entrepreneurial enterprises develop economies of scale with a complex division of labor by developing networks of connections, based on
interpersonal contacts, with complementary organizations throughout
mainland China.[17] Their middle-class religious organizations have done
the same. Their branches have a high degree of autonomy and encourage entrepreneurial local initiative. They are bound to one another out
of respect for their charismatic leaders, but instead of specific instruc-
tions, their leaders offer general guidelines that can be pursued by local
religious entrepreneurs.

How much of Buddhism and Daoism is lost in such translation into
the language and logic of a globalized network society? There are debates
within Taiwan's religious circles about this. Tzu Chi sometimes gets criticized for being "insufficiently dharmic" *(bu ru fa)*. And there does seem
to be some possibility that all of the religious movements discussed here
could dissolve into a general "new age" tissue of benign sentiment with
little capacity for philosophical depth or moral discipline. Yet even as they
adopt some of the idiom of globalized media culture, these organizations
criticize important parts of the content of that culture. All of them warn
against consumerism and stress that true happiness comes from cultivating the heart, not acquiring things. They all warn against self-indulgence
and encourage generosity. All of them—but Tzu Chi most effectively—
urge people to achieve harmony with the natural environment. Are their
efforts destined to be defeated by the seductive pressures of global consumer culture, or can they actually help to transform that culture?

"Some foreigners see Taiwan simply as a 'casino society,'" said Tzu
Chi's spokesperson (a former official in Taiwan's Ministry of Foreign Af-

fairs) to a gathering of foreign journalists in the fall of 1999. "But the way we have generously responded to our earthquake—and the way we have helped other people who have faced natural disasters around the world—shows that this is not true. We are a loving society who sees the world as a global village." There are indeed plenty of crass elements of Taiwanese society that are visible for the world to see: financial speculation, political corruption, blatant materialism, rude habits and sexual exploitation (nicely joined together in the use of scantily clad young women to sell packages of the ubiquitously chewed betel nut), and reckless destruction of the natural environment. The religious organizations we have been discussing here project an image of a better Taiwan. Because the image is not mere political propaganda, but a sincere representation of ideals actually lived out in practice by at least some members of these organizations, it has credibility both to domestic and foreign audiences. It thus has some capacity to bring into being what it imagines. The act of sincerely imagining an ideal Taiwan encourages Taiwan's citizens to live up to the ideal.

The Taiwan case shows that strict political control over religion (as exercised by the authoritarian KMT for four decades following 1945) does not necessarily either destroy religion or cause religion to react fiercely against the state once the repression is ended. It shows that, in a Chinese cultural context, it is possible for the state to win the active cooperation of religion while respecting the autonomy of religious leaders over their own organizations. It shows that Asian values can be interpreted in such a way as to support democracy rather than dictatorship. It shows that Confucianism, Buddhism, and Daoism have the capacity both to adapt to modernity and to humanize the modern world. It shows that globalization can help lead to a religious renaissance that supports dialogue among civilizations rather than clashes between them.

These findings are welcome signs of hope in a world full of troubles. I would like to conclude this book by speculating on the hopeful significance of this particular Taiwanese development of Asian values for Westerners concerned about moral dilemmas in which they find themselves.

TOWARD A HOPEFUL SOCIOLOGY

The Crisis of Modernity

As envisioned by the Western Enlightenment, the modern moral order would be based on critical reason rather than faith.[18] It would emancipate individuals from subjugation based on myth and custom, and join such individuals into associations for mutual benefit. As this moral order expanded to encompass the globe, the result would be universal peace and interdependent prosperity.[19] It didn't work out that way. For one thing, there were philosophical and practical disputes about what kinds of economic and political arrangements would best protect individual autonomy while maximizing the mutual benefits of economic interdependence. A liberal vision stressed the need for an unregulated market economy, whose invisible hand would naturally lead to the greatest benefit for the greatest number of people, and for a minimal government, freely elected by all citizens, to protect the rights of each individual to personal security and private property. A socialist vision stressed the need for economic planning to protect individuals from want and for a large centralized government led by a vanguard of the people. And there have been various mixtures of elements from these two extreme versions of political economy.

In the second half of the twentieth century, the great struggle was between the liberal and socialist visions of modernity. Both liberal democrats and state socialists could blame various dysfunctions within their societies on their need to struggle against their ideological rival and their consequent inability to extend their vision across the whole world. State socialism has collapsed, but the triumph of liberal democracy has been short lived. The whole globe is now tied together through a lightly regulated market economy and its political processes are dominated by the United States, which legitimates its projection of power through its mission of being the primary champion of the liberal democratic vision of modernity. Yet dedicated militants who resent the new global order's injustice, are repelled by its alienating fragmentation, and have contempt for its materialistic shallowness are challenging it. Even in the United States, religious fundamentalists and nationalist militarists have come to dominate a polity supposedly based on critical rationality and commerce-oriented individualism.

Liberal democracy can no longer blame its troubles on the pressures of competing with socialism. The problem may lie deeper, in the very premises of the Enlightenment vision of modern moral order. There may be something inadequate about the version of critical rationality and autonomous individualism that we have assumed to be the basis of a modern moral order. Critical reason has proven to be an incomparable instrument for the development of empirical science, effective technology, and rationalized bureaucracy. The liberation of individuals from unchosen social relationships has paved the way for the cosmopolitan, impersonal relationships of a dynamic global market economy. This has made possible the emergence of globe-spanning webs of wealth and power. What has been lacking, however, are widely shared, convincing visions of what moral limits should be placed on the pursuit of wealth and power for the sake of justice, human solidarity, and a sustainable ecological harmony.[20]

There have of course been major philosophical efforts—for example, by Emmanuel Kant, John Stewart Mill, John Rawls, and Jürgen Habermas—to find a modern, rational basis for global justice and human solidarity. However satisfying they may be for intellectuals, however, they have not inspired the widespread commitments that might effectively solve the problems of modernity. They have been too abstract to gain much of a grip on popular consciousness, even in the West. And they are too tied to Western cultural assumptions to be broadly plausible in non-Western cultures.[21]

Moreover, critical reason cannot completely substitute for myth and ritual in generating the sense of common identity that motivates the pursuit of justice. An individualism based solely on a quest for independence untempered by a sense of social responsibility cannot sustain the trust and loyalty that make social cooperation possible. Without a strong moral basis for justice and loyalty, it is impossible to sustain the institutional foundations of a liberal democratic world order.

The primary foundations for such an order are a free market economy and democratic governance. The market economy generates severe inequalities, especially when it becomes globalized. Without a shared commitment to social justice, the market will generate intense conflicts that will be difficult under any circumstances to resolve by democratic institutions, and next to impossible to resolve when such institutions are not sustained by loyalty and trust.

Into this moral vacuum have flowed religious movements. The myths and rituals at the heart of religious movements can generate moral solidarities and energize collective endeavors much more effectively than the teachings of critical intellectuals. But many of the most dynamic recent religious and moral regeneration movements have been reactionary. They negate the positive legacies of Enlightenment liberalism, the affirmation of individual dignity, the respect for diversity, the commitment to rational inquiry. They separate believers from non-believers, and place the particular over the universal, the local over the global. In religiously divided societies, they often inhibit the establishment of pluralistic democracies. In religiously unified societies, they sometimes support assertive nationalism that can threaten world peace.

Yet history shows that religion doesn't have to be reactionary. Our great historical visions of a universal moral order have their origins in religious prophesy. It is the great world religions that have taught us to hope for world justice and peace. In the contemporary world, there are also important examples of progressive religious movements, and this book offers some Taiwanese examples of them. If my account of the problems of Enlightenment modernity turns out to be correct, the disruptions caused by reactionary religion will not be solved simply by trying to substitute critical scientific reason for religion or by trying to keep religious discourse out of public life. In the long run, the only solution to the disruptions of reactionary religion is progressive religion.

But where does progressive religion come from? Sociological theories are not very good for answering such questions. Products of the Enlightenment themselves, their strength is in analyzing the power of reactionary religion and in trying to overcome it through critical thinking. At the beginning of the twentieth century, Emile Durkheim brilliantly showed how religious ritual contributed to the moral foundations of social life. His classic study, *The Elementary Forms of Religious Life,* focused on the production of sacred symbols within the small face-to-face moieties of Australian aborigine society, but he hoped to show how an understanding of these processes could give us insights into how to carry out a modern moral education that would support the moral individualism necessary to sustain a differentiated modern society.[22] However, his analysis was much better at showing how myth and ritual could create relatively small, closed groups than sustain a cosmopolitan individualism.

Max Weber showed how the Protestant Reformation led to the rationalized organization of modernity. Yet in his analysis, the religious impulse that originally led to this innovation has vanished; the outcome is an iron cage of modernity. In the future, charismatic movements may arise to challenge the alienating modern order. But to succeed, they have to develop their own rationalized forms. The outlook was not for a universal peace, but for more intense conflicts among better-organized warring gods—an unhappy prospect that has been realized all too fully today.[23]

The classics of modern sociological theory are better at showing why, in considering the role of religion in the modern world, we should look to the future with fear and resignation rather than with hope. Here I would like to build upon the classic Durkheimian and Weberian traditions in ways that can better account for the origins and potential of the small signs of hope I have seen in Taiwan.

The Axial Challenge

To understand how religious innovations can both enhance individual human freedom while integrating humans into wider, more inclusive world orders, we should look to the time when hope for such innovations first arose—the period in the middle of the first millennium B.C.E. that Karl Jaspers called the "axial age"—when there simultaneously and independently arose visions of individual self-consciousness and moral universalism in China, India, Israel, and Athens.[24]

From the legacy of the axial age, we have derived the most precious features of our modern identities: the aspiration for human dignity through a critical transcendence of our present circumstances and the affirmation of the fundamental unity of the human species. However, the cultural creativity of this time period could not be sustained. The creative tension between a critical, world-transcending universalism and a ritually sanctified particularism broke down. The axial cultures opened up new ways of imagining a wider world, but in the end those worlds were unified and dominated by worldly political power. The axial cultures devolved into universal empires that embraced the whole world known to people within those cultures. Some of the axial insights survived, but they were calcified into political orthodoxies, such as state Confucianism during the Han Dynasty. In the words of Jaspers, "There arose spiritually stable, long-enduring periods of great empires, attended by a leveling down to mass culture and by the sublime, but unfree, spirituality of conservative aristocracies. It is as though the world fell into a centuries-long sleep, accompanied by the absolute authority of great systems and mummifications." One consequence of this was a hardening of the great axial cultural traditions into mutually incompatible systems. The stage was set for what today we might call a clash of civilizations.[25]

The crisis of late-twentieth-century modernity, Jaspers thought, could be resolved in favor of human freedom only if there were something like a new axial age. Writing a few years after World War II, Jaspers saw a new world unity coming into being. There were two possible forms that this new level of global integration could take: either the form of a world *empire*, held together through force by a ruling hegemon; or a world *order*, "perennially reestablished in negotiation and decision, of states governing themselves within legally restricted domains."[26] Influenced by his mentor Max Weber, Jaspers thought the realistic prospects for a humane modernity were dismal. The world empire was more likely, its domination perhaps veiled, as in antiquity, "by figures of speech and sham contrivances from the free past." ("There was hardly ever so much talk of Greek liberty, which was again and again guaranteed by the victors, as when it was finally destroyed in favor of an imperial regime.")[27]

But Jaspers was not without hope. A world order, based on a global flourishing of freedom, was not impossible, though it would have to arise slowly "in numerous gradations of freedom."[28] A new global order, as opposed to an empire, would require the widespread, free commitment (free because based on interior conviction of self-critical, rational individuals) to transcendent norms binding everyone, no matter what his or her cultural origin. The spiritual movements of the first axial age held out hope that such commitments could be possible.[29]

The spiritual insights of the first axial age remained essential. But the demands of a new world order would require first that they be released from their mummifications. And new visions of global responsibility would have to be created. This, though, would require a fresh appropriation of the spiritual insights of the first axial age and the breakthrough to something like a new axial age. Unlike the original axial age, which saw the parallel development of several separate cultural traditions, a new axial age would have to arise through the interaction of many different traditions. The religious universalism of a new axial age would have to be an ecumenical one, which freely elicited common understandings from diverse faiths, rather than an imperialistic universalism that tried to dominate all parts of the world under a single faith. As Jaspers put it, "The universality of a world order obligatory to all (in contrast to a world empire) is possible *only* when the multiple contents of faith remain free in their historical communication, without the unity of an objective, universally valid doctrinal content."[30]

How might this happen? What would be the conditions of its occurrence? What forms might it take? Though very general, the explanation given by Jaspers for the advent of the first axial age gives us hints about where to look: the initial breakthroughs took place on the margins of powerful empires, in small states that had experienced some prosperity but which were locked in incessant competition with other states and were insecure and vulnerable. This made possible the emergence of itinerant intellectuals, not bound to particular rulers, who could critically address the insecurities of the time.[31]

This book has focused on a marginal place, Taiwan, an island that has experienced impressive economic growth and political development in the past generation, but is extremely vulnerable to military domination from the PRC and faces intense economic competition from China and other Asian developing countries. Not a bad place, perhaps, to look for moral and religious developments of potentially global significance.

I am not claiming that Taiwan is the origin of a major new global axial breakthrough. If such a breakthrough ever were to occur, it would surely be the result not of one spectacular prophetic movement emanating from single place, but of the slow coalescence of many small movements in many areas. However, we might consider the cases here as precursors of such movements, and by studying them we might get a more fine-grained understanding of the social and cultural matrix out of which axial breakthroughs can arise.

Progressive Religion in Taiwan

The movements I have described in this book all attempt to move from a particularistic to a universal moral consciousness—to make their practitioners critically evaluate their particular concerns in the light of global concerns and to see their local commitments as subordinate to global responsibilities. None of them are truly "new religious movements"—they are not radical departures from common religious practices in Taiwan. They rather represent a reform of common religious practices—a reinterpretation of them, often with the ostensible aim of recovering their original meaning. The original meaning supposedly being recovered is something like the axial Daoist, Confucian, and Buddhist meanings—an affirmation of the fundamental interdependence of all things and a call to cultivate one's moral life so as to be in accord with that interdependence.

Nonetheless, they retain a grounding in stories and rituals that identify practitioners with particular communities—particular extended-family networks, particular ethnic identities (Taiwanese), particular local communities (e.g., Taipei), and a particular nation (Taiwan). The tightness of the connection varies. The Enacting Heaven Temple represents a rather loose syncretism, a juxtaposition of high-minded Confucian morality with down-to-earth folk Daoist practice. Buddha's Light Mountain represents a carefully organized package of activities that combines the preaching of Confucian social morality mixed with Buddhist compassion and a wide variety of traditional Buddhist devotional practices. It is like a neatly arrayed spiritual supermarket (a metaphor evoked by Hsing Yun himself) in contrast to the bustling bazaar that is the Enacting Heaven Temple. Tzu Chi represents a more thorough rearranging of traditional Buddhist myths and rituals in the name of a single-minded focus on extending Buddhist compassion to the global village. Yet by no means does it leave behind the Buddhist stories and customs that most Taiwanese would have known from childhood. Cheng Yen uses Buddhist stories and parables to illustrate the challenge of compassion. Visitors to the Abode of Still Thoughts join with the resident nuns in a full range of Buddhist chanting. Other ceremonies are modifications of traditional Buddhist practices. Tzu Chi's social morality builds on a Confucian notion of expanding family loyalties to encompass an ever-wider circle of humanity. The Dharma Drum Mountain Temple focuses on an elite Chan Buddhist tradition—something that most people in Taiwan would know about even if relatively few practice it—but through its educational and media outreach it popularizes this among ordinary middle-class people.

Thus, in their teaching and practice, the religious movements we have studied expand (to varying degrees) the moral horizons of participants beyond the boundaries of family, locality, ethnic group, or nation. They articulate a moral vision for a globalized world. At the same time, they reaffirm familiar bonds. They bring about a more self-conscious, and indeed a more heartfelt, connection to family, community, and nation, even as they claim that a properly heartfelt connection should impel one beyond the boundaries of customary relationships. An important part of the appeal of these new global visions is that they reaffirm an imagined connection to the common spiritual heritage of Taiwan.

They try to avoid, however, making their religious imagination into a vehicle for collective egoism. As we have seen, they are resolutely ecumenical. Their leaders (to varying degrees) define devotion not in terms of a commitment to convert the rest of the world to their religious practice, but in terms of their capacity to affirm the worth of other religions and cultures and to engage in active dialogue with them. They zealously preach tolerance, not the passive tolerance of indifference, but an actively engaged tolerance of respectful dialogue.

Of course, members of these groups—especially the lay members—have a wide variety of motives, and some of what they speak about and do can be explained in terms of their economic and political interests. I have discussed this throughout this book. But after all economic and political interests have been accounted for, and after all the inevitable hypocrisy has been acknowledged, there remains a core of genuine idealistic religious creativity in these groups. It is a kind of religious revival that holds out much more positive hopes for the building of a free world order than do the various forms of zealous tribalism associated with religious revivals in the Middle East and America. What is the social and moral ecology out of which such a progressive revival has emerged?

The Matrix of Axial Innovation

Mary Douglas has provided a useful framework for conceptualizing the relationship between social and cultural context and the symbolic forms of religious practice, which we have alluded to from time to time throughout this book. Let us now elaborate her framework and apply it systematically. For Douglas, the structure of a society's moral order, the forms of its cosmologies, and the meaningfulness of its rituals all depend on the tightness of its group ties (which, in her shorthand jargon, she calls "group") and the clarity and specificity of its moral norms (which she calls "grid").[32] Societies strong in group are structured according to closed corporate groups which are difficult to exit and can put high levels of social pressure on their members. Societies weak in group are assemblages of mobile individuals who can voluntarily choose their associates. Societies strong in grid have clear, coherent, and well-institutionalized systems for classifying roles and statuses, rights and responsibilities. Societies weak in grid are anomic—their institutions are weak and moral standards indistinct.

Societies with different combinations of strong and weak group and grid give rise to different kinds of symbol systems. People socialized under conditions of strong grid and strong group employ a "restricted" symbolic language. They utilize multilayered, metaphorical symbols that condense the meanings gained through the common experience of relatively closed groups. Some of these condensed symbols are felt to be so intrinsically powerful that in the very act of being expressed they bring about what they signify. Such symbols are the basis for sacramental religions, based, in turn, on a strong sense of the sacredness (and thus the basic immutability) of religious institutions.[33] The Daoist purification rituals that we saw in the Enacting Heaven Temple are examples of condensed symbolic action that bring into being that which they symbolize.

People socialized under conditions of strong grid and weak group use "elaborated" speech codes. These are based on symbols with specific, clearly defined meanings, which each individual can use to communicate his or her unique interests and feelings with the hope of reaching agreement with someone with complementary interests and feelings. It leads to a religion of inner experience rather than external form and to a critical consciousness that frees individuals from the habitual following of authority, even as it allows them to calculate strategically in a complexly organized world.[34] This is the pattern of expressive individualism which the authors of *Habits of the Heart* found to be prevalent in the United

States, in a context of weak group ties and a strong grid of bureaucratic institutions.[35]

Taiwanese society used to be fairly strong in group. It was structured into extended families, lineages, and native place associations. Boundaries between ethnic groups—native Taiwanese, Mainlanders, and aborigines—were strong. With Taiwan's rapid industrialization and urbanization, such groups have greatly weakened. Increasingly, Taiwan is becoming a society of mobile individuals. There has been a vast proliferation of voluntary associations, constituting an energetic civil society. But Taiwanese group life is still significantly stronger than in the United States and Europe. Many voluntary associations (Tzu Chi being an excellent example) often imagine themselves as something like extended families rather than as associations based on quasi-contractual relationships among freely consenting individuals. There are a number of reasons for this. Taiwan's industrialization is recent. It is a small island, where people can never get too far away from their family backgrounds. The economy is built on relatively small, family-owned businesses rather than large, impersonal corporate enterprises. Because of an unfortunate history of conflicts, the boundaries between its ethnic groups are still relatively strong. Even cosmopolitan Taiwanese, who have worked or studied abroad, tend to live in ethnic enclaves abroad, with the result that, for the first generation at least, they retain a strong sense of Taiwanese corporate identity. The weakening of traditional group life has given Taiwanese both the means and motivation to seek new forms of affiliation. But they still feel the pressure and enjoy the security, of extended families and other non-voluntary corporate groups.

The religious innovators described in this book all take for granted the mobility and openness of modern Taiwanese society, but they try to convince their followers that this is not the whole story, that they are grounded in a web of transcendent connections centered on the family, and that they are responsible for maintaining these. This might be less broadly plausible in a highly individualistic society like the United States, where group boundaries are weak and families more often incoherent.

Being embedded in such corporate groups, especially extended families, keeps Taiwanese familiar with the dense, metaphor-rich symbolic forms of religious ritual. Even among professional middle-class people, for example, weddings and funerals still involve an intricate mix of ceremonies to affirm right relationships with parents and relatives and to ensure that the wedding will find its proper place in the cosmic order. In their purses and wallets, many Taiwanese with PhDs still carry talismans consecrated in their local temples, often given to them by their mothers when they were about to leave home. At the same time, educated Taiwanese become fluent in the articulated, elaborated speech codes of the "symbol manipulators" who constitute the new middle classes around the world. Perhaps it is the creative tension between these two ways of representing the world that fosters conceptions of universal community grounded not simply in the interplay of subjective self-interest, but also in a transcendent tissue of solidarity that is real but too rich to be encompassed in dogmatic doctrine.

Though stronger in group than the United States, Taiwan is weaker in what Mary Douglas would call grid. In modern American and European societies, formally organized corporations and a bureaucratic state provide a vast lattice of rules and categories that channel individual aspirations and set benchmarks for success. In Douglas's jargon, such societies are strong in grid. As Max Weber has argued, in the early stages of their development, such bureaucratic institutions may have been shaped by religious impulses. But now they are devoid of religious significance and are largely experienced as alienating.

In Taiwan, such institutions are still in the process of development, and religion is playing a role in the development. Taiwan still lacks strongly institutionalized rules for economic and political life. In its transition from an authoritarian to democratic government, the rules of political procedure are often weak and unclear. Government regulation of business is still irregular and haphazard. This situation creates felt needs for comprehensive moral visions that could guide the way toward a more firmly institutionalized economy and polity.

The religious organizations that we have studied make efforts to fill this need. In other societies, religious organizations often see themselves as a haven from what they see as impersonal, bureaucratic organizations. In Taiwan, the religious organizations that we have studied here want to help construct a better national state. They are not in any position, however, to do this on their own. They have to use powers of persuasion to find common ground in the midst of differences. This encourages what one might call an ecumenical rather than an imperialistic universalism.

It is not just Taiwan's domestic society that is suspended halfway between strong and weak group life and strong and weak institutional order. These conditions are characteristic of Taiwan's position in the international system as a whole. Taiwan is at once open to the global market economy and in the process of building strong bonds of a particular national identity, based supposedly on the uniqueness of Taiwan's history and culture. Meanwhile, Taiwan is not part of a strong grid of international relations. Its lack of international legitimacy makes it impossible for it to depend for its security on reliable treaties among fellow nation states. To get global help, Taiwan has to rely on persuasion, on the global attractiveness of its cultural ideals and political practices. As it builds a national identity, it has to celebrate the glory of its culture—including its religious culture—but to get international support it has to do so in a way that is respectful of the values of others.

Political economists say that Taiwan's status as a late developing society has enabled it to become technologically and economically innovative by leapfrogging some of the economic obstacles (like obsolete technology and deteriorating infrastructure) of earlier developing societies. Perhaps Taiwan's late development is also allowing it to be religiously and morally innovative—to give rise to quasi-axial religious innovations that combine dense, multilayered symbols with critically elaborated systems of universal classification and that inspire humans to seek a universal unity without uniformity.

I have suggested how Taiwan's social structure and institutional framework have encouraged the development of religious movements with a certain symbolic structure. But the broadly inclusive quality of these religious developments is also indebted to the content of the traditions out of which they arise. The content of Confucian, Daoist, and Buddhist traditions is more conducive than the major Western traditions to blurring the boundaries that divide people from one another.

Consider the notion of *shan*, "the good" in East Asian traditions. Its place in the universe of Confucian discourse is quite different from the notion of the good in classic Western philosophy. In both the Hebrew Bible and in classic Greek philosophy the good is the beginning and end of human destiny. In the book of Genesis, God creates heaven and earth and sees that they are good. The goodness of God (in spite of many appearances to the contrary) is arguably the central teaching of the Hebrew Bible.[36] In Aristotle's ethics, pursuit of the good is the goal of the moral life.[37] In Christian philosophy, the highest good is identified with God. In such discourse, goodness becomes absolutized. One can imagine an absolute good that is counterpoised against absolute evil.

In the Confucian tradition, goodness resists such absolutization. *Shan* is only intermittently mentioned in *The Analects*. More central to Confucian philosophy are discussions of the virtues of *ren* (human relatedness) and *yi* (righteousness) and prescriptions for practice of *li* (rituals for expressing and actualizing well-ordered human relationships). If one practices *li* and cultivates the virtues of *ren* and *yi*, one will produce things that are *shan*, and the experience of this goodness will bring surpassing joy to a person morally cultivated enough to appreciate it. Goodness represents an ultimately valuable quality of life. Yet this quality does not become the sacred foundation of a moral community. It is rather the byproduct of a way of life in which fundamentally social human beings practice the rituals of deference, differentiation of social roles, and mutual support that make a harmonious sociability possible. In the Confucian tradition, one of the fundamental purposes of this way of life is to avoid social polarization and to resolve problems without violent conflict.

In the Daoist classics, the very distinction between good and evil is questioned. "Is there a difference between good *(shan)* and evil *(e)*? . . . What nonsense!"[38] But in the religious Daoist tradition begun by Zhang Daoling in the second century C.E., the word *shan* is used to refer to the morally good acts and efficacious practices that extend life and lead to immortality.[39] Buddhists used the term to denote acts of compassion and generosity *(cishan)* that would bring good karma. But in both the Daoist and Buddhist traditions, goodness is part of the means through which one seeks the ultimate goal of attaining immortality or being reborn in the pure land. In none of these cases does good denote anything like the *summum bonum*, an ultimate goal to which all things ought to strive. In Chinese cultural traditions, there is no transcendent, supernatural good toward which humans strive. The natural good is a basic foundation for a this-worldly, open-ended human project of creating a community that recognizes its interdependence with all things.

The benefit of such moral traditions is that they give guidance and motivation for the self-transcendence necessary for human flourishing within interdependent societies—but they are not conducive to a crusader mentality. They provide fertile ground for the flexible, ecumenical universalism encouraged by the Taiwanese religious movements I have studied here.

Redeeming Modernity

The Taiwanese religious developments described here are fragile shoots that may not survive the winter of discontent that seems to be descending upon us. They are vulnerable to political forces that threaten to obliterate an independent Taiwanese culture. Like the great axial breakthroughs of two and a half millennia ago, they are an unstable mix of transcendent universalism and socially embedded particularism—products of a peculiar phase in a transition from social closure to openness. Fate may well have decreed that they fail to influence the American empire that is being built up around us, or fail to mitigate the forces of resentment arrayed against it.

No matter what happens to Taiwan and what happens to these religious innovations within the years to come, these moments of axial religious creativity offer glimpses of alternatives to the dysfunctional modernity that most of us experience, ways of softening global competition with global care, of situating the quest for individual freedom within global webs of responsibility, and of affirming global human solidarity while respecting diversity. Investigating such shoots of hope while they are still alive and understanding the social ecologies that facilitate their growth may help us to cultivate other shoots in other times and places.

Notes

PREFACE

1. Interviews conducted with directors of the Tzu Chi center in Puli in October, 1999. Unless otherwise noted, information in this book is based on interviews with members (including leaders) of the various religious organizations studied and on participant-observation ethnography. Most of the research was carried out between September 1999 and January 2000, when I was a research fellow at the Academia Sinica in Taiwan. The Chiang Ching-kuo Foundation provided funding for this project. I gathered additional data during a two-week research trip in July 2001, funded by the Pacific Rim Program of the University of California Office of the President. Able research assistance was provided by Ho Hua-chin and Kuo Ya-yu.

2. Statistics are readily available in Tzu Chi Foundation Yearbooks for 1999 and 2000.

3. At a Tzu Chi retreat that I attended in California, this was represented by having participants construct a huge heart made out of hundreds of little paper hearts.

4. Susanne Hoeber Rudolph and James Piscatori, eds., *Transnational Religion and Fading States* (Boulder, CO: Westview Press, 1997); and José Casanova, *Public Religions in the Modern World* (Chicago: University of Chicago Press, 1994).

5. For an excellent account of the rise and fall of the secularization thesis, see Casanova, *Public Religions*, 11–39.

6. A popular version is Thomas L. Friedman, *The Lexus and the Olive Tree* (New York: Farrar, Straus and Giroux, 1999).

7. An Asian spokesperson for this view is Lee Kuan Yew of Singapore. See

Lee Kuan Yew, *The Singapore Story: Memoirs of Lee Kuan Yew* (New York: Prentice Hall, 1998). This view also appears in the *Bangkok Declaration on Human Rights* (United Nations High Commission on Human Rights, 1993).

8. Lee Kuan Yew, *The Economist*, April 27, 1994, 5. Quoted in Kenneth Christie and Denny Roy, *The Politics of Human Rights in East Asia* (London: Pluto Press, 2001), 1.

9. Samuel P. Huntington, "The Clash of Civilizations?" *Foreign Affairs* 72, no. 3 (Summer 1993), 22–49.

10. A superb book on Buddha's Light Mountain is Stuart Chandler, *Establishing a Pure Land on Earth: The Foguang Buddhist Perspective on Modernization and Globalization* (Honolulu: University of Hawaii Press, 2004); an excellent comparative study is André Laliberté, *The Politics of Buddhist Organizations in Taiwan: 1989–2003* (London: RoutledgeCurzon, 2004). A magisterial study in Chinese is Jiang Canteng, *Taiwan fojiao wenhua fazhanshi: Riju shiqi* (Taipei: Nantian chuban she, 2000). When I did my research and formulated my basic arguments, these works were not yet available, but I have incorporated them into my final analysis.

11. Good exceptions are Robert P. Weller's *Alternate Civilities: Democracy and Culture in China and Taiwan* (Boulder, CO: Westview Press, 1999) and *Unities and Diversities in Chinese Religion* (Seattle: University of Washington Press, 1987); Meir Shahar and Robert P. Weller, eds., *Unruly Gods: Divinity and Society in China* (Honolulu: University of Hawaii Press, 1996); Philip Clart and Charles B. Jones, eds., *Religion and Modernity in Modern Taiwan* (Honolulu: University of Hawaii Press, 2003).

12. For a history of Taiwan's economic development, see Thomas B. Gold, *State and Society in the Taiwan Miracle* (Armonk, NY: M. E. Sharpe, 1987). For a history of political transformation, see Shelley Rigger, *Politics in Taiwan: Voting for Democracy* (London: Routledge, 1999).

13. Shelley Rigger, *From Opposition to Power: Taiwan's Democratic Progressive Party* (Boulder, CO: Lynne Rienner Publishers, 2001); Denny Roy, *Taiwan: A Political History* (Ithaca, NY: Cornell University Press, 2003).

14. A good summary of the divisions is in A-chin Hsiau, *Contemporary Taiwanese Cultural Nationalism* (London: Routledge, 2000), 3–7.

15. Robert N. Bellah, Richard Madsen, William M. Sullivan, Ann Swidler, and Steven M. Tipton, *Habits of the Heart: Individualism and Commitment in American Life* (Berkeley, CA: University of California Press, 1985); and *The Good Society* (New York: Alfred A. Knopf, 1991).

16. Robert N. Bellah, "Religious Evolution," in *Beyond Belief* (Berkeley, CA: University of California Press, 1991), 20–50. Bellah is currently writing a major book building on the insights of this classic essay (originally published in 1964). I have been deeply influenced and inspired by reading and discussing parts of the draft manuscript of this work.

17. Karl Jaspers, *The Origin and Goal of History* (New Haven, CT: Yale University Press, 1953), 1

18. Ibid., 1–21.

19. Ibid., 4.

20. Ibid., 2–4.

CHAPTER 1. THE TAIWANESE RELIGIOUS CONTEXT

1. Comprehensive surveys by Chiu Hei-yuan indicate that Christians now constitute only about 5 percent of the total population. Chiu Hei-yuan, *Taiwan shehui bianqian jiben diaocha: Disanqi disanci diaocha zhixing baogao* (Taipei: Academia Sinica, Institute of Sociology, 1998).

2. See Richard Madsen, "Confucian Conceptions of Civil Society," in *Alternative Conceptions of Civil Society,* ed. Simone Chambers and Will Kymlicka, (Princeton, NJ: Princeton University Press, 2002), 190–204. For broader and deeper discussions of the Confucian vision, see Donald Munro, ed., *Individualism and Holism: Studies in Confucian and Taoist Values* (Ann Arbor: University of Michigan Center for Chinese Studies, 1985); Wm. Theodore de Bary, *Asian Values and Human Rights: A Confucian Communitarian Perspective* (Cambridge, MA: Harvard University Press, 1998); Tu Wei-ming, "Confucianism" in *Our Religions,* ed. Arvind Sharma (San Francisco: HarperSanFrancisco, 1993); David Hall and Roger Ames, *Thinking Through Confucius* (Albany: State University of New York Press, 1987). Tu Wei-ming used the phrase "Confucian persuasion" in an entry on "Confucius and Confucianism" in the Encyclopedia Britannica, 15th ed., 1988.

3. Loren E. Lomasky, "Classical Liberalism and Civil Society" in *Alternative Conceptions,* Chambers and Kymlicka, 50–67; Chandran Kukathas, "Ethical Pluralism from a Classical Liberal Perspective" in *The Many and the One: Religious and Secular Perspectives on Ethical Pluralism in the Modern World,* ed. Richard Madsen and Tracy B. Strong (Princeton: Princeton University Press, 2003), 55–77. For a critique of classical liberalism in the modern world, see Robert N. Bellah, Richard Madsen, William M. Sullivan, Ann Swidler, and Steven M. Tipton, *The Good Society* (New York: Knopf, 1991), 82–109.

4. The National Security Strategy of the United States, issued on September 20, 2002, paragraph 1.

5. In a recent important paper on the contributions of socially engaged Buddhism to civil society in Taiwan, David Schak includes three other important Buddhist groups in addition to the three presented here: the Chung Tai Chan Ssu [Zhong Tai Chan Si]; Fuchih [Fuzhi]; and Ling Chiu Shan [Ling Qiu Shan]. He notes, though, that these three are not as important in size and influence. David Schak, "Socially-engaged Buddhism in Taiwan and its Contributions to Civil Society" in *Engaged Buddhism, Its History, Doctrines and Practices: Essays in Memory of Master Yin-shun (1906–2005),* ed. Hsu Mu-chu et al. (Hualian: Ciji daxue chuban she, 2007).

6. Dietrich Bonhoeffer, *Letters and Papers from Prison,* ed. Eberhard Bethge (London: SCM Press, 1971).

7. One can see examples of this spirit in *Rebirth: Transformations in Tzu-chi* (Taipei: Buddhist Compassion Relief Association, n.d.), a collection of testimonials about how Tzu Chi members became converted to working in the organization.

8. In a survey of socially engaged Buddhist groups done under the direction of David Schak and Hsin-Huang Michael Hsiao by the Survey Research Center of the Academia Sinica, the average level of education of Dharma Drum Mountain members was higher than Tzu Chi, which was higher than Buddha's Light

Mountain. This suggests that the popular perception of where these groups stand in the Taiwanese class hierarchy has a basis in reality. Yet it also clear that the range of individuals contributing to these averages is broad. David Schak is still carrying out analysis of these research findings and I am grateful to him for sharing with me these preliminary results.

9. There are many uncertainties about the size and composition of Taiwan's middle classes. A comprehensive discussion of the issue can be found in Hsin-Huang Michael Hsiao, ed., *Discovery of the Middle Classes in East Asia* (Taipei: Academia Sinica, Institute of Ethnology, 1993), 121–217. The discussion distinguishes between a new middle class of salaried professionals, managers, and technicians, and an older middle class composed of small business owners. In the early 1990s, when this book was published, the two groups together constituted about 30 percent of Taiwan's population. In surveys, however, about 50 percent of the population subjectively thought of themselves as middle class.

10. Pierre Bourdieu, *Distinction: A Social Critique of the Judgement of Taste,* trans. Richard Nice (Cambridge, MA: Harvard University Press, 1984).

11. The Mainlanders are those Chinese who came to Taiwan mostly after 1949, when the KMT was defeated by the Communists in China's civil war. The Mainlanders constitute about 13 percent of Taiwan's population. One marker of identity is language: Mainlanders speak Mandarin Chinese as their mother tongue, while most of the native Taiwanese speak the Hoklo dialect (commonly called Taiwanese) as their mother tongue; a minority speak Hakka (Taiwan Yearbook, 2003). In order to consolidate its control over Taiwan, the KMT systematically killed or imprisoned the Taiwanese intellectual and political elite. During the "White Terror" that began after the crackdown on Taiwanese dissent with the February 28 (1947) Incident and continued throughout the 1950s, as many as thirty thousand Taiwanese were killed and hundreds of thousands imprisoned. Understandably, many Taiwanese have harbored deep hatred toward Mainlanders. This is diminishing among some parts of the younger generation, especially in northern Taiwan, as memories of past atrocities fade and as intermarriage and mutual cultural adaptation have taken place. But a strong countervailing tendency of cultural nationalism has developed among some Taiwanese. This is more prevalent in southern Taiwan, and it fuels sentiment for Taiwan to assert its independence from mainland China. See Shelly Rigger, *Politics in Taiwan* (London: Routledge, 1999), 55–102.

12. The story of Taiwan's political development since the end of martial law in 1987 is well told in Rigger, *Politics in Taiwan,* 128–93; and Shelly Rigger, *From Opposition to Power: Taiwan's Democratic Progressive Party* (Boulder, CO: Lynne Rienner, 2001).

13. See David K. Jordan, Andrew D. Morris, and Marc L. Moskowitz, *The Minor Arts of Daily Life: Popular Culture in Taiwan* (Honolulu: University of Hawaii Press, 2004).

14. Ralph Clough, "Taiwan under Nationalist Rule: 1949–1982" in *The Cambridge History of China,* vol. 14, ed. Roderick MacFarquhar and John K. Fairbank (Cambridge: Cambridge University Press, 1991), 821–27. See also Andrew D. Morris, "Taiwan's History: An Introduction" in *Minor Arts,* Jordan, Morris, and Moskowitz, 3–31.

15. Rigger, *Politics in Taiwan*, 103–30.

16. Ibid.

17. Ibid. See also, A-chin Hsiau, *Contemporary Taiwanese Cultural Nationalism* (London: Routledge, 2000): 170–87.

18. Rigger, *Politics in Taiwan*, 103–30.

19. Ibid. Also, Rigger, *From Opposition to Power*, 119–53.

20. Charles Brewer Jones, *Buddhism in Taiwan: Religion and the State, 1660–1990* (Honolulu: University of Hawaii Press, 1999); André Laliberté, *The Politics of Buddhist Organizations in Taiwan: 1989–2003* (London: Routledge-Curzon, 2004).

21. Murray A. Rubenstein, "Christianity and Democratization in Modern Taiwan: The Presbyterian Church and the Struggle of Minnan/Hakka Selfhood in the Republic of China" in *Religion in Modern Taiwan*, ed. Philip Clart and Charles B. Jones (Honolulu: University of Hawaii Press, 2003), 204–56.

22. The election process and its associated issues are well analyzed in Rigger, *From Opposition to Power*, 173–204. The KMT constituency was split between Lien Chan, the official candidate, who got a dismal 23 percent of the vote, and James Soong, a former KMT provincial governor who had split with the KMT to form his own People First Party, who got 37 percent of the vote. Chen Shui-bian received a bit over 39 percent of the vote.

CHAPTER 2. TZU CHI

1. Chien-yu Julia Huang and Robert P. Weller, "Merit and Mothering: Women and Social Welfare in Taiwanese Buddhism," *Journal of Asian Studies* 57, no. 2 (May 1998), 379–96; Chien-yu Julia Huang, "Recapturing Charisma: Emotion and Rationalization in a Globalizing Buddhist Movement from Taiwan" (PhD diss., Boston University, 2001); Hwei-Syin Lu, "Gender and Buddhism in Contemporary Taiwan—a Case Study of Tzu-chi Foundation," *Proceedings of the National Science Council ROC* 8, no. 4:539–50; André Laliberté, *The Politics of Buddhist Organizations in Taiwan: 1989–2003* (New York: Routledge-Curzon, 2004).

2. English translations of *Still Thoughts* (*Jingsiyu*), published by Still Thoughts Cultural Publishing, Taipei, 1996.

3. See Hsin-Huang Michael Hsiao, "The Development and Organization of Foundations in Taiwan: An Expression of Vigor in a Newly Born Society," in *Quiet Revolutions on Taiwan, Republic of China*, ed. Jason C. Hu (Taipei: Kwanghwa, 1994), 386–419.

4. Hwei-syin Lu, "Gender and Buddhism."

5. The basic chronology of Cheng Yen's life is taken from Yu-ing Ching, *Master of Love and Mercy: Cheng Yen* (Nevada City, CA: Blue Dolphin Publishing, 1994) and from *Lotus Flower of the Heart: Thirty Years of Tzu-chi Photographs* (Taipei: Still Thoughts Cultural Mission, 1997). Neither of these is a completely independent source of information. Yu-ing Ching obviously wrote her story in close cooperation with the Tzu Chi leadership. Her main source for the narrative of Cheng Yen's early life is an interview with Cheng Yen's mother. Wanting to write an inspirational book, she tends to dramatize the story of Cheng

Yen's life and attributes feelings and motives to Cheng Yen that cannot be verified. *Lotus Flower of the Heart* is issued by Tzu Chi's official publishing house. Both books agree on the basic facts of Cheng Yen's career and I have found no evidence to contradict these facts. However, I have avoided reproducing here the official or semi-official accounts of Cheng Yen's inner motives and intentions. The information in this paragraph comes from Yu-ing Ching, *Master of Love*, 151–78, and *Lotus Flower*, 31–35.

    6. Ching, *Master of Love*, 181–235.

    7. See Nancy J. Barnes, "Buddhist Women and the Nuns' Order in Asia," in *Engaged Buddhism: Buddhist Liberation Movements in Asia*, ed. Christopher S. Queen and Sallie B. King (Albany, NY: State University of New York Press, 1996), 259–94.

    8. Barnes, "Buddhist Women," 236–40; *Lotus Flower*, 35.

    9. Raoul Birnbaum, "Buddhist China at the Century's Turn" in *Religion in China Today*, ed. Daniel L. Overmeyer (Cambridge: Cambridge University Press, 2003), 120–30; Don A. Pittman, *Toward a Modern Chinese Buddhism: Taixu's Reforms* (Honolulu: University of Hawaii Press, 2001). For Yin-shun's career, see Charles Brewer Jones, *Buddhism in Taiwan: Religion and the State, 1660–1990* (Honolulu: University of Hawaii Press, 1999), 124–95. Yin-shun wrote an important biography of his teacher Tai Xu. But in his own writings, Yin-shun went further than Tai Xu in secularizing Buddhism. Tai Xu had called his form of humanistic Buddhism *rensheng* (human life). Yin-shun changed this to *renjian* (the human realm). As he explained, "The Buddha was not a god, nor a demon, nor did he claim to be a son of god or the prophet of a god. He frankly stated: All buddhas and world-honored ones arise from the human realm and not from the gods.'" Quoted in Jones, *Buddhism in Taiwan*, 134. Cheng Yen, as well as the other Buddhist leaders discussed in this book, call their form of Buddhism *renjian*. This connotes the idea that Buddhist practice does not entail worshiping a quasi-deity who stands apart from the world, but rather seeks buddhahood by caring for people within the human realm. During the last years of his life, Yin-shun lived at the Tzu Chi hospital in Hualien. He died in June 2005. At the Tzu Chi headquarters in Hualien there is a large room commemorating his life with a display of his writings and a history of his life and times.

    10. Ching, *Master of Love*, 240–42.

    11. For a brief summary of the contents of the Lotus Sutra and its significance for the development of Mahayana Buddhism, see Donald S. Lopez, Jr., "Buddhism" in *Religions of Asia in Practice*, ed. Donald S. Lopez, Jr. (Princeton, NJ: Princeton University Press, 2002), 189–92.

    12. *Lotus Flower*, 38–41.

    13. Ching, *Master of Love*, 221.

    14. Ching, *Master of Love*, 225–30

    15. Ching, *Master of Love*, 234.

    16. Hsing Yun, the founder of Buddha's Light Mountain, which we will discuss in the next chapter, has very publicly expressed his devotion to his mother, and presents this devotion as an exemplar of monastic filial piety. Stuart Chandler, *Establishing a Pure Land on Earth* (Honolulu: University of Hawaii Press, 2004), 243–48.

17. Cheng Yen, *Three Ways to the Pure Land,* trans. Lin Sen-shou (Taipei: Tzu Chi Cultural Publishing Company, 2001), 19.

18. Ibid., 22.

19. Ibid., 25

20. Ibid., 195–96.

21. *Rebirth: Transformations in Tzu Chi* (Taipei: Still Thoughts Cultural Mission, 1997), 148.

22. Ibid., 155.

23. Hwei-Syin Lu, "Gender and Buddhism."

24. Richard Madsen, "Confucian Conceptions of Civil Society" in *Alternative Conceptions of Civil Society,* ed. Simone Chambers and Will Kymlicka (Princeton, NJ: Princeton University Press, 2002), 202.

25. Cheng Yen, *Three Ways,* 42–43

26. Jones, *Buddhism in Taiwan,* 137–52.

27. Christian Jochim, "Carrying Confucianism into the Modern World: The Taiwan Case" in *Religion in Modern Taiwan,* ed. Philip Clart and Charles B. Jones (Honolulu: University of Hawaii Press, 2003), 60–61.

28. *Lotus Flower,* 43–49.

29. Ibid., 54.

30. A thorough account of the work and organization of Tzu Chi commissioners is in Sheng Jen Chen, "Understanding the Buddhist Tzu Chi Association: A Cultural Approach" (PhD diss., University of Southern California, 1990), 72–79, 91–113.

31. *Lotus Flower,* 36.

32. Cheng Yen and her followers now place much greater emphasis on ecumenical cooperation than on inter-religious competition. The competitive note is more clearly sounded in the writings of Hsing Yun of Buddha's Light Temple, which we will discuss in the next chapter.

33. See Sheng Jen Chen, "Understanding Tzu-chi," 64–71.

34. *Lotus Flower,* 55–75.

35. *Lotus Flower,* 16.

36. *Lotus Flower,* 86–102.

37. *Lotus Flower,* 104–127.

38. International relief efforts are summarized in the Tzu Chi publication *Love Transcends Borders* (2000). Regular updates are available on the Tzu Chi website: www.tzuchi.org.

39. Hwei-syin Lu, "Gender and Buddhism."

40. *Lotus Flower,* 132–35.

41. Information obtained from www.tzuchi.org.

42. One consequence of these practices is that the Tzu Chi medical school has an abundance of cadavers, unlike other medical schools in Taiwan. Traditional religious beliefs have made Taiwanese very reluctant to donate their bodies to science. But sixteen thousand people have signed body donation forms for Tzu Chi. Tzu Chi actually gives some of its cadavers to other medical schools, provided they agree to treat them with the same rituals of respect as practiced in the Tzu Chi medical school.

43. See the discussion of the sociological difference between *church* and *sect*

in Robert N. Bellah, Richard Madsen, William M. Sullivan, Ann Swidler, and Steven M. Tipton, *Habits of the Heart: Individualism and Commitment in American Life* (Berkeley: University of California Press, 1995), 243–45. The classic discussion of the church-sect distinction is Ernst Troeltsch, *The Social Teachings of the Christian Churches* (1911), trans. Olive Wyon (London: George Allen, 1931); see especially vol. 1, 328–82, and vol. 2, conclusion.

44. See A-chin Hsiau, *Contemporary Taiwanese Cultural Nationalism* (London: Routledge, 2000).

45. Shelly Rigger summarizes recent Taiwan public opinion polls in this way: "Public opinion surveys reveal a broad consensus on three points. First, Taiwanese do not want to be annexed or absorbed by the People's Republic of China. . . . Second, they recognize that their fate is linked to China. Third, Taiwanese believe that foreign contacts offer protection from annexation. . . . Most Taiwanese are willing to sacrifice the prestige of formal independence to avoid armed conflict. Moreover, only a minority of Taiwanese feel a strong need for *de jure* independence." Shelly Rigger, "Taiwan in U.S.-China Relations," *The Aspen Institute Congressional Program* 18, no. 1 (2003), 25–26.

46. Followers claim, however, that it is like the architecture of the Tang dynasty (618–907), which was the last time that Buddhism was the official state religion of China.

47. David Y. H. Wu, "McDonalds in Taipei: Hamburgers, Betel Nuts, and National Identity" in *Golden Arches East: McDonalds in East Asia*, ed. James L. Watson (Stanford: Stanford University Press, 1997), 110–35.

48. See Pitman B. Potter, "Belief in Control: Regulation of Religion in China" in *Religion in China Today*, ed. Daniel L. Overmeyer (Cambridge: University of Cambridge Press, 2003), 11–31.

49. Murray Rubenstein, "Christianity and Democratization in Modern Taiwan: The Presbyterian Church and the Struggle for Minnan/Hakka Selfhood in the Republic of China" in *Religion in Modern Taiwan*, ed. Philip Clart and Charles B. Jones (Honolulu: University of Hawaii Press, 2003), 204–56.

50. Author's field notes, 1999.

51. There are many uncertainties about the size and composition of Taiwan's middle classes. A comprehensive discussion of the issue can be found in Hsin-Huang Michael Hsiao, ed., *Discovery of the Middle Classes in East Asia* (Taipei: Academia Sinica, Institute of Ethnology, 1993), 121–217. The discussion distinguishes between a new middle class of salaried professionals, managers, and technicians and an older middle class composed of small business owners. In the early 1990s, when this book was published, the two groups together constituted about 30 percent of Taiwan's population. In surveys, however, about 50 percent of the population subjectively thought of themselves as middle class.

CHAPTER 3. BUDDHA'S LIGHT MOUNTAIN

1. He makes this statement in *Foguangshan*, a promotional video produced by his organization.

2. An extremely rich study of Foguangshan and its significance in the Bud-

dhist history is Stuart Chandler, *Establishing a Pure Land on Earth* (Honolulu: University of Hawaii Press, 2004).

3. Mary Douglas, *Natural Symbols* (New York: Vintage Books, 1973), 44–58.

4. Robert N. Bellah, "Civil Religion in America," in *Beyond Belief: Essays on Religion in a Post-Traditional World* (Berkeley: University of California Press, 1991), 168–89.

5. According to Stuart Chandler, Hsing Yun was inspired to have this constructed after visiting Disneyland in 1976. Chandler, *Establishing a Pure Land,* 11.

6. In the *Foguangshan* promotional video.

7. Ibid.

8. By the 1990s, Buddha's Light Mountain had become a major tourist attraction. The Buddha's Cave and assorted gift shops were set up especially for the benefit of such tourists. In 1997, in a solemn ceremony, the temple complex was closed to casual visitors. For four years, it was open only to visitors who had registered to attend a religious function. But in 2001, at the urging of President Chen Shui-bian, the temple complex was opened once again.

9. These represent a higher level of initiation and commitment than simply taking refuge in the Buddha, dharma, and sangha, or promising to obey the five precepts (refrain from taking life, from theft, from unacceptable sex, from lying, from intoxicants). There are different sets of bodhisattva vows, but they can be summarized in the four "all encompassing vows": sentient beings without limit I vow to deliver; afflictions without end I vow to sever; approaches to dharma without number I vow to master; the unexcelled enlightenment of a Buddha I vow to attain. See Sheng Yen, *Hoofprint of the Ox: Principles of the Chan Buddhist Path as Taught by a Modern Chan Master* (New York: Oxford University Press, 2001), 58–60.

10. Fu Chi-ying, *Handing Down the Light: The Biography of Venerable Master Hsing Yun,* trans. by Amy Lui-ma (Hacienda Heights, CA: Hsi Lai University Press, 1996), 365–86.

11. Ibid., 212. According to Fu Chi-ying, "It must be noted that estimated at NT$150 billion in assets [one US dollar equals about thirty Taiwanese dollars], Fo Kuang Shan is far behind the top-ten list of Taiwan's wealthiest religious corporations."

12. Stuart Chandler provides an extensive analysis of the possible motives for this incident. Chandler, *Establishing a Pure Land,* 275–86. See also Jeffrey Toobin, "Adventures in Buddhism: What Really Happened at the Hsi Lai Temple," *New Yorker,* September 18, 2000, 76–88.

13. Fu, *Handling Down the Light,* 7–61, 483–84.

14. Raoul Birnbaum, "Buddhist China at the Century's End" in *Religion in China Today,* ed. Daniel L. Overmyer (Cambridge: Cambridge University Press, 2003), 129–30.

15. Fu, *Handling Down the Light,* 73–85.

16. Ibid., 85–101.

17. Ibid., 92.

18. Ibid., 74.

19. Ibid., 404–6.

20. Hsing Yun, *The Philosophy of Being Second* (Hacienda Heights, CA: Hsi Lai University Press, 2000), 85.

21. Hsing Yun, *Where There is Dharma There is a Way* (Taipei: Foguang Cultural Enterprise Co., 2001), 52.

22. Fu Chi-ying, *Handing Down the Light*, 133–50.

23. Ibid., 147.

24. Ibid., 273–88. But Hsing Yun notes, "Although I have relinquished my position as abbot, I cannot relinquish my obligations as Master. I remain a member of Fo Guang Shan, and to my disciples and followers I am still the Master. Whenever the Temple needs me, I am obliged to state my opinion and make suggestions. Whenever disciples entreat me, I am willing to mediate their disputes." Hsing Yun, *Where there is Dharma*, 22.

25. Fu Chi-ying, *Handing Down the Light*, 341–64.

26. Ibid., 202.

27. Ibid., 452–55.

28. Ibid., 369–70.

29. Hsing Yun himself acknowledges that he has been called a "political monk" and he vigorously defends himself. See Hsing Yun, *Philosophy of Being Second*, 34, 89, 139. See also André Laliberté, *The Politics of Buddhist Organizations in Taiwan, 1989–2003* (London: RoutledgeCurzon, 2004).

30. Hsing Yun, *Where There is Dharma*, 149–50.

31. See Richard Madsen, "Confucianism and the Globalization of Ethics" in *The Globalization of Ethics*, ed. William Sullivan and Will Kymlicka (Cambridge: Cambridge University Press, 2007).

32. Hsing Yun, *Philosophy of Being Second*, 139.

33. Laliberté, *Politics of Buddhist Organizations*, 75.

34. Hsing Yun, *Where There is Dharma*, 165–66.

35. Quoted in Fu Chi-ying, *Handing Down the Light*, 228–30.

36. Max Weber, *The Sociology of Religion*, trans. Ephraim Fischoff (Boston: Beacon Press, 1964), 95–99.

37. Marco Orru, Nicole Woolsey Biggert, and Gary G. Hamilton, "Organizational Isomorphism in East Asia" in *The New Institutionalism in Organizational Analysis*, ed. Walter W. Powell and Paul J. DiMaggio (Chicago: University of Chicago Press, 1991), 383–86.

38. Fu Chi-ying, *Handing Down the Light*, 208.

39. "Today, Hsi Lai Temple . . . is the headquarters for the spread of Buddhism in the West . . . . The seed was sown when Hsing Yun first came to America as a guest of its bicentennial celebrations. . . . The country's cultural diversity and receptiveness struck him irrevocably. . . . But most of all, Hsing Yun pondered, in contrast to the heavily armed and intrusive ways in which Christianity penetrated China in the last century, could Buddhism now be taught peacefully in the West?" Fu Chi-ying, *Handing Down the Light*, 345.

40. Hsing Yun recalls, "Forty years ago, when I first arrived in Taiwan, my living conditions were quite desperate, and I was not sure where I was going to get my next meal or bed. Someone told me, 'Since Buddhism is on the decline

and Christianity on the rise, why don't you convert to Christianity? Life will be a lot easier.' I told him firmly that 'Even if the Buddha comes to me and tells me to become a Christian, I will not!' Today, Buddhism is not only flourishing in Taiwan, it is also sprouting in Christian lands like Europe and the United States." Hsing Yun, *Where There is Dharma, There is a Way* (Taipei: Foguang Cultural Enterprise, 2001), 171.

41. Toobin, "Adventures in Buddhism," 76–88.

42. Taipei, Chinese Information and Cultural Center, December 13, 2000.

43. From the Buddha's Light Mountain website: www.fgs.org.tw.

44. Robert D. Putnam, *Making Democracy Work: Civic Traditions in Modern Italy* (Princeton, NJ: Princeton University Press, 1993), 87–90.

45. Author's field notes taken during Hsing Yun dharma talk, December, 1999.

46. Hsing Yun, *The Carefree Life: Dharma Words of Venerable Master Hsing Yun* (Hacienda Heights, CA: Hsi Lai University Press, n.d.), 46.

47. Ibid., 43–44.

48. Ibid., 47.

49. Ibid., 37.

50. Ibid., 14.

51. Ibid., 64–67.

52. Ibid., 109.

53. Ibid., 88.

54. Ibid., 88–91.

55. Ibid., 33.

56. See Anita Chan, ed., *China's Workers under Assault* (Armonk, NY: M. E. Sharpe, 2001).

57. Fu Chi-ying, *Handing Down the Light,* 240–41.

58. Author's interview, November, 1999.

CHAPTER 4. DHARMA DRUM MOUNTAIN

1. *Autobiography of Sheng Yen* (2002). Available both in Chinese and English on Dharma Drum Mountain's website: www.chan1.org/autobio.html. See also the more comprehensive account in Sheng Yen and Dan Stevenson, *Hoofprint of the Ox: Principles of the Chan Buddhist Path as Taught by a Modern Chinese Master* (New York: Oxford University Press, 2001), 1–13.

2. *Autobiography of Sheng Yen,* 2.

3. Ibid., 2.

4. Ibid., 3.

5. Ibid., 4.

6. Ibid., 4.

7. Ibid., 4.

8. Ibid., 5.

9. Ibid., 5.

10. Sheng Yen and Stevenson, *Hoofprint of the Ox,* 7, 12; *The Chung-hwa Institute of Buddhist Studies* and *The Vows of Master Sheng-yen* (pamphlets published by the Dharmapala Organization of Dharma Drum Mountain, Taipei).

11. *Dharma Propagation of Nung Ch'an Monastery* (pamphlet published by the Dharmapala Organization of Dharma Drum Mountain, Taipei).

12. Information from interviews conducted by the author, Taipei, Dec. 1999.

13. *Chung-hwa Institute,* Dharmapala Organization.

14. Dharma Drum Mountain website: www.chan1.org.

15. *Vows of Master Sheng-yen,* Dharmapala Organization.

16. Sheng Yen, *In the Spirit of Ch'an: An Introduction to Ch'an Buddhism* (New York: Dharma Drum Publications, 1998), 13–14.

17. Sheng Yen, "Human Consciousness in the Chan Perspective," *Chan Newsletter* 84 (March 1991), from: westernchanfellowship.org/dharmatalks (now discontinued).

18. Sheng Yen, "Speech for the Millennium World Peace Summit of Religious and Spiritual Leaders" (lecture, World Peace Summit, United Nations, Aug. 29, 2000), see: www.chan1.org.

19. Sheng Yen, "Interreligious Understanding and Cooperation" (concluding address, International Conference on Religious Cooperation, Sept. 20, 2001), see: www.chan1.org.

20. Sociology based on Emile Durkheim's classic theory that all societies divide the world into the sacred and profane, with the sacred being the emblem of the moral order that constitutes social life.

21. Sheng Yen, "The 'Sacred' in a Pluralistic World: Seeking Common Ground while Preserving Differences" (speech, World Economic Forum, New York, Feb. 1, 2002), see: www.chan1.org.

22. Ibid.

23. Sheng Yen, "Interreligious Understanding and Cooperation" (concluding address for the International Conference on Religious Cooperation, Sept. 20, 2001), see: www.chan1.org.

24. Sheng Yen, "Buddhist View on the Terror Attack" (interview with *Commonwealth Magazine,* Sept. 17, 2001), see: www.chan1.org.

25. Sheng Yen, "Violence and Terrorism in Religion" (speech, global conference on "The Use of Religion to Incite for Violence and Terrorism," United Nations Dag Hammarskjold Library Auditorium, May 21, 2003).

26. "Master Sheng Yen's Words on War," March 26, 2003, www.chan1.org.

27. Hsing Yun, "Commentary on Beginning of Iraq War," Foguangshan website: www.fgs.org.tw.

28. "Jet Li and Master Sheng Yen on Fame and Wealth," Sept. 22, 2003, www.chan1.org.

CHAPTER 5. THE ENACTING HEAVEN TEMPLE

1. According to a survey published in the late 1980s, there were 12,737 temples in Taiwan—3.71 temples per ten thousand persons. Li-shiang Yau and Hei-yuan Chiu, "Studies of Religious Change in Taiwan," Academia Sinica Monograph Series, no. 53 (Taipei: Academia Sinica, Institute of Ethnology, 1986), 655–85. Cited in Wu Ning-yuan, "Folk Religion in Taiwan," *Dongfang congjiao yanjiu* (Oct. 1991), 373.

2. See Lai Chi-tim, "Daoism in China Today, 1980–2002" and Kenneth

Dean, "Local Communal Religion in Contemporary South-east China" in *Religion in China Today*, ed. Daniel L. Overmyer (Cambridge: Cambridge University Press, 2003), 107–121, and 32–52.

3. See the Enacting Heaven Temple publication, *Xiaolaoyisheng* (Taipei: Xing Tian Gong Foundation, 1998).

4. Kristofer Schipper, *The Taoist Body*, trans. Karen C. Duval (Berkeley: University of California Press, 1993), 21–22.

5. For an excellent summary, see Paul R. Katz, "Religion and the State in Post-war Taiwan" in *Religion in China*, Overmyer, 89–106.

6. For the single best summary of popular Daoism in English, see Schipper, *Taoist Body*.

7. Ibid., 22.

8. Robert P. Weller, *Unities and Diversities in Chinese Religion* (Seattle: University of Washington Press, 1987), 44–45; Schipper, *Taoist Body*, 38–39.

9. The account of Xuan Kong's life is taken from a three-part article in the Temple's monthly magazine: "Lishi de yanjing—Xing Tian Gong yange," *Xing Tian Gong* 38 (Jan. 1999), 6–8; 39 (Feb. 1999), 5–8; and 40 (March 1999), 6–8.

10. "Lishi de yanjing," *Xing Tian Gong* 38:7–8.

11. Ibid., 8.

12. Weller, *Unities and Diversities*, 12.

13. Ibid., 45

14. Schipper, *Taoist Body*, 39–40.

15. "Xing Tian Gong cong zhe," *Xing Tian Gong* 38 (Jan. 1999): 8.

16. "Xing Tian Gong cong zhe," *Xing Tian Gong* 41 (April 1999); 17–20; "Xing Tian Gong cong zhe," *Xing Tian Gong* 42 (May, 1999): 17–19. The quote about purity is taken from 42:18.

17. "Lishi de yanjing," *Xing Tian Gong* 38:8.

18. "Lishi de yanjing," *Xing Tian Gong* 40:7

19. Ibid.

20. Weller, *Unities and Diversities*, 144–72.

21. Weller, *Unities and Diversities*, 45.

22. Wm. Theodore de Bary, *Asian Values and Human Rights: A Confucian Communitarian Perspective* (Cambridge, MA: Harvard University Press, 1998), 124.

23. Mencius 3A:4, quoted in de Bary, *Asian Values*, 17.

24. Tu Wei-ming, "Confucianism" in *Our Religions*, ed. Arvind Sharma (San Francisco: HarperSanFrancisco, 1995), 186–94.

25. "Xing Tian Gong cong zhe," *Xing Tian Gong* 41:19.

26. Ibid.

27. Ibid.

28. Ibid., 20.

29. Tu Wei-ming, "Multiple Modernities: Implications of the Rise of 'Confucian' East Asia" in *Chinese Ethics in a Global Context*, ed. Karl-Heinz Pohl and Anselm W. Müller (Leiden: Brill, 2002), 55.

30. Ibid., 74. See also Richard Madsen, "Confucianism and the Globalization of Ethics" in *The Globalization of Ethics*, ed. Will Kymlicka and William Sullivan (Cambridge: Cambridge University Press, 2007).

31. Weller, *Unities and Diversities.*
32. Enacting Heaven Temple, *Xiaolaoyisheng,* passim.
33. Ibid.
34. *Ziyou ribao,* Taipei, June 30, 2001, 5–6.
35. Robert N. Bellah, Richard Madsen, William M. Sullivan, Ann Swidler, and Steven M. Tipton, *Habits of the Heart: Individualism and Commitment in American Life* (Berkeley: University of California Press, 1985), 106–07.

CONCLUSIONS

1. For good but relatively brief critical accounts of the liberal vision of civil society, see the relevant sections in the volumes on civil society in the Ethikon series, especially Simone Chambers and Will Kymlicka, eds., *Alternative Conceptions of Civil Society* (Princeton, NJ: Princeton University Press, 2002); Nancy L. Rosenblum and Robert Post, eds., *Civil Society and Government* (Princeton, NJ: Princeton University Press, 2002); and Richard Madsen and Tracy B. Strong, eds., *The Many and the One: Religious and Secular Perspectives on Ethical Pluralism in the Modern World* (Princeton, NJ: Princeton University Press, 2003).
2. A good overview of the East Asian development model is Ezra F. Vogel, *One Step Ahead in China: Guangdong under Reform* (Cambridge, MA: Harvard University Press, 1989), 426–42.
3. See Fu Chi-ying, *Handing Down the Light: The Biography of Venerable Master Hsing Yun,* trans. by Amy Lui-ma (Hacienda Heights, CA: Hsi Lai University Press, 1996), 244–53.
4. See *Lotus Flower of the Heart: Thirty Years of Tzu-chi Photographs* (Taipei: Still Thoughts Cultural Mission, 1997), 16.
5. See Khun Eng Kuah-Pearce, *State, Society, and Religious Engineering: Toward a Reformist Buddhism in Singapore* (London: Times Academic Press, 2003).
6. *Lotus Flower of the Heart,* 86–102.
7. According to Fu Chi-ying, *Handing Down the Light,* 246–47, "[T]he government had no part whatsoever in the growth of Fo Kuang Shan. Not even a single tree or a blade of grass. Except, maybe, for ten years' delay in matters of official registration." But the enormous growth of Foguangshan temples, schools, and other ventures throughout Taiwan in the 1970s and 1980s has benefited from the cooperation of important government officials.
8. See Hsin-Huang Michael Hsiao, "The Development and Organization of Foundations in Taiwan: An Expression of Vigor in a Newly Born Society," in *Quiet Revolutions on Taiwan, Republic of China,* ed. Jason C. Hu (Taipei: Kwang Hwa, 1994), 386–419.
9. David Schak shows that membership in socially engaged Buddhist groups (including Chung Tai Chan Ssu, Fuchih, and Ling Chiu Shan, as well as the groups discussed here) is connected with higher levels of what the political scientist Robert Putnam calls "social capital." Membership in such Buddhist groups is correlated with higher levels of group membership in general—for example, with "a square dancing, hiking, or book reading group other than a Buddhist group in which you have participated." It is also positively correlated with having more

close friends, with giving more to charity (besides the money contributed to the Buddhist group), believing that "if you do good to people, they will do good to you," being more willing to trust others in general, having higher trust in elected officials, and with voting in general elections. David Schak, "Socially-engaged Buddhism in Taiwan and its Contributions to Civil Society" in *Engaged Buddhism, Its History, Doctrines and Practices: Essays in Memory of Master Yinshun (1906–2005)*, ed. Hsu Mu-chu et al. (Hualien: Tzu Chi University Press, 2005).

10. A-chin Hsiau, *Contemporary Taiwanese Cultural Nationalism* (London: Routledge, 2000).

11. Shelly Rigger, "Taiwan in U.S.-China Relations," *The Aspen Institute Congressional Program* 18, no. 1 (2003): 25–26.

12. Ping-Yin Kuan, Dominique Tyl, and Catalina Wei-Chi Yin, *Attitudes and Reflections toward the West, Western Culture, and Christianity in Taiwan* (Turin, Italy: Fondazione Giovanni Agnelli, 1999), 11–12.

13. Jiang Canteng, *Taiwan fojiao wenhua fazhanshi: Riju shiqi* (Taipei: Nantian chuban she, 2000).

14. Information graciously provided to me by Alise DiVido.

15. As Fu Chi-ying puts it, "The seed [for the idea of building Hsi Lai Temple in Los Angeles] was sown when Hsing Yun first came to America as a guest of its bicentennial celebrations. . . . The country's cultural diversity and receptiveness struck him irrevocably. Further, the need for a spiritual anchorage for the fast increasing number of immigrants of Chinese heritage was more than obvious. But most of all, Hsing Yun pondered, in contrast to the heavily armed and intrusive ways in which Christianity penetrated China in the last century, could Buddhism now be taught peacefully in the West?" Fu Chi-ying, *Handing Down the Light*, 345.

16. Rigger, "Taiwan in U.S.-China Relations."

17. Marco Orru, Nicole Woolsey Biggert, and Gary G. Hamilton, "Organizational Isomorphism in East Asia" in *The New Institutionalism in Organizational Analysis*, ed. Walter W. Powell and Paul J. DiMaggio (Chicago: University of Chicago Press, 1991), 383–86.

18. This section of the conclusion was originally published in *Social Transformations in Chinese Societies* 2 (Spring 2007), where it was accompanied by two critiques, written by Chan Hoi Man and Chan Shun Hing, followed by my rejoinder.

19. See Charles Taylor, *Modern Social Imaginaries* (Durham: Duke University Press, 2004).

20. See Richard Madsen, William Sullivan, Ann Swidler, and Stephen Tipton, eds., *Meaning and Modernity: Religion, Polity, Self* (Berkeley: University of California Press, 2002).

21. Richard Madsen and Tracy B. Strong, eds., *The Many and the One: Religious and Secular Perspectives on Ethical Pluralism in the Modern World*, 1–21.

22. Emile Durkheim, *The Elementary Forms of the Religious Life*, trans. Karen E. Fields (New York: The Free Press, 1995).

23. Max Weber, *The Protestant Ethic and the Spirit of Capitalism*, trans. Tal-

cott Parsons (New York: Charles Scribner's Sons, 1958); "Science as a Vocation" in *From Max Weber: Essays in Sociology,* H. H. Gerth and C. Wright Mills (New York: Oxford University Press, 1966), 129–56.

24. Karl Jaspers, *The Origin and Goal of History* (New Haven, CT: Yale University Press, 1953), 1–21.

25. Ibid., 194.

26. Ibid., 196–98.

27. Ibid., 195.

28. Ibid., 199.

29. Ibid., 195, 199–200.

30. Ibid., 227.

31. Ibid., 18. See also Robert N. Bellah, "The Axial Age," in *Religious Evolution* (unpublished work in progress).

32. Mary Douglas, *Natural Symbols: Explorations in Cosmology* (New York: Vintage, 1973), 77–92.

33. Ibid., 19–58.

34. Ibid., 40–58.

35. Robert N. Bellah, Richard Madsen, William M. Sullivan, Ann Swidler, and Stephen M. Tipton, *Habits of the Heart: Individualism and Commitment in American Life* (Berkeley: University of California Press, 1985).

36. I am indebted for this point to the distinguished biblical scholar, David Noel Freedman.

37. Aristotle, *Nicomachean Ethics,* trans. J. A. K. Thomson (London: Penguin Classics, 1955).

38. Lao Tsu, *Tao Te Ching,* trans. Gia-fu Feng and Jane English (New York: Vintage Books, 1972), 22.

39. Catherine Bell, "Stories from an Illustrated Explanation of the *Tract of the Most Exalted on Action and Response,*" in *Religions of Asia in Practice,* ed. Donald S. Lopez, Jr. (Princeton, NJ: Princeton University Press, 2002), 439–47.

Bibliography

Aristotle. *Nicomachean Ethics*. Translated by J. A. K. Thomson. London: Penguin Classics, 1955.

Barnes, Nancy J. "Buddhist Women and the Nuns' Order in Asia." In *Engaged Buddhism: Buddhist Liberation Movements in Asia,* edited by Christopher S. Queen and Sallie B. King. Albany, NY: State University of New York Press, 1996.

de Bary, Wm. Theodore. *Asian Values and Human Rights: A Confucian Communitarian Perspective*. Cambridge, MA: Harvard University Press, 1998.

Bell, Catherine. "Stories from an Illustrated Explanation of the *Tract of the Most Exalted on Action and Response.*" In *Religions of Asia in Practice,* edited by Donald S. Lopez, Jr. Princeton, NJ: Princeton University Press, 2002.

Bellah, Robert N. "Religious Evolution." In *Beyond Belief,* by Robert N. Bellah. Berkeley: University of California Press, 1991.

Bellah, Robert N., Richard Madsen, William M. Sullivan, Ann Swidler, and Steven M. Tipton. *Habits of the Heart: Individualism and Commitment in American Life*. Rev. ed. Berkeley: University of California Press, 1996.

———. *The Good Society*. New York: Alfred A. Knopf, 1991.

Birnbaum, Raoul. "Buddhist China at the Century's Turn." In *Religion in China Today,* edited by Daniel L. Overmeyer. Cambridge: Cambridge University Press, 2003.

Bonhoeffer, Dietrich. *Letters and Papers from Prison*. Edited by Eberhard Bethge. London, SCM Press, 1971.

Bourdieu, Pierre. *Distinction: A Social Critique of the Judgement of Taste*. Translated by Richard Nice. Cambridge, MA: Harvard University Press, 1984.

Buddhist Compassion Relief Association. *Rebirth: Transformations in Tzu-chi*. Taipei: Buddhist Compassion Relief Association, n.d.

Casanova, José. *Public Religions in the Modern World*. Chicago: University of Chicago Press, 1994.

Chan, Anita, ed. *China's Workers under Assault*. Armonk, NY: M. E. Sharpe, 2001.

Chandler, Stuart. *Establishing a Pure Land on Earth: The Foguang Buddhist Perspective on Modernization and Globalization*. Honolulu: University of Hawaii Press, 2004.

Chen, Sheng Jen. "Understanding the Buddhist Tzu-chi Association: A Cultural Approach." PhD diss., University of Southern California, 1990.

·Cheng Yen. *Three·Ways to the Pure Land*. Translated by Lin Sen-shou. Taipei: Tzu Chi Cultural Publishing Company, 2001.

———. *Still Thoughts*. Still Thoughts Cultural Publishing, Taipei, 1996.

Ching, Yu-ing. *Master of Love and Mercy: Cheng Yen*. Nevada City, CA: Blue Dolphin Publishing, 1994.

Chiu Hei-yuan. *Taiwan shehui bianqian jiben diaocha: Disanqi disanci diaocha zhixing baogao*. Taipei: Academia Sinica, Institute of Sociology, 1998.

Christie, Kenneth, and Denny Roy. *The Politics of Human Rights in East Asia*. London: Pluto Press, 2001.

Clart, Philip, and Charles B. Jones, eds. *Religion and Modernity in Modern Taiwan*. Honolulu: University of Hawaii Press, 2003.

Clough, Ralph. "Taiwan under Nationalist Rule: 1949–1982." In *The Cambridge History of China*, edited by Roderick MacFarquhar and John K. Fairbank. Cambridge: Cambridge University Press, 1991.

Dean, Kenneth. "Local Communal Religion in Contemporary South-east China." In *Religion in China Today*, edited by Daniel L. Overmyer. Cambridge: Cambridge University Press, 2003.

Dharmapala Organization of Dharma Drum Mountain. *Chung-hwa Institute of Buddhist Studies*. Taipei: Dharmapala Organization of Dharma Drum Mountain, n.d.

———. *Dharma Propagation of Nung Ch'an Monastery*. Taipei: Dharmapala Organization of Dharma Drum Mountain, n.d.

———. *The Vows of Master Sheng-yen*. Taipei: Dharmapala Organization of Dharma Drum Mountain, n.d.

Douglas, Mary. *Natural Symbols*. New York: Vintage Books, 1973.

Durkheim, Emile. *The Elementary Forms of the Religious Life*. Translated by Karen E. Fields. New York: The Free Press, 1995.

Friedman, Thomas L. *The Lexus and the Olive Tree*. New York: Farrar, Straus and Giroux, 1999.

Fu Chi-ying. *Handing Down the Light: The Biography of Venerable Master Hsing Yun*. Translated by Amy Lui-ma. Hacienda Heights, CA: Hsi Lai University Press, 1996.

Gold, Thomas B. *State and Society in the Taiwan Miracle*. Armonk, NY: M. E. Sharpe, 1987.

Hall, David, and Roger Ames. *Thinking Through Confucius*. Albany: State University of New York Press, 1987.

Hsiao, Hsin-Huang Michael, ed. *Discovery of the Middle Classes in East Asia*. Taipei: Academia Sinica, Institute of Ethnology, 1993.

———. "The Development and Organization of Foundations in Taiwan: An Expression of Vigor in a Newly Born Society." In *Quiet Revolutions on Taiwan, Republic of China*, edited by Jason C. Hu. Taipei: Kwang-hwa, 1994.

Hsiau A-chin. *Contemporary Taiwanese Cultural Nationalism*. London: Routledge, 2000.

Hsing Yun, *The Carefree Life: Dharma Words of Venerable Master Hsing Yun*. Hacienda Heights, CA: Hsi Lai University Press, n.d.

———. *The Philosophy of Being Second*. Hacienda Heights, CA: Hsi Lai University Press, 2000.

———. *Where There Is Dharma There Is a Way*. Taipei: Foguang Cultural Enterprise Co., 2001.

Huang, Chien-yu Julia. "Recapturing Charisma: Emotion and Rationalization in a Globalizing Buddhist Movement from Taiwan." PhD diss., Boston University, 2001.

Huang, Chien-yu Julia, and Robert P. Weller. "Merit and Mothering: Women and Social Welfare in Taiwanese Buddhism." *Journal of Asian Studies* 57, no. 2 (May 1998): 379–96.

Huntington, Samuel P. "The Clash of Civilizations?" *Foreign Affairs* 72, no. 3 (Summer 1993), 22–49.

Jaspers, Karl. *The Origin and Goal of History*. New Haven, CT: Yale University Press, 1953.

Jiang Canteng. *Taiwan fojiao wenhua fazhanshi: Riju shiqi*. Taipei: Nantian chuban she, 2000.

Jochim, Christian. "Carrying Confucianism into the Modern World: The Taiwan Case." In *Religion in Modern Taiwan*, edited by Philip Clart and Charles B. Jones. Honolulu: University of Hawaii Press, 2003.

Jones, Charles Brewer. *Buddhism in Taiwan: Religion and the State, 1660–1990*. Honolulu: University of Hawaii Press, 1999.

Jordan, David K., Andrew D. Morris, and Marc L. Moskowitz. *The Minor Arts of Daily Life: Popular Culture in Taiwan*. Honolulu: University of Hawaii Press, 2004.

Kuah-Pearce, Khun Eng. *State, Society, and Religious Engineering: Toward a Reformist Buddhism in Singapore*. London: Times Academic Press, 2003.

Kuan, Ping-Yin, Dominique Tyl, and Catalina Wei-Chi Yin. *Attitudes and Reflections toward the West, Western Culture, and Christianity in Taiwan*. Turin, Italy: Fondazione Giovanni Agnelli, 1999.

Kukathas, Chandran. "Ethical Pluralism from a Classical Liberal Perspective." In *The Many and the One: Religious and Secular Perspectives on Ethical Pluralism in the Modern World*, edited by Richard Madsen and Tracy B. Strong. Princeton, NJ: Princeton University Press, 2003.

Lai Chi-tim. "Daoism in China Today, 1980–2002." In *Religion in China Today*, edited by Daniel L. Overmyer. Cambridge: Cambridge University Press, 2003.

Laliberté, André. *The Politics of Buddhist Organizations in Taiwan: 1989–2003*. New York: RoutledgeCurzon, 2004.

Lee Kuan Yew. *The Singapore Story: Memoirs of Lee Kuan Yew*. New York: Prentice Hall, 1998.

Lomasky, Loren E. "Classical Liberalism and Civil Society." In *Alternative Conceptions of Civil Society*, edited by Simone Chambers and Will Kymlicka. Princeton, NJ: Princeton University Press, 2002.

Lopez, Donald S, Jr. "Buddhism." In *Religions of Asia in Practice*, edited by Donald S. Lopez, Jr. Princeton, NJ: Princeton University Press, 2002.

Lu, Hwei-Syin. "Gender and Buddhism in Contemporary Taiwan: A Case Study of Tzu-chi Foundation." In *Proceedings of the National Science Council ROC* 8, no. 4:539–50.

Madsen, Richard. "Confucian Conceptions of Civil Society." In *Alternative Conceptions of Civil Society*, edited by Simone Chambers and Will Kymlicka. Princeton, NJ: Princeton University Press, 2002.

———. "Confucianism and the Globalization of Ethics." In *The Globalization of Ethics*, edited by William Sullivan and Will Kymlicka. Cambridge: Cambridge University Press, 2007.

———. "Toward a Hopeful Sociology" *Social Transformations in Chinese Societies* 2, no. 1 (Spring 2007).

Madsen, Richard, William M. Sullivan, Ann Swidler, and Stephen M. Tipton, eds. *Meaning and Modernity: Religion, Polity, Self*. Berkeley: University of California Press, 2002.

Morris, Andrew D. "Taiwan's History: An Introduction." In *The Minor Arts of Daily Life: Popular Culture in Taiwan*, edited by David K. Jordan, Andrew D. Morris, and Marc L. Moskowitz. Honolulu: University of Hawaii Press, 2004.

Munro, Donald, ed. *Individualism and Holism: Studies in Confucian and Taoist Values*. Ann Arbor: University of Michigan Center for Chinese Studies, 1985.

Orru, Marco, Nicole Woolsey Biggert, and Gary G. Hamilton. "Organizational Isomorphism in East Asia." In *The New Institutionalism in Organizational Analysis*, edited by Walter W. Powell and Paul J. DiMaggio. Chicago: University of Chicago Press, 1991.

Pittman, Don A. *Toward a Modern Chinese Buddhism: Taixu's Reforms*. Honolulu: University of Hawaii Press, 2001.

Potter, Pitman B. "Belief in Control: Regulation of Religion in China." In *Religion in China Today*, edited by Daniel L. Overmeyer. Cambridge: University of Cambridge Press, 2003.

Putnam, Robert D. *Making Democracy Work: Civic Traditions in Modern Italy*. Princeton, NJ: Princeton University Press, 1993.

Rigger, Shelley. *From Opposition to Power: Taiwan's Democratic Progressive Party*. Boulder, CO: Lynne Rienner Publishers, 2001.

———. *Politics in Taiwan: Voting for Democracy*. London: Routledge, 1999.

———. "Taiwan in U.S.-China Relations." *The Aspen Institute Congressional Program* 18, no. 1 (2003).

Rosenblum, Nancy L., and Robert Post, eds. *Civil Society and Government*. Princeton, NJ: Princeton University Press, 2002.

Roy, Denny. *Taiwan: A Political History*. Ithaca, NY: Cornell University Press, 2003.

Rubenstein, Murray A. "Christianity and Democratization in Modern Taiwan: The Presbyterian Church and the Struggle of Minnan/Hakka Selfhood in the Republic of China." In *Religion in Modern Taiwan*, edited by Philip Clart and Charles B. Jones. Honolulu: University of Hawaii Press, 2003.

Rudolph, Susanne Hoeber, and James Piscatori, eds. *Transnational Religion and Fading States*. Boulder, CO: Westview Press, 1997.

Schak, David. "Socially-engaged Buddhism in Taiwan and its Contributions to Civil Society." In *Engaged Buddhism, Its History, Doctrines and Practices: Essays in Memory of Master Yin-shun (1906–2005)*, edited by Hsu Mu-chu et al. Hualian: Ciji daxue chuban she, 2007.

Schipper, Kristofer. *The Taoist Body*. Translated by Karen C. Duval. Berkeley: University of California Press, 1993.

Shahar, Meir, and Robert P. Weller, eds. *Unruly Gods: Divinity and Society in China*. Honolulu: University of Hawaii Press, 1996.

Sheng Yen, *In the Spirit of Ch'an: An Introduction to Ch'an Buddhism*. New York: Dharma Drum Publications, 1998.

Sheng Yen, and Dan Stevenson, *Hoofprint of the Ox: Principles of the Chan Buddhist Path as Taught by a Modern Chan Master*. New York: Oxford University Press, 2001.

Still Thoughts Cultural Mission. *Lotus Flower of the Heart: Thirty Years of Tzuchi Photographs*. Taipei: Still Thoughts Cultural Mission, 1997.

———. *Love Transcends Borders*. Taipei: Still Thoughts Cultural Mission, 2000.

Taylor, Charles. *Modern Social Imaginaries*. Durham: Duke University Press, 2004.

Toobin, Jeffrey. "Adventures in Buddhism: What Really Happened at the Hsi Lai Temple." *New Yorker*, September 18, 2000.

Troeltsch, Ernst. *The Social Teachings of the Christian Churches*. Translated by Olive Wyon. London: George Allen, 1931.

Tu Wei-ming. "Confucianism." In *Our Religions*, edited by Arvind Sharma. San Francisco: HarperSanFrancisco, 1993.

———. "Confucius and Confucianism." *Encyclopedia Britannica*, 15th edition, 1988.

———. "Multiple Modernities: Implications of the Rise of 'Confucian' East Asia." In *Chinese Ethics in a Global Context*, edited by Karl-Heinz Pohl and Anselm W. Müller. Leiden: Brill, 2002.

United Nations High Commission on Human Rights. *Bangkok Declaration on Human Rights*. United Nations High Commission on Human Rights, 1993.

United States Government Printing Office. *The National Security Strategy of the United States*. U.S. Government Printing Office, 2002.

Vogel, Ezra F. *One Step Ahead in China: Guangdong under Reform*. Cambridge, MA: Harvard University Press, 1989.

Weber, Max. *The Protestant Ethic and the Spirit of Capitalism*. Translated by Talcott Parsons. New York: Charles Scribner's Sons, 1958.

———. "Science as a Vocation." In *From Max Weber: Essays in Sociology*, edited by H. H. Gerth and C. Wright Mills. New York: Oxford University Press, 1966.

———. *The Sociology of Religion*. Translated by Ephraim Fischoff. Boston: Beacon Press, 1964.

Weller, Robert P. *Alternate Civilities: Democracy and Culture in China and Taiwan*. Boulder, CO: Westview Press, 1999.

———. *Unities and Diversities in Chinese Religion*. Seattle: University of Washington Press, 1987.

Wu, David Y. H. "McDonalds in Taipei: Hamburgers, Betel Nuts, and National Identity." In *Golden Arches East: McDonalds in East Asia,* edited by James L. Watson. Stanford: Stanford University Press, 1997.

Wu Ning-yuan. "Folk Religion in Taiwan." *Dongfang zongjiao yanjiu* (1991).

Xing Tian Gong Foundation. *Xiaolaoyisheng.* Taipei: Xing Tian Gong Foundation, 1998.

Yau, Li-shiang, and Hei-yuan Chiu. "Studies of Religious Change in Taiwan." Academia Sinica Monograph Series, No. 53. Taipei: Academia Sinica, Institute of Ethnology, 1986.

Glossary

CHINESE	TAIWAN ROMANIZATION	PINYIN
Names		
陳履安	Chen Lu-an	Chen Lü'an
陳水扁	Chen Shui-bian	Chen Shuibian
證嚴	Cheng Yen	Zheng Yan
蔣經國	Chiang Ching-kuo	Jiang Jingguo
瞿海源	Chiu Hei-yuan	Qu Haiyuan
何華欽	Ho Hua-chin	He Huaqin
簫新偟	Hsiao Hsin-huang	Xiao Xinhuang
星雲	Hsing Yun	Xing Yun
修道	Hsiu Tao	Xiu Dao
徐木珍	Hsu Mu-chen	Xu Muzhen
許聰敏	Hsu Tsung-ming	Xu Congmin
玄空	Hsuan Kung	Xuan Kong
玄奘	Hsuan Tsang	Xuan Zang
黃忠臣	Huang Chung-chen	Huang Zhongchen
黃叢	Huang Tsung	Huang Cong
關公	Kuan Kung	Guan Gong

郭雅瑜	Kuo Ya-yu	Guo Yayu
李登輝	Lee Teng-hui	Li Denghui
李國深	Li Kuo-shen	Li Guoshen
林洋港	Lin Yang-kang	Lin Yanggang
靈源	Ling Yuan	Ling Yuan
呂秀蓮	Lu Hsiu-lien	Lü Xiulian
盧蕙馨	Lu Hwei-syin	Lu Huixin
白丈	Pai Chang	Bai Zhang
聖嚴	Sheng Yen	Sheng Yan
東初	Tung Ch'u	Dong Chu
王錦雲	Wang Chin-yun	Wang Jinyun
王月桂	Wang Yue-Kuei	Wang Yuegui
吳伯雄	Wu Po-hsiung	Wu Boxiong
印順	Yin-shun	Yin Shun

Places

花蓮	Hualien	Hualian
宜蘭	Ilan	Yilan
高雄	Kaohsiung	Gaoxiong
埔里	Puli	Puli
臺中	Taichung	Taizhong
臺北	Taipei	Taibei
臺東	Taitung	Taidong

Buddhist Organizations and Temples

中台禪寺	Chung Tai Chan Ssu	Zhongtai Chan Si
法鼓山	Faku Shan	Fagushan
佛光山	Fokuangshan	Foguangshan
福旨	Fuchih	Fuzhi
西來寺	Hsi Lai Ssu	Xilai Si
行天宮	Hsing Tien Kung	Xing Tian Gong
農禪寺	Nung Chan Ssu	Nongchan Si
普明	Pu Ming	Pu Ming
慈濟功德會	Tzu Chi Kung Te Huei	Ciji Gongdehui

Index

Page numbers in italics refer to illustrations.